# U.S. JOURNAL

# U.S. JOURNAL

## by Calvin Trillin

E. P. DUTTON & CO., INC. | NEW YORK | 1971

Published simultaneously in Canada by Clarke, Irwin & Company Limited,
Toronto and Vancouver

Library of Congress Catalog Card Number: 76–133587

All the material in this book appeared originally in *The New Yorker*.

SBN: 0–525–22660–5

*To William Shawn*

The editor for almost all of these pieces at *The New Yorker* was Robert Bingham. The editor for all of the rough drafts at home was Alice Trillin. William Shawn, the editor of *The New Yorker,* was encouraging about trying a series like "U.S. Journal," and has made the final decision every three weeks on which story should be done. I thank all of them for their intelligent suggestions and for their patience.

# Contents

# KILLINGS

# A Stranger with a Camera

On a bright afternoon in September, in 1967, a five-man film crew working in the mountains of Eastern Kentucky stopped to take pictures of some people near a place called Jeremiah. In a narrow valley, a half-dozen dilapidated shacks—each one a tiny square box with one corner cut away to provide a cluttered front porch— stood alongside the county blacktop. Across the road from the shacks, a mountain rose abruptly. In the field that separated them from the mountain behind them, there were a couple of ramshackle privies and some clotheslines tied to trees and a railroad track and a rusted automobile body and a dirty river called Rockhouse Creek.

The leader of the film crew was a Canadian named Hugh O'Connor. Widely acclaimed as the co-producer of the Labyrinth show at Expo 67 in Montreal, O'Connor had been hired by Francis Thompson, an American filmmaker, to work on a film Thompson was producing for the American pavilion at HemisFair in San Antonio. O'Connor went up to three of the shacks and asked the head of each household for permission to take pictures. When each one agreed, O'Connor had him sign the customary release forms and gave him a token payment of ten dollars—a token that, in this case, happened to represent a month's rent. The light was perfect in the valley, and the shooting went well. Theodore Holcomb, the associate producer of the film, was particularly struck by the looks of a miner, still in his work clothes and still covered with coal dust, sitting in a rocking chair on one of the porches. "He was just sitting there scratching his arm in a listless way," Holcomb said later. "He had an expression of total despair. It was an extraordinary shot—so evocative of the despair of that region." The shot of the coal miner was good enough to be included in the final version of the film, and so was a shot of a half-dozen children who, somehow, lived with their parents in one of the tiny shacks.

After about an hour and a half, the crew was ready to leave, but someone had noticed a woman come out of one of the shacks and go to the common well to draw some water, and she was asked to repeat the action for filming. As that last shot was being completed, a woman drove up and told the filmmakers that the man who owned the property was coming to throw them off of it. Then she drove away. A couple of minutes later, another car arrived, and a man—a thin, bald man—leaped out. He was holding a pistol. "Get off my property!" he shouted again and again. Then he shot twice. No one was hit. The filmmakers kept moving their equipment toward their cars across the road while trying to tell the man that they were leaving. One of them said that the man must be shooting blanks. "Get off my property!" he kept screaming. Hugh O'Connor, who was lugging a heavy battery across the highway, turned to say that they were going. The man held the pistol in both hands and pulled the trigger again. "Mr. O'Connor briefly looked down in amazement, and I saw a hole in his chest," Holcomb later testified in court. "He saw it and he looked up in despair and said, 'Why did you have to do that?' and, with blood coming from his mouth, he fell to the ground."

Whitesburg, a town about twelve miles from Jeremiah, is the county seat of Letcher County—headquarters for the county court, the sheriff, and assorted coal companies and antipoverty agencies. Word that someone had been killed reached Whitesburg quickly, but for a couple of hours there was some confusion about just who the victim was. According to various stories, the dead man had been a representative of the Army Corps of Engineers, a Vista volunteer, or a C.B.S. cameraman—any of whom might qualify as a candidate for shooting in Letcher County. The Corps of Engineers had proposed building the Kingdom Come Dam across Rockhouse Creek, thereby flooding an area that included Jeremiah, and some opponents of the dam had been saying that the first government man who came near their property had better come armed. Throughout Eastern Kentucky, local political organizations and coal-mining interests had warned that community organizers who called themselves Vistas or Appalachian Volunteers or anything else were nothing but another variety of Communists, and even some of the impoverished people whom the volunteers were supposedly in Kentucky to help viewed them with fear and suspicion. A number of television crews had been to Letcher County to record the despair that Holcomb saw in the face of the miner sitting on the front porch. Whitesburg happens to be the home of Harry M. Caudill, a lawyer who drew attention to the plight of the mountain people in 1963 with an eloquent book called *Night Comes to the Cumberlands*. Television crews and reporters on a tour of Appalachia are tempted to start with Letcher County in order to get the benefit of Caudill's counsel, which is ordinarily expressed in a tone of sustained rage—rage at the profit ratio of out-of-state companies that take the region's natural resources while paying virtually no taxes, rage at the strip mines that are gouged across the mountains and at the mud slides and floods and pollution and ugliness they cause, rage at the local merchants and politicians who make a good living from the trade of welfare recipients or the retainers of coal companies and insist that there is nothing wrong with the economy, and, most of all, rage at the country that could permit it all to happen. "Look what man hath wrought on that purple mountain's majesty," he will say as he points out the coal waste on the side of a mountain that had once been beautiful. "A country that treats its land and people this way deserves to perish from the earth."

In the view of Caudill and of Tom Gish, the liberal editor of the *Mountain Eagle*, a Letcher County weekly, the reactions of people in Jeremiah to the presence of O'Connor's film crew—cooperation by the poor people being photographed in their squalid shacks, rage by the man who owned the shacks—were characteristic of Letcher County: a lot of people who are still in Eastern Kentucky

after years of welfare or subsistence employment have lost the will
to treat their situation as an embarrassment, but outside journalists
are particularly resented by the people who have managed to make
a living—running a country store or a filling station or a small
truck mine, working for the county administration, managing some
rental property. They resent the impression that everyone in Eastern Kentucky is like the people who are desperately poor—people
whose condition they tend to blame on "just sorriness, mostly." In
Letcher County, fear of outsiders by people who are guarding repu-
tations or economic interests blends easily into a deep-rooted suspicion of outsiders by all Eastern Kentucky mountain people, who
have always had a fierce instinct to protect their property and a
distrust of strangers that has often proved to have been justified.
All of the people in Letcher County—people who live in the shacks
up remote hollows or people who run stores on Main Street in
Whitesburg—consider themselves mountain people, and, despite
an accurate story in the *Mountain Eagle,* many of them instinc-
tively believed that the mountaineer who killed Hugh O'Connor
was protecting his property from smart-aleck outsiders who
wouldn't leave when they were told.

The mountaineer's name was Hobart Ison. There have always
been Isons in Letcher County, and many of them have managed
somewhat better than their neighbors. Hobart Ison had inherited a
rather large piece of land in Jeremiah—he raised chickens and
rented out shacks he himself had built and at one time ran a small
sawmill—but he was known mainly as an eccentric, mean-tem-
pered old man. Everyone in Letcher County knew that Hobart Ison
had once built and furnished a house for his future bride and—having been rejected or having been afraid to ask or having had no
particular future bride in mind—had let the house remain as it was
for thirty years, the grass growing up around it and the furniture
still in the packing crates. He had occasionally painted large signs
attacking the people he thought had wronged him. He was easily
enraged by people hunting on his property, and he despised all of
the local Democrats, whom he blamed for injustices that included
dismissing him from a post-office job. A psychiatrist who examined
him after the shooting said, "Any reference to 'game warden' or
'Democrat' will provoke him tremendously." Once, when some

local youths were taunting him, he took a shot at them, hitting one
in the shoulder. "A lot of people around here would have welcomed them," Caudill said of the filmmakers. "They just happened
to pick the wrong place."

Streams of people came to visit Ison in the Letcher County jail
before he was released on bail. Women from around Jeremiah
baked him cakes. When his trial came up, it proved impossible to
find a jury. The Letcher County commonwealth's attorney and
Caudill, who had been retained by Francis Thompson, Inc., se-
cured a change of venue. They argued that Ison's family relationship in Letcher County was "so extensive as to comprise a large
segment of the population," and, through an affidavit signed by
three citizens in position to know public opinion, they stated that
"the overwhelming expression of sentiment has been to the effect
that the defendant did right in the slaying of Hugh O'Connor and
that he ought to be acquitted of the offense of murder."

Harlan County is a mountain or two away from Letcher County. In
the town of Harlan, benches advertising Bunny Enriched Bread
stand outside the front door of the county courthouse, flanking the
First World War monument and the Revolutionary War monument
and the plaque recalling how many Kentucky courthouses were
burned down by each side during the Civil War. On the ground
floor of the courthouse, the men who habitually gather on the plain
wooden benches to pass the time use old No. 5 cans for ashtrays or
spittoons and a large container that once held Oscar Mayer's Pure
Lard as a wastebasket. In the courtroom, a plain room with all of
its furnishings painted black, the only decoration other than pictures of the men who have served as circuit judge is a framed
poster in praise of the country lawyer—and also in praise, it turns
out upon close reading, of the Dun & Bradstreet Corporation. The
front door of the courthouse is almost always plastered with election stickers. In the vestibule just inside, an old man sits on the
floor behind a display of old pocketknives and watchbands and bill-
folds and eyeglass cases offered for sale or trade.

The commonwealth's attorney of Harlan County is Daniel
Boone Smith. Eight or nine years ago, Smith got curious about how
many people he had prosecuted or defended for murder, and

counted up seven hundred and fifty. He was able to amass that total partly because of longevity (except for a few years in the service during the Second World War, he has been commonwealth's attorney continuously since 1933), partly because he has worked in an area that gives anyone interested in trying murder cases plenty of opportunity (the wars between the unions and the coal operators in Harlan County during the thirties were almost as bloody as the mountain feuds earlier in the century), and partly because he happens to be a quick worker ("Some people will take three days to try a murder case," he has said. "I usually get my case on in a day"). During his first week as commonwealth's attorney of Harlan and an adjoining county, Smith tried five murder cases. These days, Harlan County may have about that many a year, but it remains a violent place. The murders that do occur in mountain counties like Harlan and Letcher often seem to occur while someone is in a drunken rage, and often among members of the same family—a father shooting a son over something trivial, one member of a family mowing down another who is breaking down the door trying to get at a third. "We got people in this county today who would kill you as quick as look at you," Smith has said. "But most of 'em are the type that don't bother you if you leave them alone." Smith is known throughout Eastern Kentucky for his ability to select jurors—to remember which prospective juror's uncle may have had a boundary dispute with which witness's grandfather twenty years ago—and for his ability to sum up the case for them in their own language once the evidence has been heard. He is an informal, colloquial, storytelling man who happens to be a graduate of the Harvard Law School.

A lack of fervor about convicting Hobart Ison was assumed in Harlan County when he came up for trial there in May, 1968. "Before the case, people were coming up and saying, 'He *should've* killed the son of a bitch,' " Smith said later. "People would say, 'They oughtn't to make fun of mountain people. They've made enough fun of mountain people. Let me on the jury, Boone, and I'll turn him loose.' " Smith saw his task as persuading the citizens and the jurors that the case was not what it appeared to be—that the filmmakers were not "a bunch of privateers and pirates" but respectable people who had been commissioned by the United States government, that the film was not another study of how poor and ignorant people were in Eastern Kentucky but a film about the whole United States in which the shots of Eastern Kentucky would take up only a few seconds, that the filmmakers had behaved properly and politely to those they were photographing. "Why, if they had been smart-alecks come to hold us up to ridicule, I'd be the last man to try him," Smith assured everyone. It took Smith only a day or so to present his case against Hobart Ison, although it took three days to pick the jury. On the witness stand, the surviving filmmakers managed to avoid admitting to Ison's lawyers that it was the appalling poverty of his tenants that had interested them; they talked about being attracted by expressive family groups and by the convenience of not having to move their equipment far from the road. The defense asked if they were planning to take pictures of the Bluegrass as well as Appalachia. Were they going to make a lot of money from the film? How many millions of viewers would see the pictures of poor Eastern Kentucky people? Had they refused to move? Had they taunted Ison by saying he was shooting blanks? Did the people who signed the release forms really know what they were signing? (At least one of the signers was, like one out of four of his neighbors, unable to read.)

Except for the underlying issue of Eastern Kentucky v. Outsiders, the only issue seriously in contention was Ison's sanity. The director of a nearby mental-health clinic, testifying for the defense, said that Ison was a paranoid schizophrenic. He told of Ison showing up for one interview with long socks worn on the outside of his trouser legs and of his altercations with his neighbors and of his lack of remorse.

The prosecution's psychiatrist—an impressive woman from the University of Kentucky who had been retained by Francis Thompson, Inc.—said that Ison had grown up at a time when it was common practice to run people off of property with a gun, and, because he had lived with aging parents or alone ever since childhood, he still followed that practice. Some of Ison's ideas did have "paranoid coloring," she said, but that could be traced to his being a mountaineer, since people in isolated mountain pockets normally had a suspicion of strangers and even of each other. "Socio-cultural circumstances," she concluded, "lead to the diagnosis of an individual who is normal for his culture, the shooting and the paranoid color both being present in other individuals in this culture who are considered normal." In the trial and in the insanity hearing that had earlier found Ison competent to stand trial, Smith insisted that Ison was merely peculiar, not crazy. "I said, 'Now, I happen to like mayonnaise on my beans. Does that make *me* crazy?' " Smith later recalled. "I turned to one of the jurors, a man named Mahan Fields, and I said, 'Mahan, you remember Uncle Bob Woolford, who used to work up at Evarts? Did you ever see Uncle Bob in the winter when he didn't have his socks pulled up over his pants legs to keep out the cold? Now, was Uncle Bob crazy? Why, Mahan, I bet on many a winter morning *you* wore *your* socks over your pants legs.' "

In his summation, Smith saved his harshest words not for the defendant but for the person who was responsible for bringing Hobart Ison, a mountaineer who was not quite typical of mountaineers, and Hugh O'Connor, a stranger with a camera who was not quite typical of strangers with cameras, into violent conflict. Judy Breeding—the operator of a small furniture store near Ison's shacks, and the wife of Ison's cousin—had testified that she was not only the woman who told the film crew that Ison was coming but also the woman who had told Ison that the film crew was on his property. "Hobart," she recalled saying, "there is some men over there taking pictures of your houses, with out-of-state license." Smith looked out toward the courtroom spectators and suddenly pointed his finger at Judy Breeding. He told her that he would like to be prosecuting her, that if it hadn't been for her mouth Hugh O'Connor would not be in his grave and Hobart Ison would be back home where he belonged. Later, Smith caught a glimpse of Mrs. Breeding in the hall, and he thought he saw her shake her fist at him, smiling. "You know," he said, "I believe the idea that she had anything to do with bringing that about had never occurred to her till I mentioned it."

The jury was eleven to one for conviction, but the one held out. Some people were surprised that Ison had come that close to being convicted, although it was generally agreed that the prosecution's psychiatrist had out-talked the psychiatrist who testified for the defense. Smith believed that his case had been greatly strengthened by the fact that the filmmakers had been respectful, soft-spoken witnesses—not at all smart-alecky. "If there was anything big-headed about them," he said, "it didn't show."

The retrial was postponed once, and then was stopped suddenly during jury selection when Smith became ill. On March 24th, Hobart Ison came to trial again. The filmmakers, who had been dreading another trip to Kentucky, were at the county courthouse in Harlan at nine in the morning, ready to repeat their testimony. Although Smith had anticipated even more trouble finding a jury, he was prepared to go to trial. But Ison's lawyers indicated to Smith and Caudill that their client, now seventy, would be willing to plead guilty to voluntary manslaughter, and they finally met Smith's insistence on a ten-year sentence. Ison—wearing a baggy brown suit, his face pinched and red—appeared only briefly before the judge to plead guilty. A couple of hours after everyone arrived, Caudill was on his way back to Whitesburg, where he was working on the case of a Vietnam veteran accused of killing two men during an argument in the street, and the filmmakers were driving to Knoxville to catch the first plane to New York.

The following day, the clerk of the court, a strong-looking woman with a strong Kentucky accent, happened to get into a discussion about the filmmakers with another citizen who had come to know them in the year and a half since Hugh O'Connor's death—a woman with a softer accent and a less certain tone to her voice.

"You know, I asked those men yesterday morning if they were happy with the outcome," the clerk said. "And they said, 'Yes.' And I said, 'Well, you know, us hillbillies is a queer breed. We are. I'm not offering any apologies when I say that. Us hillbillies *are* a queer breed, and I'm just as proud as punch to be one.'"

"Not all of us are like that," the other woman said. "Mean like that."

"Well, I wouldn't say that man is mean," the clerk said. "I don't guess he ever harmed anybody in his life. They were very nice people. I think it was strictly a case of misunderstanding. I think that the old man thought they were laughing and making fun of him, and it was more than he could take. I know this: a person isolated in these hills, they often grow old and eccentric, which I think they have a right to do."

"But he didn't have a right to kill," the other woman said.

"Well, no," the clerk said. "But us hillbillies, we don't bother nobody. We go out of our way to help people. But we don't want nobody pushin' us around. Now, that's the code of the hills. And he felt like—that old man felt like—he was being pushed around. You know, it's like I told those men: 'I wouldn't have gone on that old man's land to pick me a mess of wild greens without I'd asked him.' They said, 'We didn't know all this.' I said, 'I bet you know it now. I bet you know it now.' "

# I've Always Been Clean

John Mervin, a menacing-looking young man with long unkempt hair and a shaggy beard, was arrested for murder last November, confirming the suspicions of a lot of West Chester citizens about the kind of crimes young people who looked like that were capable of perpetrating. The killing that Mervin was accused of—shooting to death an unemployed nineteen-year-old named Jonathan Henry —had taken place during what a newspaper account referred to as a "liquor and drug party." Anybody who had seen Mervin around town knew that he wore not only a beard but the jacket of an out-law motorcycle gang called the Warlocks. The lead story on his arraignment in the West Chester *Daily Local News* revealed that at the time of the killing Mervin was out on bail on a charge of assault with intent to kill—a charge resulting from an October shooting in front of a West Chester saloon.

The paper identified Mervin as a student at West Chester State College, which might be considered an odd thing for a Warlock to be, except that some people in West Chester were ready to believe almost anything about the kids at West Chester State. The type of school that used to be known as a teachers' college, West Chester State is sufficiently conservative so that someone with a beard would not have been permitted to take classes there a few years ago, but lately the townspeople have been concerned about what they often call "that small element" in the college, an element associated with drugs and demonstrations and bizarre appearance and a lack of respect for accepted values. The small element at West Chester State that worries the townspeople blends easily with a small element among their own children—the most visible result being a band of students or ex-students or drifters occupying the ledges around the steps of the county courthouse, flaunting mustaches and long hair and dirty T-shirts, staring arrogantly at the respectable citizens who walk by.

West Chester has about fifteen thousand citizens, almost all of whom consider themselves respectable. Some of them commute to Philadelphia or to Wilmington or to industries in towns in surrounding Chester County, but West Chester is too self-contained to be considered a suburb. It has a few small industries of its own, plus the legal and bureaucratic machinery that goes with being a county seat. The area that surrounds it still looks rural; the fields and barns of Chadds Ford, familiar from the paintings of Andrew Wyeth, are only a few miles to the south. The law offices clustered around the county courthouse are not in modern office buildings but in brick row houses, marked with neat white shingles. There has always been a lot of talk about history in Chester County—about when the county was founded and how many covered bridges it has and how many generations it has been Republican. But in the last year or two there has also been a lot of talk about drugs and disturbance and crime. The borough council made an effort to improve the police force, buying some new equipment and hiring the chief of county detectives, Thomas Frame, as police chief, at a considerable raise in pay. But a series in the local paper last June said that marijuana was easily available a few steps from the courthouse, the black people of West Chester continued to raise questions about equal treatment, and the kids on the ledges around the courthouse steps continued to symbolize all that menaced the traditional tranquillity of West Chester.

The arrest of John Mervin for shooting Jonathan Henry caused some angry outbursts about just how far things had gone with the "hippies." (Although motorcycle gangs have been known to break up peace demonstrations and harass flower children, West Chester citizens tend to bunch all oddly dressed people together as hippies.) Then, a few days after the arrest, Chief Frame held a press conference to announce that John Mervin was an undercover police officer, having been recruited from the Warlocks and secretly sworn in a couple of months before. The police arrested a dozen or so people, most of them from around the college, for having sold drugs to Mervin. Frame announced that thanks to Mervin's efforts the police force had gained possession of forty-eight thousand dollars' worth of dangerous drugs. Mervin, who appeared at the press conference in a neat business suit, said that the arrests resulting from his work would "nearly annihilate any drug distribution" in West Chester. The Chief, without commenting on the details of the shootings, said Mervin had "handled himself in the best manner a police officer could" and would begin to work on regular police shifts. John Mervin became a hero.

After it was revealed that Mervin had been an undercover agent, the Philadelphia *Inquirer* decided that he was not merely a student but an honor student, as well as a former high-school football star —a young man who, underneath that hippie disguise, had precisely the attributes any American parent would be proud of. In an *Inquirer* story headlined " 'HIPPIE POLICEMAN' LIVED IN DEGRADA-TION AND FEAR," Mervin said that the most difficult part of his assignment was not the physical danger but the frustration of not being able to tell his loved ones that he was actually a policeman. "They thought I had gotten into bad company," he said. They were, of course, right: by his own account, Mervin had been in the Warlocks, a group that takes some pride in being considered just about the worst company in eastern Pennsylvania, for two years before anybody approached him about being a policeman. But the stories in the Philadelphia papers made it sound as if practically anything Mervin had ever done was part of the hippie disguise that he had manfully suffered until he was at last able to throw it off, the drug traffic in West Chester having finally been annihilated. "His love of his motorcycle gained him admission into the Warlocks motorcycle gang two years ago," the *Inquirer* piece said. "And that helped him in his disguise." In a later piece, the Philadelphia *Bulletin* reported the assurance of Mervin's contact man in the police department that Mervin was "always polite, never using elsewhere words and actions he had to use as a hippie drug purchaser and twilight world character." Mervin told the *Inquirer* that his first action after his identity was revealed was to call his mother.

Although the initial reaction in West Chester to Chief Frame's announcement was overwhelming support of Mervin, the support was not unanimous. The October shooting outside the West Chester saloon had been investigated only perfunctorily by the West Chester police after Mervin was arraigned and released on bail. But the killing of Jonathan Henry had taken place in an apartment behind a restaurant-and-bar just outside West Chester, in the jurisdiction of the West Goshen Township police, who continued their investigation even after Chief Frame publicly expressed his confidence in Mervin's innocence. The district attorney's office made it clear that it was pursuing the murder charge, and eventually it even got a preliminary hearing held on the October shooting—a hearing that produced the testimony of a couple of witnesses that Mervin, after an argument at the bar, had shot his victim in the leg and then had stood over him and shot him in the back. Chief Frame hinted that the district attorney was sore at not having been informed in advance of Mervin's mission and that the other law-enforcement agencies in the county resented West Chester's success in arresting drug dealers. Frame supported Mervin's story that the October shooting had been in self-defense; after the man who had been shot in the back testified, the West Chester police arrested him, on a complaint by Officer Mervin.

Some people familiar with the drug scene in West Chester scoffed at the notion that arresting some college kids for offenses such as selling Mervin a Chiclets box full of LSD tablets had had any effect on the drug traffic. The college crowd began to tell anyone who would listen that Mervin, far from being an honor student, had for a couple of years been a motorcycle tough who bragged about his violence—a bully who had merely redirected his bullying toward coercing people into selling him drugs. Some conversations among West Chester citizens were not about Mervin's heroism but about why someone with his background was sworn in as a policeman and why he was allowed to continue after the first shooting and why he was getting such vigorous support from the police department. "I would like to know what line of duty Mervin was performing on both October 4 and November 19," someone eventually wrote to the *Daily Local News*. "Or who has something on whom?"

Black people in West Chester have the wariness that black people anywhere would have toward a policeman who shoots two people within six weeks, and they have even more reason than most black people to be worried about having an armed former member of a motorcycle gang patrolling the town in a police car. Last Labor Day, during a demonstration in the Chester County town of Parkesburg, a prominent black leader named Harry Dickinson was shot to death, and three members of a motorcycle gang called the Pagans were among those accused (but not convicted) of his murder. No Warlocks had been named by Mervin as drug dealers; when the preliminary hearing on the October shooting was finally held, there were complaints that witnesses testifying against Mervin were intimidated not only by threats of arrest from the West Chester police but by the threat implied by the presence of six attentive Warlocks in the courtroom. Liberals in West Chester were concerned about what has developed in other parts of the country into a sort of alliance between the police and the motorcycle gangs, with the gangs almost in the role of police auxiliaries in the rougher dealings with peace demonstrators and black people and students. At a West Chester borough-council meeting not long after Chief Frame's press conference, the only black councilman moved that, in line with the procedure followed elsewhere when a policeman is accused of a felony, Mervin be suspended until he was exonerated. The motion failed to get a second.

Mervin continued to ride in a police car, carrying a gun, and he began to appear with Chief Frame around the county to lecture on the evils of drugs—explaining to service clubs and P.T.A.s and high-school assemblies that "popping a pill" meant taking a tablet and that "acid" meant LSD. The forty-eight thousand dollars' worth of drugs that Mervin had captured—Frame's estimate of the retail price of the drugs Mervin had purchased for twenty-two hundred dollars in borough funds—became fifty thousand dollars at some point in the lecture series. As time went on, it was quoted occasionally as a hundred and thirty-five thousand dollars. The kids around the courthouse steps began to put on mock drug-buying scenes for the benefit of the passing citizens: "Hey, you got any grass to sell?" "No, but I hear there's a guy down at the police station . . ."

On January 26th, a Chester County grand jury indicted Mervin for the murder of Jonathan Henry. West Chester had a new mayor by then, the first Democratic mayor in a century or so, and on the evening after the grand-jury decision he ruled that Mervin had been a special officer whose duties were at an end. There was angry reaction to both the indictment and the mayor's ruling. A number of policemen staged a brief protest in which they handed in their guns —apparently symbolically, since they took them right back when Chief Frame told them to. The police started a John A. Mervin Defense Fund. A number of letters to the *Daily Local News* said that the borough was behaving shoddily by taking away the gun and the position of a man who had saved untold numbers of the community's children from the perils of drugs and had since reported attempts on his life by the murderous elements who control the drug traffic. The borough council, overriding the mayor, voted to hire, and immediately suspend, Mervin as a regular rather than special police officer—guaranteeing that a salary would be put aside for him while the cases were in court and that West Chester would have, among its other historical claims, the distinction of having hired as a policeman someone under indictment for two felonies, one of them murder. A few days later, Mervin reported that he had been shot in the thigh with a .22 while he lay watching television. The mayor felt compelled to write a letter to the *Daily Local News* stating that the decision to end Mervin's service and take away his gun had been made with the approval of Chief Frame and in the best interests of Mervin as well as of the borough. "The futile debate which councilmen and the mayor engaged in on Wednesday night regarding Mervin's pay fades into insignificance today in light of what occurred last night," the *Daily Local News* editorialized the day after Mervin was shot. "What are a few hundred dollars compared to the life of a man who risked everything in order to smash a flourishing drug ring in West Chester?"

"There are only two opinions in West Chester about Mervin," a local reporter said when Mervin came to trial for murder this month. "Either he's a trigger-happy thug who conned the cops or he's a dedicated police officer." People on both sides thought that public opinion was about evenly divided, the word of mouth against Mervin having partly undercut almost universally laudatory press notices. Some of Mervin's most vocal support was judged to be based on a fear of drugs ("Drugs have become such a fearful thing people want to stop the problem and they don't care how," Devere Ponzo, head of the Chester County Black Action Committee, has said. "If a couple of people get killed—tough"); some of it may have come from political considerations (it was thought that raising questions might have been insulting not only to the chief of police but to the Republican establishment that supported him); some of it was undoubtedly a matter of ideology (one group that backed the John A. Mervin Defense Fund—the Association of Alert Citizens, a group that grew out of an anti-sex-education organization called Taxpayers for Decency—based its support partly on the ground that, in the words of one of its spokesmen, "we support the police—period").

But a lot of the talk about the Mervin case in West Chester emphasizes, aside from any political or ideological or anti-drug feeling, how much people *want* to believe in John Mervin. Some people in Chester County (and in the newsrooms of Philadelphia newspapers) seem to have fastened on the Mervin case as a belated sign that the threatening and inexplicable manifestations of the youth culture are not true after all—that the long-haired arrogant-looking kids around the courthouse steps might also throw off *their* disguises and reveal themselves to be honor students and former high-school football stars and battlers against the deadly menace of drugs, that other mothers who are worried about their children's having fallen in with bad company might be told, as John Mervin's mother was told, that it was all an illusion. As the pool of jurors—most of them middle-aged or elderly people, virtually all of them white—walked into the courthouse on the first day of Mervin's trial, one of the usual "hippies," a thin young man with long hair, sat cross-legged on the ledge next to the courthouse steps. He stared at them with a slight smile, occasionally taking a swig of orange juice out of a quart bottle. When any of the jurors being examined said that he already had a firm opinion about the case, both the assistant district attorney and the defense lawyer assumed the opinion was that John Mervin was innocent.

The John Mervin who appeared at the trial was clean-shaven and dressed in summer-weight Ivy League clothes—a baby-faced, somewhat stout young man who answered his elders with polite "Yes, sir's" and "No, sir's." It would have taken an extraordinary leap of imagination to envision him as a hoodlum biker, dressed in a greasy Warlock jacket, swinging a chain—except, of course, to the extent that he had to wear a costume in the line of duty. (When Mervin testified that he had joined the Warlocks two and a half years before, his attorney said, "Were you engaged in any *other* activities that made you valuable as a police officer?") Mervin testified that after being recruited by Chief Frame he had let his clothing and hair become unkempt and had started attending psychedelic and exotic parties. Trying to show that Mervin had not had to play any role to be accepted in local low life, the assistant district attorney asked him if it wasn't true that as an undercover man he wore the same clothing he had worn as a private citizen, merely allowing it to get a bit dirtier. Mervin looked offended. "I've always been clean," he said. According to Mervin, Jonathan Henry had been shot as he was about to shoot a West Chester State student named Jeffrey Saltzman, whom Henry suspected of being an undercover policeman—a scene precisely like those conjured up by Chief Frame's statements that as an undercover man Mervin had constantly risked his life in "this drug jungle." Saltzman, who happens to be the son of the mayor of a tough Delaware River town named Marcus Hook and the nephew of a West Chester policeman, appeared as a defense witness to corroborate the story. He turned out to be a husky, collegiately dressed young man who also said "Yes, sir" and "No, sir." When the assistant district attorney, trying to argue that Saltzman had been a prospect for membership in the Warlocks, asked him why he had had one of his ears pierced, people in the courtroom looked flabbergasted—as if someone had, for reasons too bizarre to contemplate, asked Saltzman why he had begun talking to his friends in Urdu or why he had taken up the lute.

The witnesses against Mervin made no claim to being the type of people West Chester parents would be proud of. A West Chester State student testified that he had found Mervin's Warlock jacket in his front yard, and that Mervin, saying that Jonathan Henry had worn the jacket while assaulting a girl, had sworn vengeance. The student had long hair and a mustache; the only question he was asked by the defense attorney was one eliciting the admission that he knew some of the people against whom Mervin had brought charges of dealing in drugs. The fourth person present at the scene of the shooting—Eugene Moran, the tenant of the apartment where the shooting took place—testified that Mervin, with Saltzman's acquiescence, had shot Henry in cold blood; the assistant district attorney argued that the bullet angles supported Moran's story and made the Mervin-Saltzman version physically impossible. But Moran also admitted having told the grand jury that he remembered nothing about the crime; he said he had been threatened by Mervin and Saltzman and was terrified of talking. Moran, a thin man in his thirties who was wearing a suit that seemed too large, had been to college and was said to be fond of discussing philosophy—although on the night in question he happened to be speechless from over-consumption of Southern Comfort and water. He didn't look in the least collegiate.

Jonathan Henry, as described in court, seemed even more disreputable than those who had testified that he might have been murdered. Michael Thompson, a Warlock who appeared in a kind of Hitler mustache, took the stand to describe how he and Henry spent their days. Henry would come by for him every day about three or four in the afternoon, and then they would "just ride around, get some beer and drink, do anything we wanted to, really." Thompson said they occasionally dealt in LSD, in a minor way, for gas money. The proprietor of a bar frequented by the Warlocks testified that Henry had waved a gun around, threatening people the night before he died. Mervin testified that Henry had bragged to him about shooting someone—or, as Mervin put it, about having to "dust somebody off."

Henry, in fact, sounded remarkably like the description that West Chester State students offer of John Mervin. But after a week's testimony the assistant district attorney was under no illusions about being able to persuade the jury that John Mervin was anything but a decent young officer who had once been obliged to pretend to be like Jonathan Henry. After reminding the jury that they were not trying "the police or police in general or the issue of Support Your Local Police," the assistant district attorney further reminded them that neither sympathy nor prejudice should affect a jury's decision—and the sympathy and prejudice he was talking about was sympathy for John Mervin, a young college student, and prejudice against Jonathan Henry, a violent drug peddler. The judge repeated the admonition in his charge: "We are not here concerned with whether Henry deserved to live."

It took the jury approximately twenty-five minutes to reach a verdict of not guilty. Afterward, in the corridor, the jurors were having a final chat with each other when Mervin walked by, holding hands with a pretty girl. A number of the jurors walked up to shake his hand and pat him on the back and wish him luck. "Thank you. Thank you, sir," Mervin said to one of them. They smiled at him as he walked on down the corridor—a nice-looking, neatly dressed, polite young man who did look as if he had always been clean.

# TRAVELING PEOPLE

# A Traveling Person on a Beautiful Place

When the Boeing 747 was introduced on transcontinental air service, the great advantage I saw in it was that it didn't stop at O'Hare Airport. More planes land at O'Hare, in Chicago, then at any other airport in the world, and I'm usually on them. Reading about the immense sums that airlines were spending at Kennedy Airport for ground facilities large enough to handle a two-hundred-and-thirty-foot airplane, I even allowed myself to believe that the 747 might be *unable* to stop at O'Hare. Although the traffic at O'Hare is supposedly caused by Chicago's importance as an airline-connection point, I have come to believe that a plane that *can* land at O'Hare usually does—as if some gravitational pull were being exerted by the man in charge of keeping up the takeoff-and-landing statistics. I have also come to believe that planes land at O'Hare more often than they take off. Traveling People talk almost as much about waiting at O'Hare as we do about being stacked up over Kennedy or about narrowly escaping a violent end at the hands of a small feeder line. When the 747 was introduced, I was only mildly interested in American's claim that its plane was a beautiful place or in T.W.A.'s claim that its plane was the roomiest of all because of having seats for a mere three hundred and forty-two passengers instead of three hundred and sixty-one; the only piece of advertising copy that could have won my allegiance was "This plane will under no circumstances stop at O'Hare Airport." Even if I were riding on a beautiful place, coming within a couple of hundred air miles of O'Hare would still cause me to think of nothing but lugging my suitcase through the thirty-seven miles of corridor that the airport designer managed to place between any two airlines that could be shown to have more than one connecting flight a month. (Traveling People never check their luggage.) The thought of being able to frolic in the aisles of a T.W.A. 747 where nineteen seats might have been means nothing to a man who is sitting in one of O'Hare's bleak waiting rooms thinking about how he could have at least watched a travelogue if he had been stuck in the Minneapolis-St. Paul airport, or could have at least played the pinball machines if he had been held over in New Orleans. (Traveling People don't demand the Bright Lights.) One night, when I fell asleep on a flight that I thought went nonstop from Denver to New York, I was shaken awake at about 2 A.M. by a hostess who told me we were at O'Hare and that because of some mechanical difficulties we had to change to another aircraft. (Hostesses never call airplanes airplanes.) I walked into the empty corridors of O'Hare and, in one of those sudden realizations that can come in the middle of the night, I knew that it was my one and true home. I stop in New York to see my family, and I visit other cities, but I always go back home to O'Hare to sit in the black chairs in the waiting rooms and try to find something of interest in the Chicago *Tribune*. T.W.A. has been talking about starting 747 flights there this spring.

I discovered that fact when I decided to investigate the 747 on behalf of other Traveling People, by flying on one to Los Angeles and back. There has been a lot of talk lately, particularly among radicals, about people searching for a sense of community, and it has caused me to realize that I feel a sense of community with lecturers and sales representatives and auditors from the regional office and attenders of conferences and management consultants and, of course, people who spend a lot of time crossing state lines in order to incite riots. Many of them are unable to investigate the 747 for themselves because many Traveling People don't like to ride in a new airplane until it has been tried out on the general public for six months. When I announced my travel plans to a friend of mine, who is a Traveling Person and a strong believer in the six-month theory, he told me that, by coincidence, he had to go to Los Angeles himself at about the same time. "It's too bad we can't go out on the same flight," he said. "But a rule's a rule."

A Traveling Person ordinarily demonstrates no strong preference among airlines except for regularly swearing off one line or another forever—a permanent boycott that lasts until the Traveling Person, having to go someplace only the offending airline goes, grudgingly checks in, half hoping for an unconscionable delay that he can add to his list of atrocity stories. Three airlines have nonstop flights between New York and Los Angeles—flights that have in common, among other things, an embarrassing paucity of passengers. As it happens, there are not now enough people traveling between New York and Los Angeles to justify larger (and more expensive) planes, particularly considering the fact that those who do go— mostly Traveling People—would grumble at having less frequent flights. But when one airline tries to soak up a large share of the peak-hour market with a 747, the competition has to match it with a 747, providing even more superfluous seats. The marketing vice- president of T.W.A., which started transcontinental 747 flights in late February, told me that, as a matter of survival, American and United obviously had to order 747s because T.W.A. had ordered them.

"And why did T.W.A. order them?" I asked.

"Because Pan Am ordered them," he said, looking unhappy.

I shook my head in sympathy. A couple of days before, in a *Wall Street Journal* article about widespread financial problems in the industry, I read that T.W.A. had switched to domestic china for its first-class passengers in order to save on import duty. American, the only other airline that offered me 747 service to Los Angeles, also has some call on a Traveling Person's sympathy: like United, it has not received delivery on its 747s, and the one beautiful place it operates was leased from Pan American. There is something poi- gnant about calling somebody else's beautiful place your own, but there is something even more poignant about scrimping on the china. I decided to fly T.W.A.

As part of its attempt to win the competition for the New York-

Los Angeles market—or at least to destroy itself in the attempt less abruptly than its competitors do—T.W.A. offers all passengers a choice of two films, a marketing device that American has countered by offering even coach passengers a choice of three main courses. (Among airline marketing people, there is a theory that passengers may be lured by offering them alternatives, even if, as in the case of the food traditionally served in the coach section, all of the alternatives are likely to be unpleasant.) The "mature" movie on my flight was "Butch Cassidy and the Sundance Kid," which I had seen, and the "general audience" movie was "Downhill Racer." When I told the reservations clerk that I preferred a seat in the "Downhill Racer" section, I thought I caught a trace of condescension in her "All right, sir." Who among Traveling People sees the general-audience movie except prigs and sissies?

"General audience?" the T.W.A. man at the color-keyed general-audience desk said when I arrived at the gate at Kennedy on the agreed afternoon.

"I've seen the mature movie," I said, trying to sound casual about it. "I've already seen it."

He looked me up and down as if he could tell a confirmed general-audience type by appearance alone. I thought about telling him that I had also seen "Midnight Cowboy," which happens to be rated X, but instead I said, "Also, I'm interested in skiing." A lie.

I don't think he knew I was a Traveling Person, because I was going coach class and had checked my suitcase—both of which customs are about as popular among Traveling People as the DC-3. The man at the special 747 check-in counter had assured me that the use of containers and two carrousels made unloading a 747 just as fast as unloading any other plane, but he could see the dread in my eyes—the knowledge that anyone who checks a suitcase to Los Angeles may wait an extra hour at the Los Angeles airport only to find out that his suitcase is safe at O'Hare. But I do know some salesmen—members of my community—who *have* to check sample cases that are too large to be carried aboard. I've had many pleasant conversations with them—leisurely discussions over pre-cooked steak about such matters as whether Newark tends to close during snowy weather before LaGuardia—and I felt obligated to look into the baggage-checking operation on their behalf. There are also a number of Traveling People who sometimes find themselves traveling in the coach section, ordinarily because the first-class seats have all been taken by other Traveling People. The *Aviation Week* report on American's first 747 flights to Los Angeles said that one delay in loading had been caused by an unmovable knot of passengers whose first-class reservations had not been honored because of overbooking. I could sympathize with those who failed to get justice done—who snatched up their under-the-seat one-suiters and shouldered their blue plastic clothes bags and walked into the plane knowing they would have to make do with coach.

Because of the preference of Traveling People for first class, anyone who wants to stretch out over surrounding seats in a 747 is actually better off in the coach section—at least until the summer, when airplanes are full of people who pay for their own seats, nondeductibly. In the coach section, I was alone in my row of what I had taken to be four-abreast seats until I read in the T.W.A. brochure that it was "a double set of two-abreast seats." To a Traveling Person, the inside of a 747 looks like the inside of an ordinary airplane that is somewhat bigger than life-size—like a conventionally proportioned baby who happens to be five feet six. There are some minor novelties—overhead racks that close during the flight, protecting a passenger's raincoat from the curious stares of strangers, and one of those nozzle-like multi-beverage dispensers that I have always associated with bad bars, and a personalized inflatable lumbar support, which, I'm embarrassed to say, does not seem to inflate to the contours of my personal lumbar. But a Traveling Person feels at home immediately. The lady on the public-address system who claims to be the flight service director sounds exactly like a hostess. The captain uses his familiar Midwestern accent in the familiarly comforting way to make announcements like "We're doin' real fine up here; we hope you're doin' real fine back there." Traveling People have easily adjusted several times to a plane that seems double the size of the last plane, but if the captain's voice ever came over the public-address system in a Brooklyn accent there would probably be panic in the aisles.

The double aisles in a 747 do lead people to walk around and chat for a while after takeoff, but, possibly because there are about sixty first-class seats available, there weren't very many Traveling

People in the coach section to chat with. I thought about sneaking up to first class to tell a salesman or two a feeder-line story that I had just remembered from a conversation I once had with a Dow recruiter. I didn't think the people in coach—family groups, soldiers, a couple of children with flash cameras—would appreciate it. As the Dow man tells it, one of those six- or eight-passenger planes that seat a passenger next to the pilot was over the airport, and there was trouble getting the landing gear down. Finally, the pilot turned to the Dow executive sitting next to him and said, "Could you get the manual out of that pocket on the door there and look under 'L'?"

The irony of my embarrassment about the movies, it occurred to me as I sat staring at a mural of a Spanish castle that divided me from some of the mature-movie people, was that I have never remained awake through an entire movie on an airplane. Traveling People often fall asleep on planes—having maneuvered a rental car over an unfamiliar and unmarked route to the airport, tossed the keys to the rental-car clerk while rushing to the airline counter, tried to make last-minute phone calls in a booth crammed with the two armloads of belongings that a non-checker has to carry aboard, and then settled into a period of imposed peace that is presided over by a calm man with a Midwestern accent. The movies add to the peacefulness, particularly if the airline uses a series of small screens —screens that make the experience so much like watching the late-show television movie in bed that I always fall asleep within ten minutes, vaguely wondering whether somebody remembered to put out the garbage. After dinner, a hostess walked to the mural, flipped open a panel to get to a crank, and cranked the Spanish castle away, exposing a movie screen. Another hostess announced that we should turn the controls of our head sets to Channel 1 for our movie or to Channel 12 if we wanted to hear the movie being shown in the next compartment—the custom of providing passengers with alternatives apparently having extended to a consideration of those people who happen to enjoy looking at one movie while listening to the sound track of another. Even on Channel 1, the sound track of "Downhill Racer" sounded like another movie— one of those Second World War films in which the radio operator is trying to pick up Battalion to call for reinforcements but can only get static. The hostess announced apologetically that the sound system was broken and could not be repaired during flight. "Typical, typical," the man in front of me said to himself, and I realized, as I drifted off to sleep, that there was at least one other Traveling Person in the coach section.

When I woke up, we were about to land in Los Angeles. I looked at my watch and saw that we were right on schedule at fifteen minutes after midnight—New York time, of course. Although Traveling People are beyond superstition and long ago conquered any fear of flying, I happen to know that setting my watch ahead during a flight could cause a crash. Or at least not setting it ahead has always prevented one.

After a day in Los Angeles, I still couldn't get over the presence of my suitcase. Occasionally, I would open the closet door of my hotel room and gaze at it, amazed and grateful that it had actually been at my assigned carrousel by the time my rental-car agreement was filled out. The Los Angeles radio reported that one 747 departure to New York had been delayed by a bomb scare, reminding me that on the way into the plane at Kennedy a man just outside the door had been pointing an odd-looking device at everyone's under-the-seat one-suiter. (The mysterious destruction of 747s would be embarrassing to the airlines, of course, since the investigating detectives, after consideration of who might have a motive, would obviously confront the vice-presidents for finance of T.W.A., American, and United and accuse them of conspiring to have the deeds done.) The announcement of the bomb scare was quickly balanced by an advertisement for American's 747—a soothing voice stating that every morning at eight-forty-five a beautiful place leaves for New York. (Eight-forty-five is, oddly enough, precisely the moment T.W.A.'s beautiful place leaves for New York—oddly enough because Los Angeles has only one runway available to beautiful places.) I had a reservation on T.W.A.—first class—but on coast-to-coast flights I'm always ready to defect if another airline offers a movie that might keep me awake longer. The girl at American told me that I could have a coach seat any time but first class was sold out for the next two weeks.

"Two weeks!" I said.

"Well," she said, in an attempt to explain, "it's a new luxury."

I called T.W.A. and asked for the seat closest to the 747's most renowned architectural feature—the spiral staircase that leads from the first-class section to an upstairs bar. Some friends of mine who had taken the 747 to Los Angeles went first class and had warned me that the bar, which holds only fifteen people, is quickly filled to capacity. I looked forward to the upstairs bar as a place where Traveling People could get together, have a drink, and talk about Quality Courts or Best Western Motels or Holiday Inns. I had saved a good stack-up story for the trip. A lecturer told me that he was once on a plane that circled over Los Angeles for three hours, got low on fuel, landed at San Diego, refueled, and started circling over Los Angeles again. I was in a conversational mood. I had decided that I could report to the salesmen about bag-checking facilities without taking the chance of checking my suitcase on the way back to New York, the trip out having provided what social scientists call a fifty-per-cent sampling. I wasn't worried about bombs, because the management had provided me with a number of small, manageable anxieties to take my mind off bombs: Will I get to the bar before fifteen other people do? Will they limit passengers to two drinks even at the bar? Will the sound on the movie work? Have I been spotted as someone who preferred the general-audience movie twice in a row? Is the T.W.A. terminal at Kennedy any more likely to have enough cabs for three hundred and forty-two people than it is to have enough cabs for three hundred and sixty-one people?

As soon as the seat-belt sign went off, I bolted for the spiral staircase. I was the first one in the bar, and I felt a great sense of accomplishment. A Traveling Person gets that way. I know salesmen who would rather beat everyone to the rental-car counter than make a sale. After a few minutes, I still seemed to be alone. I looked at my watch. It was eight-fifty-five in the morning. What was I doing in a bar at eight-fifty-five in the morning? Finally, a young couple came up and looked out the window of the bar at the view, the way people used to look out from the observation bubbles on the tops of cross-country trains. "Will you *look* at that view!" the man said to his wife, apparently having seen something from twenty thousand and fifteen feet that he couldn't see from twenty thousand. They weren't Traveling People. I waited a few more minutes, and nobody came. Then a little girl came up the spiral staircase and took a picture of us with her flash camera.

# World's Strongest Man

Paul Anderson, World's Strongest Man, lives in a little town named Vidalia, Georgia. Atlanta is about a hundred and seventy miles away, and Anderson drives there routinely to catch airplanes. He enjoys highway driving. When he has a speaking engagement in some town like Jackson, or even Shreveport, he sometimes drives all the way there, gives his speech, and drives all the way back. On the front seat of his car he has an attachment called a car desk—a kind of tin cabinet that provides a flat surface for a clipboard and a place to lock up a tape recorder. Often, thoughts come to him while he's driving, and he scribbles them down, or talks them into the tape recorder. Occasionally, he thinks of a poem, and pulls off the highway for a while to write it. One morning this month, Anderson arrived at the Atlanta airport from Vidalia before nine, stopped to pick up a valet-parking attendant, and then drove on to the departure area, where a redcap greeted him by name and took his suitcase. Anderson doesn't carry much equipment with him. He takes along a dumbbell bar, and he asks the sponsors of his appearance to round up some weights for it at a local gym. He also carries a couple of one-inch boards and a twenty-penny nail to drive through them with his bare hand. A full-size barbell with weights would present a problem for air travel, and Anderson has found that lifting part of the audience is much more impressive than lifting a barbell anyway; he sends ahead a plan for building a wooden platform that will seat eight people. When he used to demonstrate his strength by hoisting a huge barbell above his head, someone would invariably come up at the end of the performance, lift one end of the barbell off the ground, and proclaim that it wasn't terribly heavy after all. "I can't understand that," Anderson says. "When a violinist gets through with a concert, nobody comes up and starts playing his violin."

Anderson is five feet ten and weighs about three hundred and seventy-five pounds; he is never mistaken for anyone else. In Atlanta, he was wearing a lightweight blue suit, a white turtleneck shirt, sunglasses, and a pair of black Western-style boots. As he walked through the terminal, just about anyone who glanced at him kept looking. At first glance, he looks like a huge fat man. He has an immense, soft-looking stomach, and he walks with a rolling gait somewhere between a swagger and a waddle—probably because of the fact that his thighs are thirty-six inches around, about the size of the average man's waist. But at second glance, when the thickness of his neck and the breadth of his back become apparent, it is obvious that he is not exactly a fat man. Some people recognize him as Paul Anderson, World's Strongest Man. He usually chats in a relaxed way with those who approach him. He has the accent common to people who were raised around north Georgia and east Tennessee, and he sometimes sounds very colloquial—talking about being "just an old country boy" or mentioning a family that was "so sorry they wouldn't take a good lick at a snake"—the way Southern politicians sound when telling stump anecdotes to reporters, or the way James Dickey sounds when introducing a poem to an audience of New York intellectuals.

"Any athlete has a great ego and wants to be recognized," Anderson has said, but he would be much happier if fewer of the people who recognize him asked him how much he can lift. "That's the first thing everybody asks," he says. " 'How much can you lift? How much can you lift?' If I tell them—six thousand two hundred and seventy pounds—they don't believe it, and then they get mad.

They say, 'I just asked a simple question.' " Sometimes when attendants at a filling station notice the name on his credit card, they ask him to lift up one end of the car. Like the Fastest Gun in the West, the World's Strongest Man has a talent that ordinary men want to see proved. Anderson might be plagued by drunks approaching him in bars to hurl arm-wrestling challenges except that, being a strict Christian of the anti-saloon turn of mind, he doesn't frequent bars. Once, in Beirut, Lebanon, a local champion insisted that Anderson try out a form of wrestling in which the opponents lock fingers and try to pull each other over a table. Handicapped by the language barrier, Anderson confused the game with an old high-school pastime that called for twisting rather than pulling, and he broke the Lebanese champion's finger. Anderson was in amateur competition for only a couple of years—during which time he won the heavyweight weight-lifting championship at the 1956 Olympic Games, in Melbourne—but, he says, "I stay ahead of the whole amateur world. Just ego, I guess. But when I'm introduced as the World's Strongest Man I want it to be true." Only rarely does anybody object to the title. "I've had people to write after I've been on TV and say, 'He's not the World's Strongest Man, someone else is,' " Anderson says. "But it's always someone who can bite a dime in two, or something. In the legitimate weight-lifting world, they know who can lift what."

Anderson boarded a jet for Indianapolis. He had a speaking engagement at Marion College, about eighty miles from there. Being the World's Strongest Man, like being the Fastest Gun in the West, is not easily translatable into a trade. In fact, Anderson had a few false starts after he gave up his amateur standing in 1956, to begin a night-club act. He says that it was "a real good act, with a comedian as m.c. and professional choreography and all," but that Las Vegas and Reno were about the only places that could handle such an act at the time, and, as a Christian, he didn't feel particularly comfortable in a night club anyway. He also wrestled for a while, and even had a fling at boxing—a fling that the press, to Anderson's irritation, tended to treat as something of a joke. In recent years, he has been making personal appearances, mostly at colleges and churches; occasionally he does a television commercial. He estimates that he makes about five hundred appearances a year. He slips easily into his stage presence—a dramatic delivery in the style of a revivalist sermon or a Fourth of July oration. Occasionally, in ordinary conversation, he'll explain that something he saw or something he read in the newspaper got him to thinking and that he sat down—or pulled off the highway—and wrote a poem about it, and that "it went something like this." Then he'll lean back a bit, gaze out into space, and begin to recite something like

> Satan said, "I am so successful because I have disciples who are constantly on the public scene."
> He said, "To gain converts I use my Communist leaders, the young atheist, and often some movie queen."

Those who engage Anderson for the evening get not only a dramatic speech and an even more dramatic demonstration of strength but also an opportunity to support a worthy cause. In Vidalia, Anderson presides over the Paul Anderson Youth Home. His contract with the local businessmen who serve on his board of directors calls for him to donate all of his earnings—which he estimates at about forty thousand dollars a year—to the home, which, in turn, pays his living expenses and a stipend of two hundred dollars a month. Anderson has always wanted to provide a real home, rather than an institution, for teen-agers who would otherwise have to go to a reformatory or who merely have no other home. In Vidalia, he, his wife and child, two other couples who work for the home, and fifteen or so teen-age boys live more or less like an exceptionally large, well-provided-for family. The Andersons themselves live in a large farmhouse that has been modernized and redecorated. There is a second house and a modern brick "cottage" for the boys, as well as a swimming pool, two patios, fifty-six acres of land, some horses, a makeshift gymnasium for Anderson's weights, and an office in a mobile home that somebody donated. Olympic medals and weight-lifting plaques hang in the dining room of the Andersons' house, where the boys eat in shifts; on the walls of the office are a resolution of congratulations from the Georgia state legislature, a certificate for winning the Olympic championship, and a framed letter from Toccoa, Georgia, where Anderson used to live, that begins, "Dear Paul: The congregation of the First Baptist Church unanimously voted an expression of commendation for your refusal to give testimony for VODKA, as explained in a story by Furman Bisher in the Atlanta paper."

Anderson is away from the home more than he's there, and he usually tries to save some days in January to catch up on his paperwork. The offer from Marion College did not include as much money as he likes to make on a trip that requires most of two days. But the Marion athletic director had been persistent, and he seemed to be a committed Christian and someone interested in the Fellowship of Christian Athletes, an organization that Anderson is sufficiently fond of to have honored with a poem. Also, Anderson likes to speak, particularly to college students. He has even gone to Daytona Beach during spring vacation "to witness to the kids on the beach," accompanied by a few fellow-athletes and a jazz band. "Some of them were hollering and raising a lot of Cain, and all such," he says. "But those kids are searching, and when someone with the other side of the picture comes along, projecting the real meaning of Christ, they'll listen."

Anderson is a Methodist himself, but not an advocate of the social gospel that some Methodists emphasize. "Christ said the poor will be with us forever," he says. "He didn't try to overthrow the Roman Empire. He preached love and salvation. When I see a preacher walking up and down the street with a sign, I know he failed in the pulpit. If you project Christ, the social problems take care of themselves." He is critical of church groups that have supported civil-rights workers—he believes that people in the South (or in South Africa, for that matter) ought to be left to take care of their own problems—although he says he is personally not interested in the color of a man's skin. (The Paul Anderson Youth Home is all white except for a Nez Percé Indian, but Anderson's wife works with some women from her church on an integrated preschool program for poor children in Vidalia.) Anderson is an outspoken believer in respectable appearance and respect for authority and, particularly, love of country. The boys at the home are clean-cut, well dressed and well-mannered. Anderson believes that too many of the old virtues have been forgotten.

The Marion *Chronicle-Tribune* had an item announcing that Paul Anderson, "billed as the World's Strongest Man," would be in town that night to provide "a 'kickoff' for a basketball tournament" of Wesleyan-affiliated colleges. Marion is the international headquarters of the Wesleyan Methodists—a denomination that split off from the regular Methodists in the nineteenth century in order to pursue a zealous abolitionism but that eventually became more conservative than the other Methodists, particularly in matters of personal conduct. Anderson had driven from Indianapolis to Marion in a rental car, eaten lunch at his motel, and gone to sleep. When the Marion College athletic director, a very serious-looking young man named Paul Mills, came by to pick him up that evening, he had changed into a white polo shirt and a black warmup outfit with his initials on it. He still wore his boots.

Anderson had thought that the program was going to be in a gymnasium, but it turned out to be in a church—a modern brick building next to the campus. There were already some people in the pews when Anderson arrived, unloaded his equipment, glanced casually at a lifting platform that had been built to his specifications, and began to load weights on his dumbbell bar. One man came up for an autograph—Anderson signed "Your friend in Christ, Paul Anderson"—and a husky young man was brought up by Mills and introduced as a fellow weight lifter.

"Could I ask how often you work out?" the young man said. "Three times a week?"

"No, about once a week," Anderson said. "Being a little older—and a little stronger, it seems—I get a lot more out of a workout." Anderson's study of strong men has led him to believe that he will not have his greatest strength until the age of about forty, a theory that gives him four years to become even stronger.

"Did you bulk up like Randall—eat two dozen eggs, and that sort of thing?" the young man asked.

"Well, not to be egotistical, Randall bulked up when he saw me," Anderson said. "He figured I had a lot of bulk and lifted a lot of weights, and he thought he'd bulk up and then *he'd* lift a lot of weights, too, but it didn't work out that way. He never told me what he ate, but I heard he was drinking sixteen quarts of milk a day."

"Too bad you can't get back your amateur standing," the young man said, after he had found out how Anderson had been doing in the three Olympic lifts.

"Well, I don't want to do that, really," Anderson said. "I got this home to support. Really, I am an amateur in a way. I never used any of the money for myself."

The program was sponsored by T-CAY-O—the church's College Age Youth Organization. At times it seemed to be a pep rally and at times a church service. The T-CAY-O Brass—a combo of three trumpets, three trombones, a piano, and a set of drums—played a couple of numbers, the kind of songs that are sometimes heard at outdoor bandstands in the summer. Then the T-CAY-O adviser, a small man who was wearing a bright-red vest, came to the pulpit and said, "In keeping with the motto of Marion College, 'First Things First,' we felt it was only appropriate that at the start of our athletic endeavors we should start with an evening of honoring our athletes and the Lord Jesus Christ—not in that order, of course." The congregation sang two hymns, led by a member of the soccer team; members of the various teams and alumni of the various participating colleges were asked to stand, and then Mills introduced Anderson, saying that the World's Strongest Man would "share some of his experiences, demonstrate the strength that the Lord has given him and the power within his own soul." Anderson first demonstrated the strength. Including a few jokes in a running description of what he would attempt to do, he began by wrapping a nail in a handkerchief and driving it through the two boards. He did a few side presses with a dumbbell, after pointing out that the side press was the specialty of the old-time strong man Louis Cyr, who used a little less weight. Then Anderson invited eight young men to sit on the homemade platform, squatted under it, placed his hands on his knees, and, after a couple of starts to get the proper balance, lifted it several inches off the ground. The congregation gasped.

After a prayer, a collection, and a couple of songs by the T-CAY-O Ensemble, Anderson returned to the microphone to give his speech. He emphasized the necessity of becoming involved—with the community and with Jesus Christ. "Three billion people or more on the face of the earth and they call me the Strongest Man in the World," Anderson said. "I say these things not to impress you but to make a point. The point is this: my athletic career is thrilling —it's a thrill to be an Olympic champion—but the greatest thing in my life is being a Christian, having the opportunity to stand up and witness for Jesus Christ." He told the audience how much they had to be thankful for in America, how much poverty and suffering he had seen in places like India and Korea. He ended with a poem— one that he has recorded, on his own Strength label, and sent to friends. By way of introduction, he told how he usually drives by the White House when in Washington, and how, on one occasion, he had been sickened at seeing there a group of protesters. "The worst-looking people I ever saw," he said. "Dirty. Filthy. They have the right to protest, but I don't think they knew what they were protesting." He had driven on to Arlington Cemetery, he said, thinking of the protesters, and at Arlington he had pulled over to the side of the road and written some rhyming words, and some of them went something like this:

> I hear an awesome moan, and for the knowledge of its source I do not have to crave.
> It's an unknown soldier or some past patriot turning in his grave. . . .
> They are tormented by those who belong to a strange and modern cult,
> Whose morals and lack of patriotism would men like Hale and Henry insult.
> This group tells us that we need a new standard of freedom and for our traditions we should not fight.
> By them we are told there is no God and that no one has seen the light.
> So say these "children of the flowers," "hippies," and "smokers of the pot."
> But if they would study our glorious heritage, I am sure that they would learn a lot. . . .
> These pacifists seldom bathe or groom and grow extremely long hair.

I just wonder if they know why Washington crossed the Dela-
ware. . . .
Some of them, bordering on treason, their draft cards they do
burn.
Could they be ignorant that to the Philippines MacArthur did re-
turn?
As they picket our Selective Service, displaying their lack of guts,
Are they aware that, when asked to surrender at Bastogne, Mc-
Auliffe answered "Nuts"? . . .

Anderson is particularly appalled by hippies—"young people
who were taught they came from animals and grew up to live like
animals"—but he also finds himself becoming irritated quite often
with such conventional segments of society as the press. "It seems
like when anyone on the conservative side becomes prominent—if
he believes in the old-fashioned idea that this is a republic rather
than a democracy—he's attacked as a fanatic or radical," he says.
"That's how the other side operates." Anderson himself tries to be
affirmative rather than negative. "I'm no fanatic," he has said,
"but, well, I'm sort of a patriot."

# Always Be Polite

Arthur Shaw arrived at the Yale Student Placement Bureau at eight-thirty in the morning. He makes it a practice to arrive at a placement office about half an hour before his first appointment, giving himself time to arrange his forms in a convenient spot on the desk, place his watch where he can glance at it quickly during an interview, and put his nameplate—"Art Shaw, Dow"—where students can see it, so they won't have to grope for his name. Also, he prefers to arrive before the demonstrators do. He expected some demonstrators at Yale. In the normal routine, a few days before a Dow Chemical Company recruiter is scheduled to arrive on a campus Shaw's secretary phones the placement office to confirm the date and to find out how many students in each discipline have signed up for interviews. These days, just as routinely, Shaw, who is both a recruiter and the supervisor of recruiting for the Northeast, gets on the telephone himself at one point to find out if a demonstration is likely. He asks about the university rules that will govern the demonstrators' behavior, he makes certain that the university president has been informed, and he says, as diplomatically as possible, that although Dow will be happy to abide by any arrangements the university makes, it has been the recruiters' experience that a demonstration often gets out of hand if the demonstrators are permitted inside the building. If it seems likely that there will be a particularly vehement demonstration, Shaw arranges for someone from Dow's public-relations department to be present, thus permitting the recruiter to concentrate on his interviewing without distractions from reporters.

Three campus policemen were standing just inside the door of the Yale Student Placement Bureau when Shaw arrived, but there were no demonstrators. Ordinarily, demonstrators are not certain enough of Shaw's identity to say anything when he walks in anyway, although he looks suspiciously like a Dow recruiter. A serious-looking young man of twenty-five, with close-cropped red hair, he was wearing heavy horn-rimmed glasses, a neat three-button business suit, a button-down shirt, and a striped tie. He had a wedding ring on one hand and a state-university class ring on the other, and he was carrying a gray fiber-glass attaché case that looked almost too thin to hold anything. In the room assigned to him, on the ground floor of the placement office, Shaw and a university official cleared some supplies out so he could bring in a chair for the interviewees—the room considered least vulnerable to harassment from outside happened to be only five by eight—and Shaw arranged things on the desk to his satisfaction. Just before nine, a Student Placement official told him that pickets had gathered in front of the building; there were about thirty-five of them, huddled under umbrellas against a cold drizzle that had begun to fall, and holding signs like "Better Dying Through Chemistry." Shaw thanked his informant courteously, but he seemed only mildly interested.

In half-hour interviews from nine to eleven, Shaw talked with four students about working for Dow. He called each of the students by his first name, and he repeated the name often as—in a friendly but businesslike way—he asked about outside interests or outlined the first few years of a typical new employee in marketing or told of the pleasures of life in Midland, Michigan, where Dow has its corporate headquarters. The subject of demonstrations came up only at the close of an interview, when Shaw would smile and say that he hoped the student hadn't had too much trouble getting in.

Shaw's last appointment before lunch was with a young man who had been described to him as the undergraduate leader of the Yale chapter of Students for a Democratic Society, but the S.D.S. man did not appear. Shaw joined two or three placement officials in a larger office and spent some time going through résumés of prospective summer employees with a woman in charge of summer placement (who said that she had phoned the S.D.S. leader and informed him that not keeping appointments was bad manners). There were still campus policemen in the hall, but someone said that the demonstrators had been gone for an hour—they were driven away when the drizzle turned into a driving rain—and everyone seemed relaxed.

Suddenly, flames shot up in the hallway outside the office. The placement officials rushed to the door. A wastebasket had been placed in front of the door, and its contents were blazing. A few feet from the basket stood a young man—thin, blond, collegiately dressed. He had a book of matches in his hand. His face was slightly flushed. He looked rather frightened.

"Why'd you do this?" a young assistant dean asked him, in a calm voice. "I'm curious about the symbolism." A campus policeman, looking perturbed, had dragged over an extinguisher and was putting out the fire. Shaw had remained inside the room.

"Fire and fire," the young man said. "I think the symbolism is pretty good."

At lunch, the assistant dean told Shaw and a recruiter from a management-consultant firm that a talk with the young man had convinced him that the wastebasket fire had indeed been meant as a piece of symbolism, rather than as a way of harming anybody. "It was obviously an act of conscience," the dean said. "He just felt he had to burn some Dow literature. He's a nice kid."

Shaw did not seem as impressed by the symbolism as the dean was—a check before lunch had indicated that the fire consisted of all of the mechanical- and chemical-engineering booklets he had placed in the waiting room—but he didn't disagree.

"It's funny," the recruiter from the consulting company said. "We do a lot of consulting for the Defense Department. I guess nobody knows."

"Don't let it out," Shaw said.

In the afternoon, Shaw began another series of interviews—describing plant sites and travel requirements and salaries, and asking if there were any questions about Dow.

"There's one thing," the first interviewee of the afternoon said, somewhat hesitantly, at the close of the interview. "If I were in marketing, and so on and so forth, is there a chance for a draft deferment, and so on and so forth?"

"Well, we've been real successful so far in getting our people deferred, Dave," Shaw said. "Both technical and non-technical. Of course, no company can guarantee anything on this."

The student looked impressed.

Shaw's schedule showed that the second appointment of the afternoon was with a Miss Alexander, a graduate student in American studies. She turned out to be a friendly-looking, dark-haired girl who began the interview by commiserating with Shaw on the weather he was having during his trip to New Haven. Shaw said he was just happy to be there. Then Miss Alexander said she was wondering why bona-fide, tuition-paying students had been refused entrance to the building by campus police, and Shaw said she would have to ask the university officials.

"Could you tell me, Miss Alexander," he went on, "if you're interested in Dow workwise?"

"I'd be more interested in working for Dow if it weren't doing something criminal," she said. "I was wondering if a Dow employee could be prosecuted as a war criminal ten or fifteen years from now, under the precedent of Nuremberg." She didn't sound at all angry. She had a slight smile on her face, like the fixed smile of a lady trying to be polite while having tea with people she doesn't know very well.

"I assume you're talking about napalm," Shaw said.

"That, and crop defoliates," Miss Alexander said, almost pleasantly.

Shaw said that he didn't consider the situation analogous to that of the manufacturers prosecuted at Nuremberg, and they spoke for a while about whether a distinction could be made between napalm and such weapons as tanks and guns—or between gas pellets for concentration camps and howitzers.

"We are supplying the government with material, and the government decides how to use it," Shaw said. "I guess I'm saying that Dow made a decision to support our government and the long-term aims of our government, and I support this."

"Do you think this is what the German manufacturers thought?"

"I don't know what they thought," Shaw said. His voice was even, and he didn't sound offended. "Let's come back to Dow and you. Are you interested in Dow as an outlet for employment?"

"I'm interested in the moral position of working for Dow," Miss Alexander said, and she handed Shaw a picture of a burned baby. "I'm curious what goes through the head of a Dow employee when he sees some of these pictures."

Shaw said that while the picture was indeed horrible, war was horrible, and there was no pleasant way to die.

"Don't you think it's different?" Miss Alexander asked. "Don't you think there's a distinction when you use this against civilians?"

"I guess I'll have to say that the Secretary of Defense, Mr. McNamara, assures us that the product is used only against military targets," Shaw said.

"Does the company really believe this?" Miss Alexander asked. She still had a polite smile on her face.

"Well, Miss Alexander," Shaw said, "I guess I can only say that I feel as an employee of Dow that we're doing the right thing and that we've made the right decision. I'm proud to work at Dow."

Miss Alexander asked if there might ever be a time when Dow would dissociate itself from a government contract if the contract proved particularly repulsive, and Shaw said he couldn't speak for the company in that area, since he was at Yale only to discuss specific employment.

"Can you see any time that anything would be so repulsive to you personally that you couldn't work there?" she asked.

"Well, that hasn't come up," Shaw said. "I haven't thought of it. I'm not concerned about this possibility. I'm not concerned."

After about fifteen minutes, Shaw said that there seemed little more to discuss, and he asked Miss Alexander if she would be interested in an application.

"Yes, I would," Miss Alexander said, politely. "And, in case you don't have the S.D.S. statement, I'll leave you this." She smoothed out a mimeographed sheet that she had read from at one point during the interview—it was entitled "Dow's Four Horsemen: Destruction, Famine, Pestilence and Death"—and, apologizing for the fact that it had been smeared by the rain, gave it to Shaw.

"Real fine," Shaw said. "Thanks. Here's an application."

Miss Alexander took the application, thanked Shaw, and left the room.

GALES FERRY, CONNECTICUT

WEDNESDAY

Before driving out to the Dow plant at Gales Ferry, near Groton, Shaw called company headquarters in Midland from his motel to check on a recruiting trip scheduled for the New York State University at Buffalo the following week. Buffalo appointments had been postponed once, when there was reason to believe that recruiters might be in physical danger, and the university was still sufficiently concerned about maintaining order to request that Dow send an extra recruiter, so interviewing could be completed in one day. Shaw decided that he ought to consider sending a man from public relations with the recruiters to Buffalo.

Two of the plant managers at Gales Ferry had gone to the University of Connecticut as recruiters in October—the university had asked them to withdraw after students refused to let them enter the interviewing offices—and Shaw met with them in the morning to get their impression of the recruiting process in general and to "kick around a couple of ideas about napalm." One of the men gave a dispassionate account of being greeted by a mock funeral at Brown earlier in the week, and Shaw told about his interview with Miss Alexander. He predicted that more protesters might begin to show up on interviewing schedules—one recruiter at M.I.T. had been faced with seven in nine interviews—although most colleges are stricter than Yale about limiting interviews to students in the disciplines the recruiters are interested in, and radical chemical engineers are not easy to come by. He said a recruiter had no choice but to talk with a protester as long as employment was being discussed. "She was cagey enough not to ask why we're murdering babies," he said. "She was shrewd enough to ask questions like 'What moral decisions have you made about working at Dow?' or 'Could a person who works at Dow be prosecuted as a war criminal?'—really bordering on legitimate questions." The man who had been at Brown said that newspapers in recruiting areas ought to be informed of the company's policy on napalm in advance, and Shaw said that all local newspapers were sent a press kit just before any Dow recruiting visit.

There was also a meeting with some young men who were about to be used as recruiters for the first time. Shaw, who wrote his Master's thesis in business school on college recruiting, spoke about the advisability of going over résumés the night before, about how to fill out the interviewer's report, about the necessity of writing thank-you letters to placement officers, and, eventually, about napalm. "I think it's reasonable to assume that almost every campus will have a demonstration of some sort," he said. "Our approach as recruiters is, first of all, to avoid any direct confrontation. They want you to talk about Dow policy, but in my case I know I'm neither authorized nor qualified to discuss Dow policy. You should maintain a businesslike, professional attitude. Always be polite. If pressed by reporters, try to refer them to the corporate public-relations group in Midland. Basically, your approach should be that you're there as the guest of the university and the only reason you're on campus is to recruit. Remember, they won't get a statement from you if you don't want to give them a statement. In the final analysis, the things you have going for you are common sense and a cool head. As these kids say, don't lose your cool."

STORRS, CONNECTICUT
WEDNESDAY

Late in the afternoon, John Powers, the student-placement director of the University of Connecticut, gave Shaw the résumés of the students Dow would be interviewing the following day, and assured him that although demonstrators (or "the beatniks," as he called them) would probably be present, the university was now committed to the students' right to meet with bona-fide recruiters. "Let me tell you something," he said. "And I'm not being facetious. This is the best thing that ever happened to the placement office. You usually have to knock kids on the head to get them in here. Last year, we used to have six kids on a schedule. Now the schedules are full—twelve, thirteen people. The demonstration was not the only reason, but it was the biggest single reason. I'm beginning to think: Give me publicity—good or bad, just so it's publicity. Maybe your company will find the same thing in the long run."

"Well," Shaw said, "we *are* less of an unknown quantity now."

THURSDAY

Shaw and another recruiter, who had flown in from Midland, chatted in an interviewing room until just before nine, and then Shaw went to the door to call in the other recruiter's first appointment and to leave for some courtesy calls on university officials. Shaw and the other recruiter planned to fly to Midland together in the afternoon. When Shaw opened the door, he found twenty or so demonstrators sitting on the floor of the hallway. Only one person seemed seriously intent on blocking the door—a thin young man with a blond mustache, who sat directly in the doorway, his back to the room. He had the look of somebody consciously not speaking, as if he had taken a vow of silence. The student with an appointment jumped over the young man into the room, and Shaw tried to leave. "Excuse me," Shaw said, but the young man with the mustache swayed in whichever direction Shaw tried to move, and two other people were tentatively blocking his path with a banner that said "Dow Lights the Way for L.B.J. in S.E. Asia." Shaw went back into the room. He makes it a practice not to push people out of the way. (At Boston University, not long before, when a student lie-in covered the entire floor space in front of the interviewing room, Shaw declined to leave until a dean advised him that the only alternative was to spend the night. At that point, Shaw, after consultation with a Dow public-relations man, removed his shoes and walked out on top of the students into several inches of snow; he was accompanied by the dean and two policemen, who, apparently working without benefit of public-relations consultation, left their shoes on.)

A reporter for the campus paper had managed to get in with the interviewee, and began to ask Shaw questions while, a few feet away, the recruiter was asking the interviewee what type of job he was interested in. The door would not quite close, and the sound of conversation was coming in from the hallway.

"Did you expect trouble?" the reporter asked Shaw, holding a clipboard ready for the answer.

"We never expect any trouble," Shaw said, trying to keep his voice down. "We did expect a student demonstration."

In a few minutes, the provost and three other university officials arrived and picked their way through the demonstrators into the room. They greeted Shaw cordially, and he told them how happy he was to be at Connecticut. The other recruiter continued his interview. The provost led Shaw and the rest out of the room—everyone stepping over the young man in the doorway—and asked the dean of students to remain outside the door and make certain that students with appointments could get in. Shaw finished his talk with the student reporter in another room—he said he was neither authorized nor qualified to comment on company policy—and then he went to make his courtesy calls.

# Up with People!

Anyone who spends much time with the militantly wholesome young men and women who appear in *Up with People!*—a road show that ordinarily bills itself as "the world-famous Sing-Out explosion"—becomes accustomed to confessions of sinful pasts. I first read of the show when it was appearing in St. Louis and the *Globe-Democrat* ran an item headlined " 'UP WITH PEOPLE' PERFORMER RESCUED FROM FATE OF HIPPIES." The performer, shown in a picture, was a husky Negro from Baltimore described as a quarterback on his high-school football team, and he appeared less likely to end up in the East Village smoking pot than on the back cover of *Ebony* holding a bottle of Coca-Cola. But he told the interviewer that he had actually participated in anti-Vietnam war demonstrations and sit-ins, and that, at the rate he had been going, he might have drifted into hippiedom if *Up with People!* hadn't set him straight.

The first *Up with People!* performer I met in person told a story almost as shocking. My wife and I had gone to Long Island to see an outdoor performance of the show at a Catholic military academy, and after forty-five minutes of exuberant singing to the beat of a set of drums and four or five guitars, the first half ended with a chorus of the theme song:

"Up! Up with people!
You meet 'em wherever you go!
Up! Up with people!
They're the best kind of folks we know.
If more people were for people,
All people everywhere,
There'd be a lot less people to worry about,
And a lot more people who care!"

"Fair enough," my wife said. She had also reacted favorably to a song that went "We ain't great, we just concentrate on doing away with greed and hate." She expected the young man who announced intermission to say that the cast would take a short rest and be back, but instead he said that the cast would be right out to meet the audience. Thereupon, all the young people onstage—about a hundred and twenty of them—leaped from the risers they had been standing on and poured out toward the audience at a dead run. I could sense that my wife was about to bolt, but we held our ground. A blond young man managed to stop just before he crashed into us, stuck out his hand, introduced himself, and asked us how we liked the show.

My wife said something about admiring the performers' enthusiasm—even during numbers when nobody left his place on the risers the stage had been constantly alive with perfectly coodinated arm and body movements—and I asked the young man how he had happened to become involved in *Up with People!*

"Well, I was pretty much of a bum," he said. I looked at him more closely. He had short blond hair and the same broad smile that all of the performers had managed to retain even while singing. "I came home from college last year and I had long hair and rode a motorcycle and everything," he went on. "My mom took one look at me and told me to get a haircut."

"What did you do?" I asked.

"Well, I got a haircut, of course," he said. "But I was leading an aimless life."

"Some bum!" my wife said later. But after spending a few days with Cast B of *Up with People!* (it is one of three casts currently touring the country) I have decided that the blond young man did have a reasonably degenerate past, as *Up with People!*

pasts go. *Up with People!* is sponsored by Moral Re-Armament—which preaches that the world can be changed if every individual changes his own life and begins to aim at absolute standards of honesty, purity, unselfishness, and love—and there are not many reformed souls, even clean-cut sixteen-year-old reformed souls, who are unable to find something in their past to have reformed from. Looking back on his life, the typical *Up with People!* performer is at least contrite and occasionally appalled. It is not unusual to hear a cheerful and ostensibly well-behaved girl confess to such sins as cheating in high school, uncharitable behavior toward sisters and brothers, or sloppiness around the house.

"When I look back on what I was like then, I'm just disgusted," an awesomely polite young lady told me before one performance.

"You mean drinking and smoking and carrying on and all?" I asked.

"Well, I didn't drink or smoke," she said. "But I just did whatever the group did. I went to church, for instance, but it was strictly Sunday-go-to-meeting. It didn't mean a thing." She seemed to be suppressing a shudder.

I talked with one boy in the cast who managed to make regular high-school attendance sound vaguely degenerate. "I just went because it was expected of me," he said.

Although the *Up with People!* cast members who swoop off the stage toward the audience are friendly to anybody they happen to come across, they are primarily interested in inspiring other young people to form their own local sing-outs or to join one of the national casts—to become part of what they have just heard called "a tough, spirited force of men and women whose enthusiasm and purpose will rocket us into a new era." The show's managers say that the last time Cast B came through Chicago in September, it inspired the formation of seventeen local sing-outs by concentrating on playing high-school assemblies—or, as they would put it, by "reaching over eighty thousand students in seventy-two assemblies in five days." (*Up with People!* people are fond of statistics; as often as possible the cast is quartered in private homes, and an adult manager of the show once told me, in describing an *Up with People!* visit to Panama, "We lived in over six hundred homes in eleven cities in ten days.") Cast members often say that *Up with People!* is a demonstration, rather than a musical show, and its publicity sometimes refers to it as a revolution—"a revolt against the cynicism and moral relativism which have diluted the country's traditions." It is based on a philosophy that can easily be expressed in song lyrics. In "Freedom Isn't Free," the audience is told, "You got to pay a price,/ You got to sacrifice/ For your liberty." In another number, the young singers, their smiles temporarily replaced by thoughtful looks, ask, "What Color Is God's Skin?" and answer, "It's black, brown, it's yellow, it is red, it is white,/ Every man's the same in the good Lord's sight." The history of the country, *Up with People!* lyrics say, was based on faith and hard work, and, as for the future, when young people jar the world out of its "psychedelic stew" they will be able to go "harder, faster, higher in space/ Deeper in the sea,/ The greatest generation in history./ And banish forever hatred and fear,/ Famine and greed,/ Every last problem of humanity." Songs are sung celebrating the heroism of Paul Revere, Joan of Arc, and the 9th Infantry Division ("The Fighting Falcons —anytime, anywhere, bar nothin—/ Will show aggressors 'round the world that Uncle Sam ain't bluffin' "). One day, I asked one of the adults from Moral Re-Armament who travel with the cast how he accounted for the strong support among the youngsters for the American action in Vietnam. "Well," he said, "these kids know that freedom isn't free. You have to pay the price. You have to sacrifice." I caught myself about to start humming. *Up with People!* tunes are very catchy.

To a number of middle-aged citizens these days, the spectacle of a hundred and fifty or so joyful, clean-living, permanently smiling young people—the boys in neat blazers, the girls in jumpers down to their knees, and all of them singing songs of faith and patriotism —must seem like a mirage. When *Up with People!* comes into a town, it sometimes receives all of the enthusiasm that local business leaders have been saving for any indication that the country may not really be doomed to fall into the hands of a generation of radicals and hopheads. Cast A stopped in Dallas this fall, and the Dallas *Times Herald* ran a front-page editorial urging every citizen to attend. The *Times Herald* called the show "the antidote for hippies and peaceniks," but those who participate in *Up with People!*

believe it is far more than that. An article in "Sing-Out"—a book-let that provides local groups with the words, music, and motions to *Up with People!* songs—says, "A girl who gave up a $9,000 scholarship put it this way: 'This is a small price to pay for a part in saving civilization.' "

Although traveling with a musical show might strike some teen-agers in the audience as a pretty romantic business, the most common remark of cast members about their participation is that they are willing to make the required sacrifices because of the urgency of the situation. They announce at every show that they receive no salary (in fact, those parents who can afford it are asked to contribute the cost of keeping a performer on the road) and that many of them have given up lucrative jobs or the joys of attending their home-town high schools (tutors oversee high-school corre-spondence courses on the road). Cast members also refrain from smoking, drinking, and dating while on the road, but they insist that this is no sacrifice; *Up with People!* struggles hard to avoid being labeled goody-goody, but absolute moral standards are abso-lute moral standards, and one of the song titles clearly states that "You Can't Live Crooked and Think Straight." Perhaps because *Up with People!* seeks to save civilization by means that are, in the customary terms of programs and issues, ineffable, it spends a lot of time assuring its audiences and its cast members that the effort is vital and that everything is going according to plan. The conversa-tion of the performers is filled with anecdotes not only about the changes in their own lives—how they now make their beds when at home, how there is now more understanding in their families—but also about the changes wrought by *Up with People!* around the world. The triumphs are announced at cast meetings before major performances, and all of the cast members know precisely the same anecdotes about how left-wing Japanese students changed their view of America after seeing the show, or how tension in Panama was reduced by a few performances, or what the President of Venezuela had to say in praise of *Up with People!*, or how important generals have kept a close watch on the considerable impact that forty-one *Up with People!* draftees have made on the United States Army. Any place that *Up with People!* has visited tends to sound like a battleground in the struggle. Performing in Germany is referred to as performing "on the border between East and West Germany," and singing in Korea is always mentioned as singing "along the Thirty-eighth Parallel in Korea"; the show always seems to have arrived in a foreign country "just weeks after violent demonstrations"; the names of Negro urban areas are normally preceded by "the streets of," so that cast members talk of having sung in "the streets of Watts." The constant repetition of how many hundreds of sing-outs have been formed and how many thousands of young people have become involved and how many millions of people have seen the show since *Up with People!* was founded two years ago creates a kind of cycle: people ought to see or join or support *Up with People!* because it is the most important force for changing the world, and it is the most important force for changing the world because people see or join or support it. The promoters of *Up with People!* seem to be able to mine a blurb out of any comment that falls short of direct slander. In the tradition of the Moral Re-Armament newspaper advertisements that used to be dominated by a picture of the movement's founder, the late Frank Buchman, chatting intimately with some famous world leader, *Up with People!* performers rarely mention the cast's trip to Germany without recalling an audience with Konrad Adenauer or discuss the cast's previous visit to Chicago without also saying, "We were invited in by Mr. Allyn, the owner of the White Sox." African members of the cast occasionally mention the involvement of Jomo Kenyatta's nephew, and in sing-out literature any picture of one dark-haired young *Up with People!* participant is accompanied not only by her name but by a title: "Granddaughter of Cecil B. deMille."

When part of Cast B performed at a high-school assembly in Cicero—a Chicago suburb once renowned for the presence of gangsters and more recently noted for the absence of Negroes—the audience applauded the singing of "What Color Is God's Skin?" but reserved its loudest cheers for mentions of Vietnam. Singing songs of racial tolerance has never spoiled the reception given *Up with People!* by conservatives; the show's first record album carries blurbs by John Wayne, Pat Boone, and the late Walt Disney, and one of its songs is dedicated to Patrick J. Frawley, Jr., who is the president of the Schick Safety Razor Company and a perennial backer of ultraconservative causes. *Up with People!* sings out for a world that has no barriers of race or class, but demonstrations designed to break down the barriers are ordinarily dismissed by cast members as "too small an answer" or lumped together with riots and drugs and peace marches as "negative." A description in the "Sing-Out" booklet of the young people who began *Up with People!* says, "Tired of protesting against what is wrong or demonstrating for their rights, they resolved that theirs would be the road of remaking the world. They decided, whatever the cost, they wouldn't stand still." The likely result of applying the *Up with People!* version of not standing still to a specific political situation was brought out at the Cicero assembly by a young African from Rhodesia, where a white minority rules through a regime that the rest of the world has not recognized as the legal government. "I came from the part of Rhodesia where all the trouble is usually engineered," he said. "I was waiting to throw stones at white men and burn white men's houses. Then I met this force and I saw that it is not the color of a man's skin that counts but his character." Although *Up with People!* avoids the shrill anti-Communism and puritanism that once characterized Moral Re-Armament statements—a *New York Times* advertisement in 1963 listed first among things that Moral Re-Armament opposed "sexual deviants in high places who protect potential spies"—it presents conservative supporters with the prospect of thousands of young people decrying the methods customarily used by young people to challenge the status quo, all the while singing "Freedom Isn't Free," making their own beds, inspiring each other with testimonials on how they are changing the world, and looking forward confidently to the day when nations will get along because they practice absolute morality and trust each other.

"But aren't there real issues separating people and countries, even if they trust each other?" I asked one young man after a discussion of what the future could hold.

"Have you heard about what happened in Panama after *Up with People!* was there?" he said.

A theater performance of *Up with People!*—the full cast assisted by dramatic spotlighting and a thunderous band—is a rousing show. I saw Cast B at the Auditorium Theatre, a recently refurbished rococo building that looks more like the Chicago Opera House than the Chicago Opera House does, in a performance for delegates to the Forty-sixth National 4-H Club Congress. In the ornate lobby, smiling cast members sold *Up with People!* albums and Moral Re-Armament books, and passed out programs that enclosed reprints of a *Reader's Digest* article on *Up with People!* and envelopes for contributions to Moral Re-Armament.

The huge auditorium was almost full when the cast burst onto the stage. The entire chorus simulated a train while singing "The Sing-Out Express," a boat while singing "Showboat, Go-Boat," and a horseback ride while singing "The Ride of Paul Revere." A group of young men pretended to swing picks or shovel coal or haul barges during a song about the value of hard work, and another group marched in place while the soloist shouted cadence in "The Fighting Ninth." The performers clapped in time or waved or rocked from side to side during some of the livelier songs, folded their arms in front of them for an Indian number called "The Great Spirit," and pointed sternly at the audience during the singing of "Which Way America?" The transitions between songs—a new group standing in front of the risers, a different trio standing in front of a microphone—were instantaneous. There were several black faces in the group (three or four of them African rather than American Negro), and there were Japanese, Latin Americans, Finns, Swiss, and American Indians in native costumes. For "What Color Is God's Skin?" the lead singer stood in the opening of a V formed by a point of three whites and balanced arms of two blacks, two American Indians, and two Japanese. The theater was illuminated not only by constantly changing spotlights but by the flashbulbs of 4-H delegates, who regularly crept down the center aisle wearing badges that identified their home states and carrying Instamatic cameras.

During the testimonials that customarily come near the end of the show, the audience applauded a girl who said that "without involvement we're a frustrated and explosive element in society," and gave a standing ovation to a young man who described how *Up with People!* had changed the image of Americans in Venezuela. The show ended, as it often does, with the audience cheering wildly. The lead singer asked everybody to join in one one or two last choruses of *Up with People!* Almost everyone sang along enthusiastically, trying to follow the hand movements being made by those onstage. Then the cast ran out to meet the audience.

# Hero Investigator

Like many people who travel as part of their daily routine, Herbert Eyman is rarely seen shuffling and reshuffling train schedules or straining for a look out of bus windows to make certain he is going in the right direction. Eyman knows by now that there will always be another train along, and that the bus will probably take him somewhere he eventually has to go. In his territory—the United States and Canada—he is unlikely to become lost, for he has been almost everywhere at least once. Eyman has spent twenty-five years on the road—patiently waiting for trains and sitting unconcernedly in buses that seemed to be going in the wrong direction—looking for heroes. When he arrived at Pennsylvania Station on a Friday morning in late spring and found that it would be an hour before another train left for the South Shore of Long Island—where, three months before, a man was said to have entered a burning rest home and carried a helpless patient to safety—he was undisturbed at the delay. Eyman walked from the ticket window to the coffee shop—a handsome, elderly-looking man with a prominent nose, white hair combed straight back, and a very slight stoop that sometimes makes his movements seem birdlike. He was dressed in a black suit, black tie, and a spotless white shirt. He carried a black notebook.

Eyman ordered coffee, lit a cigarette, and flattened out a sheet of paper on the table in front of him. Carrying a man out of a burning building is what Eyman's employers—the managers of the Carnegie Hero Fund Commission—sometimes refer to as "a simple fire case." Eyman has investigated dozens—perhaps hundreds—of fire cases. Except for the water case, they have always constituted the most common act of heroism. Eyman no longer really needs to follow the investigative outline called for by the Commission's Manual of Instructions for Field Representatives—he knows whom he has to talk to and what questions he must ask—but he finds that the outline imposes a discipline that keeps him at the heart of the case. The evening before—in his room at the Bristol Hotel, on Forty-eighth Street, where he stays when he is in New York—he had made an outline, folding a sheet of paper in quarters to provide four miniature pages, as the Manual suggests, and writing in neat longhand the name of the rescuer, Adrian Hoek, and the rescued, John Hughes, with notations under each that the name must be accompanied by address, date of birth, height, weight, and occupation. On the appropriate tiny page, in the required order, he had listed all of the information the Commission would require about the act of heroism—including a description of the scene where the act took place, with relevant measurements, and an indication of what the weather was like, what Hoek was wearing, and how familiar he was with the scene. Eyewitnesses to the act would have to be interviewed if any could be found. It would have to be ascertained, quite specifically, whether or not Hoek had risked his life; as Eyman has explained to those who ask about the standards of the Commission, "a life risk is the minimum for a Carnegie award." He would have to learn the financial circumstances of the rescuer; if Eyman's employers are satisfied that an act of heroism is authentic and that the person who performed it could use money for a worthy cause, they may award the hero not only a medal but up to a thousand dollars in cash. The Commission has an endowment of about twelve million dollars.

In listing people he would have to see, Eyman had used the abbreviations recommended by the Manual: RR for the Rescuer, QD for the Rescued, EW for Eyewitness, and RPR for Reporter, the person who brought the case to the Commission's attention. On the back of the outline he had made a preliminary sketch of the rest home, based on information furnished by the RPR, and as he sipped his coffee he looked it over, studying the route from the back bedroom, where the Rescuer was reported to have found the Rescued, to the back door. Eyman likes to have the scene of the act well in mind before interviewing anybody. The outline he studied had been done on a piece of stationery from the Midtown Motor Lodge in Kinston, North Carolina. Near Kinston, several months before, three passersby had rescued a man who was trapped in the cab of a burning truck.

Field representatives work a five-and-a-half-day week. Assuming that the Hoek case was likely to take up Friday and Monday, Eyman figured he would remain in his room at the Bristol Saturday morning to catch up on paperwork. In addition to case reports, he has to fill out expense statements, requisition forms for office supplies, and a daily report, which must list, among other things, the mail he has received from the Commission's office, in Pittsburgh, the mail he has sent to the office, the people he has interviewed (their names followed by the appropriate abbreviation), and the miles he has traveled by various means of conveyance.

He was also thinking of using the half day for one of the calls he had to make on people in the area who are beneficiaries of pensions from the Commission. There was a woman in Yonkers whose daughter, a switchboard operator, had died in a fire while remaining at her post to warn other people in the building. A woman in Babylon was getting a pension because her husband had died while rescuing a man who had been overcome by poison gas while working in a sewer. Eyman also had to visit a woman in Bay Shore whose husband had been killed many years before while performing an act of heroism that Eyman no longer remembered; he had not investigated that case originally himself. He would probably use Saturday afternoon and Sunday to write letters. Eyman gets most of his reading done on trains, and, his health having been imperfect for several years, he has given up some of the pastimes he used to enjoy on the road, such as going to ballgames (he was once a sports reporter) or prospecting for stones to cut and polish on the machinery he keeps at a sister-in-law's house in Pittsburgh. Occasionally, people ask him if he finds the life lonely. Except for

three weeks' vacation every year, he moves constantly from hotel
room to hotel room. He has not maintained a permanent home
since he joined the Commission. "You get a rhythm of life," he
says when the question comes up. "You get used to traveling. You
have the challenge of the case to spur you on. If you're interested in
meeting new people, your life is full. You work right along."

When the train from New York arrived early that afternoon in Sayville, a town about halfway along the southern shore of Long Island, a dozen people stepped down to the platform. All of them
except Eyman seemed to melt away before the train pulled out of
the station. He walked to an outdoor telephone booth, where he
called Charles Stevenson—John Hughes' son-in-law, the man who
had reported Hoek's act of heroism to the Commission—and announced that he had arrived to begin the investigation. As he
waited for Stevenson, Eyman glanced at the white stucco waiting
room and at the tree-lined streets in front of him. He could not
recall investigating any cases in Sayville in recent years, but the
ride from New York had brought a number of heroic acts to mind.
In New York itself, he has investigated every type of case listed in
the Manual: the water case, the fire case, the suffocation case, the
moving-vehicle case, the electric-shock case, the high-elevation
case, the homicidal-attack case, even the enraged-animal case. At
Bay Shore, Eyman had been reminded of an engineer who, having
realized that his brakes would not stop the train before it hit a child
who was playing on the tracks, had climbed onto a platform on the
front of the engine, leaned out as far as he could in front of the
train, and scooped up the child. In the investigation, Eyman had
decided that a life risk was involved; the engineer could have been
knocked to the tracks himself by the impact of meeting the child.
The memories jogged into Eyman's mind by the station signs of
Long Island towns were of facts brought out in his investigations;
like most people, Eyman has never actually seen anybody risk his
life in an act of heroism.

Stevenson drove up within three or four minutes. When they
shook hands, Eyman called him General Stevenson—a retired attorney, he had been a National Guard major general and, at one
time, the adjutant general of the State of New York—but Steven-

son did not have a particularly military bearing. He is a short,
stocky man with a friendly manner and a slight Brooklyn accent.

"You fellows always just call up that way, without notice?" Stevenson asked as they drove toward the Great South Bay, down a
wide residential street with old oaks whose branches nearly met
over the center of the road. "I guess that's the way to get the real
story."

Eyman smiled and nodded. "How's Mr. Hughes getting along?"
he asked.

"Oh, Mr. Hughes is surviving," Stevenson said. "He's in the
Suffolk County Infirmary at Yaphank now. My wife will probably
be going over to see him later this afternoon. He's not really what
you'd call senile, but he's approaching that state. He's living in his
childhood a lot." A block before the Bay, Stevenson turned left and
drove to a small salmon-colored bungalow. In the living room, he
showed Eyman to an easy chair, handed him an account of the case
to read, and, explaining that Mrs. Stevenson was at church polishing brass with the Altar Guild, went to the kitchen himself to get
some soft drinks. The account—in the alumni bulletin of Stevenson's
West Point class, the class of 1924—emphasized the coincidence
that Adrian Hoek, the man who had rescued Mrs. Stevenson's
father, had a son who was married to the Stevensons' daughter. Eyman studied the newsletter. The Commission considers a
man responsible for his own family; no award is given to someone
who risks his life saving his children, say, or his wife. In a case
where the Rescued and the Rescuer are distantly related, Eyman is
responsible for reporting just how close they were, so that those on
the Commission can judge whether or not the Rescuer had some
personal reason for performing the act. The inscription on a Carnegie Medal reads, "Greater Love Hath No Man Than This, That a
Man Lay Down His Life for His Friends." But it is a man's willingness to lay down his life for strangers that is most treasured by the
Commission. If a hero has a compelling reason for rescuing a person—that he is obligated to the person, perhaps, or that he values
the person's life above his own—he has not really performed what
Eyman has called "an act with no thought of self, an act of pure
nobility, if you will." The purity of a heroic act would also be miti-
gated, of course, by the hero's being prudent enough to take special

precautions for his own safety. In addition to finding out what special value Adrian Hoek placed on the life of John Hughes, Eyman would have to find out how cautiously Hoek had made his assault on the burning rest home. The clippings sent to the Commission by Stevenson had mentioned Hoek's being a volunteer fireman in West Sayville. A rest home in Bay Shore was clearly outside his area of responsibility—policemen and firemen are almost never given Carnegie awards for heroism in the line of duty—but his fireman's training might have reduced the risk. Eyman would have to find out if Hoek had covered his face with a wet cloth before dashing into the building, and if he had known enough to crouch near the floor, keeping below the smoke.

"I got out the clippings, in case you didn't see them," Stevenson said when he returned to the living room, carrying ginger ale and coffeecake. He handed Stevenson a picture spread on the fire from the New York *Daily News,* along with a clipping from a local newspaper detailing Hoek's role, as president of the Great South Bay Baymen's Association, in protesting the Brookhaven Town Board's leasing of clamdigging rights to a man from Huntington. Eyman seemed only casually interested in the clippings. He has never depended on newspaper reports. Stevenson sat opposite Eyman, looking prepared to answer questions. There was an awkward silence. Eyman rearranged the clippings on his lap and drew an ashtray closer to him. Finally, he asked if there had been any witnesses to the act.

"There might have been a bus driver," Stevenson said. "There's a school-bus garage in back of the rest home, and some of the drivers assisted with the rescue. Four people died in the fire, you know, and I think two more ladies died within a week. I don't have to tell you: the primary reason was smoke inhalation. If my father-in-law had one good whiff, that would have been curtains, because he had this difficulty with his lungs."

"Is there a foundation still there that we can look at?" Eyman asked.

"The building is still standing," Stevenson said.

Eyman looked surprised. He felt Hoek's case growing weaker. If the fire had not been serious enough to destroy the building, perhaps the fire department could have brought it under control before it reached the back bedroom. But the smoke might have been sufficiently deadly to constitute great peril even if the flames never reached the back of the house, and, as a man with fire training, Hoek might have known it. The Commission is anxious to know not only whether or not the hero placed his life in peril but also whether or not he *knew* he was placing his life in peril. Eyman never expects to find an easy answer to the second question. Cases that contain objective evidence that the hero was aware of his peril are so rare that they stand out in Eyman's mind. He often mentions a Florida water case concerning the rescue of an immense fat man who enjoyed floating and dozing in the ocean. The day the fat man neglected to consider tides and was washed out to sea, there were only two people on the beach to hear his cries—a two-hundred-pound college football tackle and a ninety-eight-pound girl. The tackle immediately ran into the water, but when he had gone about chest deep he suddenly realized what he was about to do—he saw the posibility of getting caught in the undertow himself, perhaps, or realized that the fat man might panic and pull both of them under —and he came back to the beach. The girl swam out and brought in the fat man. In his investigation, Eyman had concluded that the girl could not have witnessed the return of the tackle and remained unaware of the peril she would face if she tried to rescue the fat man.

"Perhaps we could go along with your wife if she's planning to visit her father this afternoon," Eyman said.

"I'm not really sure you would find it profitable to go to Yaphank," Stevenson said. "Mr. Hughes probably doesn't remember anything about it. We have trouble getting him to remember what happened yesterday. His childhood in Wales, or South America when he was in business there—that's a different matter."

"If there's any chance at all that he would remember, I ought to talk to him," Eyman said. "He might be the only person who could say for certain that Mr. Hoek was in the room."

Stevenson eventually agreed that they could pick up Mrs. Stevenson at the church, drive to the infirmary at Yaphank, and then drop Eyman at Adrian Hoek's house. Eyman felt pleased with the logistics of the investigation. He usually begins a case by talking to the RPR precisely because the person who took the trouble to report an act of heroism is likely to have enough interest in it to provide some guidance, and perhaps even some transportation. The Commission encourages its field representatives to make their way as frugally as possible.

On the way to pick up Mrs. Stevenson, the General told Eyman some of the facts about St. Ann's Episcopal Church that he had learned in preparing a history of the church on the occasion of its centenary. It is a small country church, built of fieldstone, next to a peaceful meadow. Mrs. Stevenson had just finished her polishing when her husband and Eyman arrived, and she insisted that Eyman come in to see the church interior. Mrs. Stevenson—a nice-looking, talkative lady with gray hair and bright-blue eyes—seemed perfectly willing to have Eyman interview her father. "He really isn't well," she said, in a chatty tone. "He comes and goes. Arteriosclerosis, you know. He's such a sweet old man. Everyone talks about how he cooperates over there. I'm still shocked from the fire. I had just seen those four little old ladies and kissed them goodbye the night before." Eyman nodded, and Mrs. Stevenson switched the subject to brass polishing, saying she was going to get some non-tarnish polish for summer. She picked up her bucket of equipment, and they walked toward the door.

Stevenson drove out through the St. Ann's cemetery so that Eyman could see the graves of some of the founders. "I thought I'd like to be buried here, but I might as well be buried at West Point," Mrs. Stevenson said cheerfully. "It ruined my life—all those Guard meetings—so I might as well end up there." Mrs. Stevenson did most of the talking on the way to Yaphank. She spoke of her father —whom she often called Taid, the Welsh word for "grandfather" —and about the problems of being ill at an advanced age. "I think he's failing, you know," she said. "When he came there, they spoke about physical therapy, but they haven't taken him down to therapy yet. What's the use, with all that's wrong with him? They're able to keep people alive now. They're able to keep these poor little people alive for ten or fifteen years, if you call it being alive. I don't know if it's better or not."

Eyman half nodded. He was concentrating on asking about Hughes's weight and his date of birth.

"This Suffolk County Infirmary is a marvellous place," Mrs. Stevenson said as they drove down the Sunrise Highway. "He gets the finest care. All kinds of drugs. It's been a drain at times. It's certainly changed our retirement. For a while, it was costing fifty dollars a month just for one kind of drug. The place that burned down was expensive, but it was a nice place, too. In the place we had to put him for a few weeks after the fire I had to go over and bathe and shave him every day myself. I took nurse's training years ago. I thought I might as well be doing something while Charlie was at all of those National Guard meetings. With the drugs they have now, they can really keep people alive past—well, their ability to live."

"The Suffolk County Infirmary *is* a fine place," Stevenson put in. "There should be more like it. At *that* place, Taid might live to be a hundred."

"Oh, no, I don't think so, Daddy," Mrs. Stevenson said to her husband. "He's failing."

The Suffolk County Infirmary is a large, well-maintained brick building on spacious grounds. In an auditorium on the first floor, a dozen or so patients, most of them elderly people in wheelchairs, were watching slides of a hospital outing while a volunteer played songs like "School Days" and "Take Me Out to the Ball Game" on an organ. Hughes was reading a Bible when Eyman and Mrs. Stevenson came into the room he shared with another man. Although the left side of Hughes's body was paralyzed—he had to lift his left arm with his right, and his mouth showed signs of a stroke—he did not give the appearance of being old and helpless. A large man who laughed often, he seemed bright and alert, despite his incapacities. "I got out by the skin of my teeth," Hughes said, after confirming that Hoek had rushed into his bedroom and carried him to safety. "I thought he was going to rough me up." Mrs. Stevenson had to shout at her father sometimes to make herself understood, but they seemed to have an easy, joking relationship. Before she left, she said something to him in Spanish and laughed and bent over to hug him. She said she would be back the following day. Hughes's roommate—a large, shambling old man with huge, gnarled hands—had been standing next to his own bed watching the conversation. "My name is Larkin. I'm a clam-digger by trade," he suddenly announced. "I wish my daughter would come that often. I wish I had a daughter like that."

"He's such a gentle little man," Mrs. Stevenson said of her father during the drive back toward Sayville. "Everybody there says how sweet he is. He used to call this the Jack Hughes Turnpike, because we'd come this way when we used to pick him up at the other place on Sundays and bring him to our house for the afternoon. He used to like to sit in the yard and eat ice cream and watch the kids. They still haven't taken him to physical therapy, Charlie. I think they know he's licked."

There was an hour or so before Hoek would be in from clamming, and Stevenson used the time for a ride, occasionally pointing out a church that was founded before or after St. Ann's, or a housing development that was formerly the site of a great estate. Mrs. Stevenson talked of the scene after the fire. Some of the old ladies had been intent on saving their clothing, and hours after the fire had been brought under control there were suitcases on the front yard and clothing flapping from the bushes under the windows. Mrs. Stevenson, who believes she has extrasensory perception, said she had been positive on the afternoon before the fire that something awful was about to happen. "It was Sunday, and I had the strangest feeling when I came home from church," she said. "I knew something was wrong. I called up my son and my two sisters. When the phone rang at seven-twenty that next morning, I said, 'Charlie, there it is. I know that's it.' Oh, look Charlie! Strawberries!"

The car had passed a roadside fruitstand. "It's early," Stevenson said. "They must be Georgia strawberries."

"Florida, I think," Eyman said. "I had occasion to be in Georgia a few weeks ago, and I don't think their strawberries were due for market before the end of this month." Near Atlanta, several months before, a high-school boy had taken a girl in his class on her first horseback ride, and the horse had bolted toward a highway the moment she mounted. The boy gave chase, caught up just as the runaway was about to cross the highway, and managed to turn it onto a bridle path that ran along the road. There was only room for one horse on the path, though, and the boy and his horse continued across the highway, where they were hit by a car and killed. The case had struck Eyman as somewhat old-fashioned. He rarely gets runaway-horse cases anymore.

Stevenson drove past the canal in Islip where Hoek docks his clamming boat. Hoek ordinarily would go nowhere near the rest home in Bay Shore on the way to his boat, Stevenson explained, but that Monday morning the canal was iced in, so Hoek was using a brother's boat, which happened to be docked in Bay Shore.

"It was just one of those flukes," Mrs. Stevenson said.

"There's Mr. Hoek's church," Stevenson said. They were driving through West Sayville and had just passed the First Reformed Church, a neat red brick building with white columns and a white steeple. The houses lining the street looked relatively old, small, and well kept. "Every one of those houses is owned by a Dutchman," Stevenson said. "They've all been here for years."

"They're thrifty, clean people," Mrs. Stevenson said. "They do the right thing."

"They're what you might call hard-core Americans," the General said.

"They do the right thing," Mrs. Stevenson repeated. "They might get killed doing it, but they always do the right thing."

Stevenson turned down Rollstone Avenue, where the signs in front of the houses had names like Van Wyen, Van Essendelft, De Ruiter, and Oeser. The Hoek house was made of weathered shingles and had an old-fashioned porch. The Hoeks were waiting in their living room—a comfortable-looking room that contained such reminders of Hoek's calling as a clock in the shape of a boat's wheel, two or three seascapes, and a bookend in the form of a boatman wearing a yellow slicker. The Stevensons made the introductions, exchanged a few words, and left. Mrs. Hoek—a plump, cheerful woman—offered Eyman the most comfortable chair and took a chair herself on the other side of the room. Hoek sat across from Eyman. A short, powerful-looking man, his face weathered and creased by years on the Bay, he had been in from clamming for a while and had changed into a blue suit for the interview. He sat rather formally, a slight smile on his face, as Eyman asked if he would mind telling the story in his own words first, and then answering questions about it while Eyman took notes.

"When I went into the house, I could feel the oxygen being burned up, and I thought, 'My God! I have to get Taid out!' " Hoek said, after explaining that he had been driving nearby when the fire bell went off.

"And you were trapped once," his wife reminded him.

Hoek didn't seem to hear her. He continued the story, describing to Eyman how he went into Hughes's bedroom, found Hughes eating breakfast, dragged him from the bed, and headed for the kitchen door. "This fellow was there when I got him back to the kitchen, and I said, 'My God! Help me with this man!' I kept him low. The smoke was very bad. I felt filled with smoke up to here." Hoek drew his hand across his thick neck. "I upchucked after I got out."

When Hoek had gone through the story once, Eyman pulled out his notebook and laid it on a table in front of him, with his investigative outline next to it. "I'm going to take some notes now," he announced. "The questions won't be chronological; they follow a report form. Now, your correct name is . . ."

"Adrian Peter Hoek."

"If you did get a medal, would 'Adrian P.' be the way you would prefer to have it written?"

Hoek smiled and shrugged. He looked at his wife. "I suppose so," he said. Eyman asked Hoek's address, date of birth, height, weight, and occupation. Mrs. Hoek occasionally offered an opinion about the answers until the questions turned to the actual act of heroism. Then, when she corrected her husband's estimate of when the fire bell went off, Eyman cautioned her formally against consultation.

Hoek answered questions about the construction of the building, about the wind and temperature, about what he and Hughes had been wearing, about how often he had visited Hughes. "When you saw it was the Senior House on fire, was your thought that you'd get anyone, or you'd get him?" Eyman asked.

"Get him. Blood is a little thicker than water, you know," Hoek replied, not realizing that he was affecting the purity of the act.

Hoek answered questions about his service with the West Sayville volunteer fire department, but even before he had outlined his years of experience both he and Eyman seemed aware that they were not in a layman's discussion. They spoke of how the stairwell was acting as a flue, of whether or not the flames were hot enough to pop out the windows, of the progress of the flames along the ceiling, of smoke too thick for anyone who was not wearing a Scott Air-Pak. Hoek seemed to have no doubt that Eyman would understand his description of conditions in the kitchen when he said, "It was a perfect setup for a back draft."

Eyman patiently went through the progress Hoek had made from the back door to the bedroom and back again, ascertaining such facts as which hand Hoek had used to swing Hughes's legs off the bed and precisely how far from the ceiling the smoke had extended. Eyman tends to distrust numerical estimates given by people who have been in a crisis—the Manual for Field Representatives warns that most people overestimate, and it includes a list of American running records, a chart transferring currents from miles per hour to feet per second, and an equation for converting statute miles into knots—but Hoek's estimates sounded authoritative.

Finally, Eyman paused, and with considerable formality said, "This series of questions has to do with your own evaluation of the risk involved in the act."

Mrs. Hoek laughed nervously. Hoek nodded a few times. He was still smiling.

"Do you feel you risked your life?" Eyman asked.

"I sure did," Hoek said. "I broke a promise to my wife, too. She said, 'Ade, don't you ever go into one of those homes.' "

"But I didn't want those poor people to perish," Mrs. Hoek said, half disclaiming her warning.

"A back draft," Hoek said. "A back draft and I'd have been caught and roasted."

Eyman asked the Hoeks a series of questions about their financial position and about what they would do with a cash gift if one happened to be awarded them; then, his interview complete, he accepted Hoek's offer of a ride to the Sayville station.

On the train back to New York, Eyman decided that he had probably been correct in estimating that he could finish up the Hoek case on Monday. He would have to visit the scene of the fire, and interview the bus drivers and, possibly, some of the Bay Shore firemen. He expected the bus drivers to be rather hostile witnesses. Eyman has found that people who were at the scene of a heroic act themselves are often reluctant to talk about the heroism of someone else. He also expected hostility occasionally from fire departments, jealous of their own responsibilities in removing people from burning buildings. Eyman finds that most people are cooperative, although perhaps not as gracious with their time and cooperation as the Stevensons. Only rarely does he, to his dismay, come across people who "think of 'hero' as a dirty word, who believe that a person who puts his life on the line for somebody else is a sucker." Not long before Eyman went to Sayville, a college boy had refused to cooperate with the investigation of his own act of heroism, believing it would lower him in the eyes of his friends. "He saved three lives, too," Eyman said later. "A boat broke apart and he held them to it. It was a wonderful act, fraught with peril."

Reflecting on the day's investigation, Eyman thought Hoek's case was fairly strong. The relationship between Hoek and Hughes was obviously not close enough to be disqualifying, and Hoek's fire training had actually made his act more heroic, since a layman might have been unaware of the peril that a back draft could bring. Still, there would probably be a lack of eyewitnesses, unless the man who met Hoek at the kitchen door could be found. Eyman would put it all in his report, for the Commission to decide. Three or four times a year, when the Carnegie awards are given out, Eyman is mailed a list of the recipients. He acknowledges receipt of the list in his daily report, and glances through the names. But he is working on another investigation by then, and that one is followed by another, and he has difficulty remembering which of the heroes he investigated were found deserving of a Carnegie medal and which of them were not.

# THE SOUTH

# Historical Note

During the two or three months of the Freedom Rides, in the spring of 1961, about two hundred people were arrested for disturbing the peace of the Trailways Bus Terminal in Jackson, Mississippi, by not observing the waiting-room segregation that Jackson authorities considered the equivalent of peacefulness. According to the terms of their bonds, all of them were required to return to Jackson that August for arraignment—creating a reunion of peacedisturbers that included, among others, national civil-rights leaders, Negro college students from the Southern sit-in movement, and some unkempt Northern white supporters who were usually referred to by white people in Mississippi as "beatnik types." Arrangements were made to transport some of the accused from New York and back on a chartered bus. On the way back North, seventeen of the Freedom Riders, most of them beatnik types, announced that they planned to stop off in Monroe, North Carolina, to help out a civil-rights movement led by a Monroe Negro named Robert F. Williams. They had been recruited in Jackson by an intense civil-rights activist named James Forman. A former schoolteacher in Chicago, Forman had worked for a while at Tent City, in Fayette County, Tennessee, a community formed by Negroes thrown off farms because of their efforts to vote; then, accompanied by a field worker for the Southern Christian Leadership Conference, he had gone to look into the situation in Monroe, a town that pickets at the United Nations had called "America's Angola."

In the early sixties, there was a lot of concern in the civil-rights movement about the form protest took—a concern based largely on the premise then widely held that Negroes had to retain the support of Northern white liberals and Southern white moderates and any other white people who could qualify as what editorial writers in those days liked to call Men of Good Will. (In fact, the Freedom Ride itself was a form that had offended some Men of Good Will—partly on the ground that many of the Freedom Riders confirmed the segregationists' vision of civil-rights activists being outside agitators.) Nonviolence was the strongest tenet of the movement at that time, and Williams, while serving as the president of the local branch of the N.A.A.C.P., had publicly renounced nonviolence. In 1959, after two white men on trial for assaulting Negro women had been acquitted in Monroe, Williams was quoted as saying that Negroes might have to meet "violence with violence" and "lynching with lynching"—a remark that caused the N.A.A.C.P. national office to suspend him from his presidency. At the time of the fiftieth annual convention of the N.A.A.C.P. that summer, the national office published a pamphlet justifying its actions. The necessity of absolute nonviolence was reasserted by such luminaries of the movement as Daisy Bates of Little Rock, and Martin Luther King, Jr. The convention upheld the suspension by a vote of seven hundred and sixty-four to fourteen. Williams continued to carry on what he often referred to as an arms race with the whites, and he continued to be something of an embarrassment in other ways. It was a policy of virtually all civil-rights leaders in those days, for instance, to avoid close association with anybody whose presence might lend weight to the routine Southern charge that the civil-rights movement was a ruse concocted by the Communists, and Williams had been associated with an assortment of Old Left radicals and Harlem black nationalists at least since he came to public attention, in 1958, with the "Kissing Case." (Two Negro boys, aged eight and nine, had been confined in the state reformatory for allegedly forcing a seven-year-old white girl to kiss one of them. The N.A.A.C.P. was slow to act, perhaps because of a

reluctance to speak loudly about interracial sex, even of the pre-
pubescent variety; Williams and a New York lawyer began a publicity campaign that caused more reaction in Europe than in the
United States; and the boys were finally freed after Harry Golden,
North Carolina's best-known white liberal, interceded with the
governor.) A vocal supporter of Fidel Castro long after it had been
decided that Cuba was in the Enemy Camp, Williams had used
visits to Havana as occasions for denouncing American racism. It
was said that he had flown a Cuban flag in his front yard until a
Negro paratrooper on leave tore it down. At a time when the basic
loyalty of American Negroes (and whites) to Cold War foreign
policy was taken for granted, *The Crusader,* Williams' newsletter,
said, "No Afro-American should be asked to fight in a white man's
conflict of conquest cloaked in the phoney respectability of a crusade for freedom."

Williams' efforts in Monroe appeared to be totally unsystematic.
He seemed to have lost interest in school integration after a mild
pass at it, for instance, and most of his energy seemed to be taken
up in protesting the kind of personal harassment that Negro civil-
rights leaders, and even a number of Southern white liberals, accepted as an inevitable hazard of their activities. With Charlotte
only about twenty-five miles away, Williams had access to active
white liberals who would have been the natural allies of most Negro civil-rights leaders. But the Charlotte liberals believed that Williams' advocacy of violence played into the hands of the segregationists, that his handling of the Kissing Case had made it into a
bad parody of the Scottsboro Case, and that his criticism of America while visiting a country considered its enemy amounted to dis-
loyalty. (Attempting to illustrate just how extreme Williams' language had been, Golden told an out-of-town reporter in 1961 that
the Cuban speeches had definitely included such phrases as "America is a prison.") James Farmer, who was then the national director of the Congress of Racial Equality and a leader of the Freedom
Rides, advised the Freedom Riders on the bus to the North not to
stop in Monroe. They decided to stop anyway.

Contrary to what a Northern reader of *The Crusader* might have
gathered, there were many places in the South much more oppres-
sive for Negroes than Monroe—although that distinction might

have been lost on the Negroes who lived there. Monroe was not, as Williams later wrote, the site of "the southeastern regional headquarters of the Ku Klux Klan," but the Klan had definitely surfaced in surrounding Union County during the fifties. A town of about eleven thousand people, not far from the South Carolina line, Monroe in 1961 was interested mainly in luring more industry to bolster an economy that was principally agricultural, and those who ran the city were not anxious to have it identified with Angola, except to whatever extent Angola is anti-union. They were in the habit of explaining to visitors that Negroes had always voted in Union County—Williams, in fact, had once run for mayor of Monroe—and that Monroe had Negro policemen and some Negro representation on county boards. But Charlotte journalists familiar with Union County would have agreed with Williams' later statement that "its spirit is closer to that of South Carolina than to the liberal atmosphere of Chapel Hill which people tend to associate with North Carolina."

Monroe's vision of itself as a decent enough place that had the bad luck to have spawned Robert Williams was reinforced by the arrival of the Freedom Riders—a sudden invasion of beatnik types. Forming an organization called the Monroe Non-Violent Action Committee, the Freedom Riders and Williams' local followers, mostly Negro teen-agers, began to picket the Union County courthouse. The leaflets they handed out listed four issues: "1) Unfair protection under law for Afro-Americans and their property; 2) The policy of the tax-supported Industrial Development which invites industries to Union County and imposes discriminatory labor practices; 3) Arbitrary and cruel administration by the Welfare Department that has deprived destitute Afro-Americans of relief; 4) Separate and unequal recreational facilities." (Williams had originally asked for a separate pool for Negroes or, at least, use of the town pool on certain days. Finally, he marched to the town pool, and it was closed; the manager said the chlorinator was broken.) But the only issue that either side discussed seriously was the issue of Robert Williams himself. There was no chance that the whites in charge were going to discuss recreational facilities with a man who flew the Cuban flag, and *The Crusader* was much more concerned with whether Williams' house had been shot at and whether Castro had been unfairly treated than it was with the welfare situation.

In 1961, of course, issues such as job discrimination and welfare would have been beyond the scope of the discussion even in cities where the Negro leader was considered responsible and the whites in power were considered progressive. The national goal in civil rights, to the extent that a goal existed, seemed to be the token integration of public schools and certain public facilities in the large cities of the South and an increase of Negro voting in those places where a Negro could register without risking his life. In the same week that the picketing of the Union County courthouse came to a climax, nine Negroes were enrolled in previously all-white high schools in Atlanta—seven years after the Supreme Court had ruled segregation in schools unconstitutional. It was considered a triumph. In an editorial of unqualified congratulations, *The New York Times* said, "Atlanta has provided a new and shining example of what can be accomplished if the people of goodwill and intelligence, white and Negro, will cooperate to obey the law and to benefit the children, regardless of color." It was taken for granted by almost all white Americans that some of the injustices practiced against Negroes in the South (injustices in the North being virtually unacknowledged) were semipermanent fixtures of American life—distressing but difficult to do anything about, like a three-and-a-half-per-cent minimum rate of unemployment. For half a dozen years before 1960, General Eisenhower had assured the citizenry that morality could not be legislated—an assurance that state politicians took not as a signal to repeal the laws governing divorce and drinking and gambling but as a signal that the federal government wouldn't bother them about segregation. The Kennedy Administration had made it known that it considered further civil-rights legislation unnecessary, and had appointed a number of openly white supremacist federal judges in the South to preside over the efforts to bring change through the courts. A suggestion made around that time by the federal Civil Rights Commission that the lever of withholding federal funds be used to stop illegal discrimination was not taken seriously by the Administration or Congress. In theory, the nation was in favor of change—but not strongly enough to accept any measures that might bring it about right away.

On a Sunday, a week after the picketing of the Union County courthouse had started, a crowd of about a thousand hostile whites gathered in the courthouse square to jeer. One car circled the courthouse carrying a sign that said "Open Season on Coons." About the time the pickets broke up for the day, part of the crowd surged toward some of them. Before order was finally restored in Monroe by the state police, several hours later, there had been dozens of pitched battles, some of them with guns, a number of the Freedom Riders had been arrested, and a policeman had been wounded. When a white couple from rural Union County drove into the Negro neighborhood during the disturbance, they were taken from their car into Robert Williams' house and held for a few hours. By the next morning, Williams had disappeared. Kidnapping charges were brought against him and two local followers, one of the Freedom Riders, and a Negro woman from Harlem. Whatever capital Williams had retained in the civil-rights movement was dissolved by the kidnapping charge. A day or so after Williams had disappeared, the Reverend Wyatt Tee Walker, then the executive director of the Southern Christian Leadership Conference, arrived in Monroe to see what could be done about the legal charges against the Freedom Riders who had been arrested during the Sunday disturbances; they had, after all, been picketing partly at the instigation of an S.C.L.C. field worker. But, despite the arguments of Forman and others that Monroe should be turned into what people then called "another Jackson," Walker made it clear that the S.C.L.C. would become involved only to the extent of providing legal aid for those already arrested. Walker was not completely unsympathetic to Williams—"Whatever Williams is Union County has made him," he said—but before he left town he told reporters that he, too, had advised the Freedom Riders to stay away from Monroe.

A few weeks later, Williams showed up in Havana, and from there he eventually moved to Peking and then to East Africa, publishing a somewhat more extreme form of *The Crusader* as he went. Forman became the executive director of the Student Nonviolent Coordinating Committee, but S.N.C.C. also decided not to become involved in Monroe. There was not much written about Monroe in the years that followed. In fact, for long periods during the next two years—the periods between some trouble during an attempt to register voters in McComb, Mississippi, and the S.C.L.C.'s unsuccessful desegregation campaign in Albany, Georgia, and James Meredith's enrollment at the University of Mississippi—there was not much written about race. Just before the forces of Martin Luther King, Jr., met the forces of Bull Connor in Birmingham in the spring of 1963, the country seemed to have almost forgotten about Negroes and civil rights. In those years, of course, most white people had never heard of Robert Williams or Monroe. (The organization formed in New York for the Monroe defendants, a small operation dominated by white radicals of the Old Left, had the tone but not the volume of the old Scottsboro committees.) But Williams continued to be something of a hero to black nationalists and black revolutionaries—although Harold Cruse, in his book *The Crisis of the Negro Intellectual,* points out that Williams' actions in Monroe were neither nationalistic nor revolutionary, since his announced goal was integration and the force he advocated was to be used not against established authority but against white vigilantes. In February of 1964, the defendants other than Williams were finally brought to trial and convicted. (Their conviction was set aside by an appeals court.) The trial took place at a time when the civil-rights movement was still confident of making progress in a nonviolent and biracial way, and *The New York Times* reporter who covered it wrote that it demonstrated "that the Monroe situation was an aberration in the civil-rights movement."

In a town like Monroe, a chlorinator that breaks down as the swimming pool is approached by Negroes is not easily repaired. Now, eight years after Williams' swimming-pool demonstration, the town pool remains closed. Whites swim at a place called Bundy's Private Swimming Pool, behind a used-car lot on the double lane that goes to Charlotte. The federal courts have ruled that places like Bundy's Private Swimming Pool are public accommodations, which, under the Civil Rights Act passed after Birmingham, can be compelled to end racial discrimination, but nobody in Monroe has ever filed a suit. Negroes in Monroe are somewhat better off economically than they were in Williams' day. The industrial-development commission eventually attracted enough plants to soak up most of the available white labor, and in the last few years the textile plants in particular are, in the words of the man at the industrial-development commission, "having to go to women and colored more." The white people in Monroe are quick to tell Northern visitors that the plants are integrated and that the schools are so thoroughly integrated that the former Negro high school has been closed. (Its closing and the pace of integration were helped along by a mysterious fire.) There is still no swimming pool for Negroes, but some people talk about including one in a recreation center that may someday be built at the site of the old Negro school. White people in Monroe still blame Williams for bringing the town a bad name, but—hating a bad name worse than they hate Williams—they wouldn't welcome having him back for a trial.

Williams, of course, returned to the United States last month, as president of a separatist group called the Republic of New Africa. Upon landing in Detroit, he was arrested on a fugitive warrant stemming from the kidnapping charge, and released on bond. James Farmer, who didn't want the Freedom Riders to go to Monroe, is now in the Nixon Administration, an Assistant Secretary in the Department of Health, Education, and Welfare. Wyatt Tee Walker has a large church in Harlem and is an adviser to Governor Rockefeller on urban affairs. Harry Golden still lives in Charlotte and supports what remains of the integration movement; he resigned from S.N.C.C. when it issued what he considered anti-Semitic statements during the time of the Arab-Israeli war, in 1967. James Forman is now a spokesman for a group demanding that American churches pay black people half a billion dollars in reparations. The same people still run the national office of the N.A.A.C.P., and they say that their policy on violence has not changed. If they were again to read in *The New York Times* of a branch president calling for Negroes to meet "violence with violence" and "lynching with lynching," they would suspend him. Of course, it is unlikely that a statement so commonplace would make *The Times*.

# The New Morality of Lester Maddox

Late last fall, all members of the Georgia legislature received letters signed by Governor Lester Maddox appointing them to the Governor's Youth Council on Alcohol, Tobacco and Health and asking them to sign a pledge card that said, "I will not partake of or use alcoholic beverages or tobacco in any form. I understand that should I violate this Pledge my membership will cease and terminate." Charles Pou, the political editor of the Atlanta *Journal,* later wrote that one Atlanta legislator was planning to send the pledge card back to Maddox with an explanatory note saying, "I go along with you on the no-smoking part of the pledge card and wish I could sign it. It might help me. However, as long as you are governor I'm afraid I can't quit drinking."

There are many Georgians, particularly in the cities, who would agree that the very idea of Lester Maddox being governor cannot be borne without the help of strong spirits, he is, after all, a man who was not taken seriously in Georgia politics even in the days when a willingness to orate about the unspeakable evils of forced race mixing was being accepted as one qualification for public office. As a result of Maddox's election, however, it has become increasingly difficult for a troubled citizen to get a drink, especially on Sunday. Georgia governors have never been anxious to endorse

sin, but in the amount of energy devoted to stamping out sinfulness
—the smoking, drinking, staying-out-late, church-skipping kind of
sinfulness—Maddox has outdone them all. An authority on such
matters—Bishop W. R. (Billy) Rogers, the Theocratic Party candidate for President—came through Atlanta last winter, marched
three or four times around the Fulton County Courthouse (for the-
ological reasons not made completely clear to accompanying reporters), and said, "I think Georgia has the best governor in the
country." The Atlanta *Journal* cautioned those who dismissed
Bishop Rogers as a man who would never be President. "After
all," the *Journal* said in an editorial, "we live in the only state in
the union where something of this kind has happened. In moments
of deeper brooding, we feel that you should not be surprised if, in
1968, the nation comes under the guidance of President Billy Rogers."

Although, according to Maddox, legislators received the pledge
cards by mistake—one of those administrative mishaps that have
drawn attention to Maddox's governorship in much the same way
that shrill anti-integration advertisements used to draw attention to
his fried-chicken restaurant—thirty or forty thousand young people
in Georgia have received them on purpose. "When it comes to alcohol," the head of the Georgia Council on Alcohol Problems says,
"the Governor's witness has been particularly effective." At his first
press conference as governor, about a year ago, Maddox said that
hard liquor would not be served in the governor's mansion as long
as he was the tenant. A couple of months after that, he announced
that Atlanta night clubs and bars would have to stop serving liquor
at midnight on Saturday nights. (They had been serving until two
in the morning, on the shaky premise that the state law allowing
cities to set their own mixed-drink regulations superseded the state
Sunday-closing law—an interpretation that forced beer drinkers to
switch to Scotch-and-soda after midnight.) During an interview
with the Governor on WRNG, an Atlanta talk station, someone
phoned in to ask if eliminating the two most popular drinking
hours of the week might cost Atlanta some convention business.
"People in conventions are not out drinking on Sunday and cutting
up," the Governor said. "This is some of our beatniks, some of our
long-haired, short-skirted people that don't have anything else to

do on Sunday morning." Last month, the night-club owners were reminded by the Governor that December 31st was Sunday, New Year's Eve or no New Year's Eve. The Governor said that a good place to celebrate the arrival of the new year was in church. "There's no law against serving out the gospel," he remarked, "even after midnight."

Shortly before Maddox declared the governor's mansion dry, he announced that he would hold a daily prayer meeting in the capitol. A worshipful citizen can still show up at the Governor's outer office at eight-fifty-five in the morning and—in the company of a couple of dozen secretaries and a few of their bosses—hear a minister who reads from the Scriptures, invokes the Lord's blessing on the Governor and the citizenry and the boys in Vietnam, and gives everyone a spiritual push toward the day's work ahead. It is likely that the Governor expects these sessions to be of practical as well as inspirational benefit, since he has often mentioned the role of the Deity in making him governor in the first place ("Even a dropout like Lester Maddox can become governor, with God on his side"). Maddox believes in giving credit where credit is due. "The American free-enterprise system could never have been established if it were not for the birth of Christ," he said in a speech last month to the Macon Association Brotherhood Rally at the Log Cabin Baptist Church. Citing the expansion of the Christmas season and the increase in sales volume, he went on to say, "Other holidays have not expanded like Christmas. And the reason for it is found in a name—the name of Jesus. There will be more automobiles, more shoes, more record-players, more television sets, more ties, more shirts, more dresses, more cosmetics, more watches and diamonds sold in the name of Christ this year than any other name."

In his State of the State speech to the Georgia legislature last week, Maddox became most animated when he presented his plans to make gambling a felony rather than a misdemeanor and to close forever the clip joints in southeast Georgia that have preyed on Florida-bound motorists who stop for a little gasoline or a jar of pecans and can't resist a small game of chance. (The clip joints, he said, in a slip of the tongue that conjured up the old Pickrick Restaurant newspaper ads, were giving "a black face to the State of Georgia.") It is normal for Georgia governors to deplore the clip joints and the local officials who permit them to operate, but Maddox flew down to give his personal warning to anyone he could find on the premises. ("As far as I know, Governor," one of those cornered was quoted as saying, "there's nothing been going on here.") The Governor had been particularly upset when a New Hampshire couple, having reported to the Savannah Better Business Bureau that they had been fleeced in McIntosh County, were advised to return and lodge a complaint, followed the advice, and were arrested for gambling. Maddox has said that he is against any kind of gambling at all—including, to the delight of the newspapers, church bingo. The year he came into office, some three hundred Georgians had placed themselves in a somewhat suspicious position concerning the state gambling laws by purchasing gambling stamps from the federal government, which has no law against gambling but does have one against gambling without a federal gambling stamp. Maddox has resolved to rid the state of all gambling stamps, although there is a strong tradition in Georgia that enforcement of gambling laws is a local matter, and most of the stamps are purchased for the slot machines of country clubs and veterans' groups and fraternal orders whose memberships include those officials charged with protecting the county from the evils of wagering. The extent to which local control in such matters has been respected in Georgia was dramatized by Maddox's predecessor, Carl Sanders, who, in an effort to put the highway clip joints out of business, stationed state police in front of each joint to warn tourists that they were about to be bamboozled.

When Maddox announces a crusade against some type of wickedness, though, people in Georgia tend to take him at his word. He practices what he relentlessly preaches. He has issued a memorandum to his own staff banning miniskirts—although lay authorities on the subject claim that there were no authentic miniskirts to be banned—and he fired his executive secretary when it came out that the man had purchased liquor for some underage college students. The Governor himself does not smoke or drink or blaspheme—although in one public appearance, finding himself momentarily in short supply of statesmanlike phrases or temporarily in the clutches of the Devil, he did say that the federal government could take its school-aid money and "ram it." Early in his crusade against drinking on the Sabbath, he demonstrated his seriousness by having agents of the Georgia Bureau of Investigation raid an Atlanta night club that was serving liquor after midnight on Saturday (the percentage of beatniks to conventioneers was not reported); most Atlanta night clubs now quit serving at midnight on Saturday. There are far fewer gambling stamps in Georgia than there were in the last fiscal year—though an increase in federal raids suggests that some people have given up the stamps rather than the gambling—and the Governor has announced that if local officials do not close down the remaining stamp holders next month he will use the Georgia Bureau of Investigation to do it. Most people think he will. The G.B.I. has already been used for gambling raids—last spring, in Bainbridge, Georgia. Those caught in the act were two Elks Lodges, four veterans' organizations, and the Loyal Order of Moose.

Maddox has occasionally been criticized for devoting too much of his attention to purifying the populace. The Roman Catholic Archbishop of Atlanta said last summer that the rags worn in the slums were of considerably more importance than the alleged miniskirts worn in the capitol, and that a moderate amount of drinking and gambling would probably not lead automatically to eternal damnation. (There was a rebuttal from a minister at Maddox's church, the North Atlanta Baptist; he said, "Neither I nor Governor Maddox . . . take our faith from a foreign power.") It is more common, however, for Maddox's detractors to express thankfulness that so much of his energy is devoted to public morality rather than to matters where real harm could be done. "Let's hope he keeps the miniskirt issue going," I was told by a citizen who has little faith that the Governor's administrative experience in the restaurant business will see him through in the capitol. "We're getting off cheap." The Governor's detractors see no harm in discouraging young people from smoking or in discouraging drivers from drinking; some of them believe that Maddox may even be doing a small service by demonstrating the absurdity of having puritanical laws in an increasingly liberated society—or, more likely, by demonstrating that the society is really not nearly as liberated as the national celebration of hippies and swingers may indicate. Georgia legislators joke about the illegality of matching for Cokes, and Georgia newspapers occasionally carry facetious letters about the Governor's crusades, but Georgia politicians have no illusions about the voters being willing to make it legal for a man to place a bet on a horse race or sleep with someone who is not his wife or practice his trade on Sunday or walk into one of the showy restaurants on top of Atlanta's skyscrapers and have a glass of beer with his Sunday supper.

There is no widespread concern that the state is being neglected while the Governor cracks down on slot machines in the Elks Lodge and drafts messages against miniskirts and makes speeches about the possibility of building a prayer room in every Georgia school (modeled after the prayer room in the Georgia capitol). Maddox has made some good executive appointments, and in legislative matters he has considerably less to do with running the state than past governors had. Until recently, the governor of Georgia was practically an absolute monarch; he personally chose the Speaker of the House and he personally controlled the spending of great sums of state funds, unrestricted by legislative appropriation. The Georgia legislature only meets for forty or forty-five days a year, and many legislators have been noted for devoting most of that time to acquiring sufficient expertise for an eloquent denunciation of Atlanta sin when they returned home. There has been some movement toward "legislative independence" in Georgia in recent years, and it was greatly accelerated when the 1966 elections became tied up in court for lack of a clear majority. The House itself decided who would be Speaker, and eventually it decided who would be governor. Lester Maddox was not ideally suited to reestablish executive control. In a state where one-party, non-ideological politics have made the use of political power a personal and complicated art, Maddox was a protest-vote symbol suddenly transformed into a chief executive—a man almost completely without contacts in any part of the Georgia political structure and completely without experience in manipulating the levers available to the governor. He remains, in many ways, as puzzling to rural legislators as he is to Atlanta businessmen. Apparently, he has difficulty remembering names—an almost unheard-of affliction in Georgia politics—and legislators speak of this phenomenon with awe, as if discussing a man who eats with his toes or rides a bicycle facing backward. (The Governor has in fact posed for pictures riding a bicycle facing backward.) "Do you know what he calls me?" I was asked by a state senator from Savannah named William Searcey. "He calls me buddy boy." Senator Searcey looked out to space for a while and shook his head. "Buddy boy," he repeated.

Maddox has some conventional legislative goals, of course, but it is difficult to imagine him giving directions to the Speaker of the House—a man who knows everybody's name, and has for years— or swaying votes with the kind of exquisite grasp of political tactics that has been the gift of some Georgia governors. As governor, he still seems like the outsider candidate. He still says "Yes, sir" and "No, sir" to reporters and aides. When an assistant asked him recently if he had made a telephone call to an industrial concern that was rumored to be interested in a Georgia plant, he said proudly, "I talked to the president himself." After a few minutes in his presence, a visitor considers it amazing not that Hubert Humphrey met with Maddox but that Maddox restrained himself from asking for the Vice-President's autograph. Some of the people who were most appalled or embarrassed at the thought of Maddox being elected governor now speak of him not altogether unkindly as a man out of his depth, bewildered by the machinations of statecraft and politics. But Maddox sounds completely confident when discussing his role in improving the moral climate of the state—and even of the country. "King David obeyed God and the people were blessed; when he did otherwise, they suffered," he said recently. He is aware that the legislative session is marked by a good deal of drinking and cutting up on Sunday and every other day, and that, as they say in Georgia, "a lot of counties vote dry and drink wet." But he thinks that he can place limits on such misbehavior, and he is convinced that the people—the kind of people who come to talk to him two Wednesdays a month, when the governor's office is thrown open to the public—believe in what he is doing. "I hope we can expand from where we're at and have other people speaking up for improving the moral climate of their place," he says. "If not, this country is going to cease to be a major power." On Christmas Eve, he announced plans to organize a nationwide demonstration "for God and liberty." Next Christmas, he predicted, a quarter of a million people will demonstrate in Atlanta alone—including "many school bands, nationally prominent singers, and religious leaders" —and twenty million people will take part across the country. "If, as the Governor of Georgia, I take my stand—for faith in God— then others are going to do this," Maddox said last week. "It encourages the fellow down the line. He might have been afraid that people will snicker or scoff if he says these things, but because it is being said by Lester Maddox, these people won't be afraid to speak out."

# A Hearing on Hunger

"We are a private group, a citizens' group," the chairman said when he opened the hearing, at about ten o'clock in the morning. "We have no official status, and this hearing this morning is one group of citizens talking to another group of citizens." The chairman introduced the members of the panel, identifying each one with a foundation or a university or a law firm or an anti-poverty project, and explained that they were members of a citizens' board formed in Washington to gather information for a report on the extent of hunger and malnutrition in the United States. "We're here simply to find out from you some of the kinds of information that data and statistics do not reveal," he went on. "And we're also here to give some of you the opportunity to tell your stories."

The first witness was Mrs. Jessie May Dash, a tall Negro woman whose right eye was almost closed, as if it had been swollen shut from some accident long ago and had never reopened. As she answered the questions of the panelists, a court reporter took down her testimony on a stenographic machine, glancing idly around the auditorium as he worked. The auditorium, on the third floor of the new State Board of Health building, was very modern. There were no windows. The walls were of smooth wooden paneling broken at intervals by vertical strips of gray brick. The aisles were carpeted in blue, and matching material covered the seats—soft seats that could be swung backward and forward, like those in an expensive movie theater. The lighting was indirect and gave off a slight hum. A plaque on the back wall said that the auditorium had been dedicated by employees of the State Board of Health in love and affection to George Sewall Thomas Peeples, M.D., the State Health Officer from 1954 to 1967, in recognition of a life devoted to the health of the citizens.

Mrs. Dash told the panel that she was from Orangeburg County. She said she had twelve children, and no husband, and an income of about thirty dollars a week on the weeks she got some help from one of her sons. She had been unable to get on the welfare rolls. The panelists—five men and one woman—sat in leather swivel chairs behind a long table and took notes on yellow pads. The chairman asked Mrs. Dash why she had been turned down by the Welfare Department. "They was wantin' to know where my husband was, and I didn't know," Mrs. Dash said. "So they never got it straight about that." After some questions about the types of food she was able to buy, Mrs. Dash was asked if she had ever had any children who died. She looked up at the ceiling for a moment, as if trying to remember, and finally said she had had one child who died of pneumonia. As she was testifying, more citizens came into the auditorium, mostly in large groups. Eventually, there were perhaps a hundred and fifty people in the auditorium. Almost all of them were Negro women. Some of them had their heads wrapped in bandannas, but most of them had hats on. They all appeared to be wearing their best clothes, and as they sat in the blue theater seats listening to Mrs. Dash discuss her breakfast menu of bologna and grits, they looked at first glance like a Negro women's club listening to a travel lecture.

A young doctor took the stand—a white general practitioner from Beaufort County, on the coast. He said that he had been studying parasites for several years, that up to ninety per cent of the Negro children in some areas of Beaufort County suffered from parasitic diseases, and that he had attributed the deaths of eight children to parasitic diseases up until a couple of years ago, when, for reasons he didn't mention, he quit keeping count. He used medical terms to answer some of the panelists' questions, speaking clearly and precisely, but toward the end of the testimony, trying to explain the nutritional problems of Beaufort, he suddenly said, "There just ain't no damn sense in this country having hungry people, and we got a bunch of them."

"We're going to move on to another county now—Dorchester," the chairman said after the doctor had left. "I understand Mrs. Victoria DeLee is here."

A thin, gray-haired woman in a black dress with an imitation-fur collar stood up and started talking about the water in Beaufort County. When the chairman asked if she was Victoria DeLee— another woman had stood up in the back of the room—she said that her name was Mrs. Arimethea McKey and that she had brought some of the water with her. She picked up a paper bag, withdrew a large jar filled with murky brown liquid, and carried it to the witness table. Thumping on the jar for emphasis, she told a complicated story about an unsuccessful attempt by the people in her area to organize themselves into a water district. Finally, one of the panelists agreed to talk with her about the legal problems during the lunch break.

The real Mrs. DeLee—a large woman who was also wearing a black dress—came to the witness table and said that she lived in Dorchester County and that she tried to help out in the community. A panelist asked her what the situation in Dorchester was like. "May I say the whole situation in entire Dorchester County, it's terrible," Mrs. DeLee said. She spoke deliberately, in a strong, slightly husky voice. Some of the women in the audience smiled and nodded when she explained that a woman who had been deserted was denied welfare unless her husband could be found and she was willing to swear out a warrant against him. "It's terrible," Mrs. DeLee repeated. "It maybe seem jokey."

Several of the panelists smiled when Mrs. DeLee said that the welfare situation had improved slightly after she got some pamphlets from Washington and "scared the Welfare Department of Dorchester County." She reported less progress in an attempt to convince the schools that they should maintain a full free-lunch program. "We've been fightin' the schools in Dorchester County from 1964 up until now," she said. "And we have never yet got the schools straightened out. It's terrible."

One question reminded Mrs. DeLee of a particular family in Dorchester County, and she told the story of the family to the panel, speaking very slowly, with her arms folded on the witness table. It was the story of a mother and children so hungry that the children once went to a neighbor's field and "digged the whole field of potatoes from the back up to the front and eat the potatoes— even pull 'em up before they had anything on 'em." As Mrs. DeLee spoke, the panelists stopped taking notes, and the audience seemed to grow quieter. In the long pauses between sentences, all that could be heard was the hum of the lighting and the soft tapping of the stenographic machine. "The Welfare Department wouldn't give her nothin'," Mrs. DeLee said. "She was in childbirth. And before she had this child, she couldn't go to the doctor, because she didn't had any money to pay the doctor with. The law is in Dorchester County you got to go to the doctor four times before you can get a card to have a baby, before a nurse can put their hands on you. And she couldn't go to no hospital because she didn't even first been to the doctor. And when this baby was fixin' to be born, the nurse couldn't even go to touch the lady. And we went to the doctor and the doctor wouldn't even give the nurse a slip to deliver the baby. And the baby born a part of the way. And these children were there sittin' around. And they was cryin'. They didn't had anything to eat. The woman was in the bed. Havin' this baby. And she were cryin'. Nothin' to eat. We went to the Welfare Department and we *insisted* that they come down there. And they come. When they come, this baby was part the way born. And the other part wasn't. And this lady stayed there a half a day, just like this. And the doctors in Dorchester County wouldn't even give the nurses a slip to deliver this baby. And this baby born by itself and just laid there. And nobody was allowed to touch it. We went back and got the Welfare Department and finally we got the sheriff. Went and got the sheriff. Got the city police of Ridgeville. Got the sheriff and all of 'em. And we said we was going to call Washington. Then the lady come down. And the lady give this woman help. Eight head of kids in the house at the time."

Other witnesses continued the story that Mrs. Dash had begun when the hearing opened. Mrs. Huggins, of Clarendon County, was asked how she managed to provide food for seven children on thirty-one dollars a month, and she said, "Some of my friends come in and they bring some." Mrs. DuBois, of Bulloch County, Georgia, was asked what her children did when the other children at school ate lunch, and she said, "They say they just go out in back." Miss Bolden, of Jasper County, was asked if diarrhea was a frequent occurrence among her children, and she said, "I don't understand." Mrs. Huggins, of Clarendon County, was asked if her children were healthy, and she said, "Yes, sir, they healthy." Mrs. DuBois, of Bulloch County, was asked what she had served for supper the previous evening, and she said, "We doesn't eat any supper."

Those who had come to testify were guests of the hearing for lunch. They stood quietly in line in the basement cafeteria of a nearby Negro high school, and then sat at the long wooden tables and ate a turkey lunch. Some of the women didn't finish their meal and wrapped a roll or a piece of cake in a paper napkin to take with them.

For the afternoon session, the court reporter with the stenographic machine had been replaced by a blond young lady wearing a shocking-pink dress and a bouffant hairdo. Instead of typing on a machine, she used a masklike device that permitted her to repeat whatever was said into a recording machine without disturbing the proceedings. She sat with her legs crossed, holding the device up to her face, as if she were very calmly taking oxygen.

There were far more witnesses than could be heard. Miss Geddis, of Dorchester County, was asked about her ailments, and she said she had "high blood and low nerves." Mrs. Haynes, of Chatham County, Georgia, was asked if she had applied for welfare, and she said, "I been down there a couple of times, but it haven't worked out." (". . . it haven't worked out" came the nearly inaudible echo from the blond's mask.) Although the chairman had explained that the panelists had conducted hearings in other parts of the country and would be conducting one in another city the following day, the witnesses tended to refer to their county welfare representative by name or to identify a community as being "way out on Two Notch Road, down this side of Camden," as if the panelists were completely familiar with a world that ended at the county line. At the close of each witness's testimony, the chairman would thank the witness for coming in, and compliment her on being able to manage as well as she did, and tell her he hoped that at some point the country—or somebody—would find a way to help her with her problems.

Early in the afternoon, the chairman called on a nutritionist from the state university. The nutritionist stood at the witness table, holding the table microphone in his hand; when the chairman asked him to say a few words about nutrition, he turned and faced the audience, rather than the panel, as if he were delivering a lecture. He discussed the "bio-medical data" gathered from a study made in Greenville of "the low-income pregnant mother." It was not long after the turkey lunch, and a lot of the women in the audience looked sleepy as the nutritionist began. Mrs. Dash, who occupied an aisle seat right in front of him, had pushed back her theater chair and was resting her head on the back. Soon she was asleep, her mouth wide open. A number of the other women fell asleep, too.

After the nutritionist had spoken for a while, one of the few men in the audience got up and said, "What the people need is food. They go down to the welfare and the welfare beat 'em around the mulberry bush."

"This is entirely out of the university's category," the nutritionist said. "We're people connected with education."

The man in charge of services for the State Board of Welfare testified next. He said that of the forty-six counties in the state thirteen participated in the federal food-stamp program. The chairman asked him if he would be able to offer any explanation of why the state had one of the lowest rates of participation in the country.

"No, sir," the welfare man said pleasantly. "I wouldn't."

A woman in the audience, trying to explain to the welfare man that the initial price of food stamps was more money than a lot of people had, asked if it could be possible that a family of eleven would need sixty-seven dollars in order to buy stamps worth a hundred and nine dollars in food.

The welfare man said that it depended on the family's income.
One of the panelists noted that the worst welfare problem appeared to be caused by the requirement that a deserted woman find her husband before welfare was granted.

"That's not part of our eligibility requirements," the welfare man said.

"Not part of it?" a panelist asked incredulously.

"No."

"Not part of it in Dorchester County?"

"No."

"Yes, it is!" a woman from the audience shouted, standing up. " 'Cause I'll be a witness for that!"

"It may be a factor," the welfare man finally said. "But it's not the whole story."

Toward the end of the afternoon, only about thirty people remained. The chairman called a witness from Georgia, but another woman walked down the aisle and explained that two elderly women had been waiting all day to testify and were now about to reboard the bus that had brought them from Hilton Head Island. One of the elderly women then sat down at the witness table and the other one stood in the aisle behind her with the Georgia witness. Soon, a small line of people waiting to testify had formed in front of the witness table. The women from Hilton Head spoke with strange, singsong, almost European accents, which forced the blond court reporter to lean forward intently. After the first woman had testified, a man in the audience stood up and—speaking in the same singsong accent—began telling the story of a Hilton Head woman, Sister Bertha Perry, who had been unable to come to the hearings. He said that Mrs. Perry had been receiving forty dollars a month in welfare for herself and her four children but that the money had recently been cut off. When he had finished reciting the details, he said, "That's a report." The panelists asked a few questions, and then started to move on. The man remained standing. "What I must tell that lady?" he asked. "Come and see you herself?" The panelists looked puzzled. Then one of them took Sister Perry's name.

The second elderly woman from Hilton Head said her name was

Esther Simmons. She was wearing a very long cloth coat, a long scarf, and a black cloche hat with black bangles hanging from it. She was almost toothless, and she seemed to be grinning slightly as she talked. The panelist who questioned her—the only woman on the panel—spoke clearly into the microphone and asked Mrs. Simmons to do the same. Mrs. Simmons rested the microphone on her upper lip and rolled it around while the questions were being asked. She told the panelist that she had been cut off welfare. "I went down to the oyster factory and I reckon I made about two, three dollars one week," she said. "And somebody tell them I makin' six dollars a day."

"The only thing we can suggest is that you go back to the welfare —you and the other people who have been here," the panelist said. "Tell them your story again. Tell them you have certain rights that they must respect. And if they say they won't put you on welfare, tell them you'd like to appeal your case, and ask for a form to fill out and send it to the State Director of Welfare."

"Yes, ma'am," Mrs. Simmons said, still grinning and holding the microphone to her mouth.

The panelist thanked her for coming, and Mrs. Simmons said thank you and walked up the aisle with the other elderly woman to board the bus to Hilton Head.

# Turks

The Turks who live in Sumter County aren't really Turks. But then, in a way, people are whatever they're called. In the city of Sumter, about ten or fifteen miles from where the Turks live, a white citizen may joke about their being a mixture of all sorts of things, and then describe one as "more your pure Turk." A school official I talked with in Sumter County spread his arms out in a V in front of him and said, "Right here, all within ten miles of where you're sitting, is the only Turkish community on the continent of North America. Oh, there may be a Turk who has come over and lives in New York, or something, but this is the only Turkish community." The Sumter County Turks have nothing in common with a Turk who has come over to live in New York. They know nothing about cooking shish kebab or hating Greeks. Their closest known ancestral link with Turkey is not precisely with Turkey: it is said that the founders of the community—two men who, having fought with General Thomas Sumter during the American Revolution, were given land by the General around his plantation—were an oddly named Frenchman called Scott and Joseph Benenhaley, who is usually identified as a Moor or an Arab. Some Sumter County Turks look rather like Arabs. But some look rather like American Indians, some look rather like Cape Coloreds, some look exactly like the Scotch-Irish farmers who have traditionally snubbed them, and some look rather like—well, like Turks.

Throughout the Southeast, there have always been communities of people who constitute a third race, usually discriminated against by whites and almost always segregating themselves from Negroes —dark-skinned people of mysterious origin who are called names like Brass Ankles or Wesorts or Red Bones or Buckheads. Most of the groups apparently descend from remnants of Indian tribes that long ago intermarried with whites and with freed or escaped slaves. In a book called *Almost White,* an anthropologist named Brewton Berry refers to them as mestizos, and includes the Turks among groups whose names—Moors, Greeks, Portuguese, Arabs, Guineas —seem to reflect attempts by the locals to account for a dark and exotic appearance. Oxendine and Lowry, two names that are common among the Sumter County Turks, are also common among the twenty or thirty thousand people in Robeson County, North Carolina, known as Lumbee Indians. There are still a lot of Turks named Benenhaley, but there are also Turks named Hood and Ray. There may be no more reason to believe that the Turks are Turkish than there is to believe that the Brass Ankles have brass ankles, but the name has become part of their identity. "The men are mostly of the small-farmer or tenant class and most of them are poor," an article in the Columbia *State* said in 1928. "They are not aggressive and seem to accept their lot with truly Eastern fatalism." In recent years, newspaper reporters trying to be respectful have occasionally called the Turks "people of Turkish descent." The Turks would just as soon not be called anything at all. They have never taken much interest in whether or not they are "of Turkish descent." In South Carolina, talk about the descent of dark and mysterious people can lead to only one suspicion—the suspicion that the Turks have always despised and dreaded. "I always knew I wasn't colored," I was told by one member of the community, a woman who might have been taken for an Indian or a gypsy. "And I never paid any attention to none of that other stuff."

The one racial fact that every Turk is certain of is that he is, in the words of one Turk I spoke with, "as white-blooded as any man who walks the earth." He is also certain that his neighbors are always ready to believe he is part Negro. Around the time of the First World War, Sumter's great-grandson, stating that he was passing on what his father had learned from the General himself, wrote that the Turks were definitely without Negro ancestors, Benenhaley having been "a Caucasian of Arab descent" who married a white woman. It is said that the General himself guaranteed the Turks' right to serve on juries by walking into a courtroom and publicly shaking hands with a Turk who had been challenged. Turks always voted in the Democratic primary, and fought in wars as white troops. There was even an element of whiteness in the way they were segregated: they attended a special school for Turks only but were taught by white teachers, and after 1904 they had their own church, the Long Branch Baptist, but always retained white pastors (before that, when they attended High Hills Baptist with Negroes and whites, they sat downstairs with the white people—on their own side of the aisle). Whites didn't marry Turks, and Turks didn't marry Negroes—or, it is said, were ostracized if they did. Before the Second World War, Turks married almost exclusively within their own community; among the three hundred or so Turks in Sumter County, there are only a half-dozen surnames. As a third racial element, with a tenuous grasp on whiteness, the Turks never knew when they might be rebuffed. But as a rural people with their own church and school they presented few opportunities to those who might rebuff them. Their neighbors knew them as poor people who were usually law-abiding and who loved to hunt and fish and who distrusted outsiders. The box for Race on their birth certificates said "Turk."

During the war, what is now Shaw Air Force Base was established on thousands of acres of land near General Sumter's old plantation—including part of the land Turks had always farmed. Shaw provided steady employment for the Turks, and some of them apparently lost the truly Eastern fatalism necessary for accepting their lot as poor, uneducated country folk. A few years after the war, the Turks asked that their children be admitted to Hillcrest, the local white high school. There was no question of the Turks' separate facilities being equal; their school only went through tenth grade. The school board found it politic to make the Turks sue for admission, but the suit was not seriously contested.

The Turks' children did not have an easy time at Hillcrest; some social events were canceled or arranged in a way that made it possible to exclude Turks. It seems to have been the kind of reaction that had traditionally caused the Turks to withdraw into their own community, but a couple of years after the Hillcrest integration they asked that their children go to the regular white grade schools as well. A federal district judge ordered the Turks into the grade schools in September of 1953. The white children boycotted classes, and the judge withdrew the order. The case went back into court, and, with one thing and another, the Turks were not admitted until eight years later.

For the Turks, it was an unpleasant eight years, full of experiences that must have reinforced the strong feeling among them that it's always better to leave well enough alone. The hearings and depositions of the case brought to the surface that pseudo-anthropology which has always thrived among white Southerners the way voodoo thrives among Haitians. The school board presented depositions from local people stating that the Turks "are dark-skinned and have other features different and distinct from the white race and are not considered white people in the community in which they reside." A member of the school board testified in a deposition that a Turkish officer from Turkey who was training at Shaw Air Force Base had been taken by him to see some of "the race alleged to be Turkish" and that the officer "upon leaving told this deponent that these people were not of the Turkish race." A deposition defending the Turks reported that a local physician who had been "making a scientific study of this group of people" believed that "they are Caucasians, although from what he is able to learn they were originally of Arab descent," and went on, "Like the upper classes of India, who are definitely Aryans, their color is not as fair as the North European people, but color alone does not determine race. None of their features are negroid." (An earlier defender, the writer of the Columbia *State* article in 1928, had said, "Their skin, though dark, is thin, showing a rosy tint in the cheeks of the young people. Their features are decidedly Caucasian, their ankles and wrists slender, and their insteps arched. No flat feet, flat noses, thick lips, or curly hair are found among them.") The school-board lawyers dug up old census reports to show that some Turks were once listed as "free colored persons," and attempted to show through an old will that they were, as one deponent put it, "tainted with Negro blood."

It was not just that the Turks were accused of being Negroes. As the case progressed, they seemed to be put in the position of having to behave like Negroes. After the Supreme Court desegregation decision of 1954, their suit became increasingly similar to the kind of suit they would have joined their white neighbors in denouncing— the kind of suit by which Negroes tried to "force their way into the schools." The Turks wanted to be in the white schools *because* they were white. When they finally won, it didn't seem like a victory. One of the Turks who instituted the suit told me that he thought it had probably caused his people to think less of him, and that he has tried to avoid talking about the subject ever since. The Sumter lawyer who finally won the decision—Ira Kaye, who is now with the Office of Economic Opportunity in Washington—is one of the few outsiders who have ever amassed any trust among the Turks, but his plans to push for changes in birth certificates and investigations of job discrimination were not pursued by his clients after he left Sumter. The Turks are happy to have their children in the white school, but would just as soon forget how they got there.

The area where the Turks have always lived, between Dalzell and Stateburg, is still rural in some ways. There are country churches, stores with gas pumps outside of them, farms planted in soybeans and peanuts and cotton, and even an old plantation house or two. But a lot of the land between Dalzell and Stateburg is now within the fence that surrounds Shaw Air Force Base, and that fence is itself surrounded by trailer camps and beer joints, strung along like an outer perimeter of defense. The tract housing that goes along with Shaw reaches almost to the Long Branch Baptist Church. The church's two red brick buildings look rather new and bare, like a lot of the church buildings that accompany tract housing, but the cemetery in back looks like a traditional country cemetery—old headstones, many of them inscribed with the name Benenhaley, shaded by gnarled, moss-covered trees. Hillcrest School also has a new-looking building, and its sixteen hundred students now include not only Turks but a couple of hundred Negroes. Its former building, just across the highway, is now the Thomas Sumter Academy, an all-white private school of the kind that has been started around the South in recent years by people who feel so strongly against sending their children to school with Negroes that they're willing to pay money to avoid it.

The lot of the Turks who attend high school has been helped by the tendency of local whites to send their children to the Academy, leaving Hillcrest largely to airbase children, most of whom are not endowed by inheritance with a precise knowledge of how Turks are to be treated in Sumter County. "We've had very few of them to go ahead and graduate," a county school official told me, but of the relatively few Turks who became seniors at Hillcrest this year one boy is near the top of his class and two girls have been accepted at a nearby college. Some of the Turks are still poor, and most of them are uneducated. Those who work at Shaw work mainly as unskilled employees in places like the warehouse or the motor pool. But steady employment at Shaw and at some of the factories in Sumter has given many Turks a kind of economic security that would have been unimaginable before the war. A few of them, perhaps combining a job at Shaw with running a trailer park or some housebuilding, have done fairly well, and now live among the careful knickknack cabinets and tinted wedding pictures of the emerging middle class.

There is undoubtedly less discrimination against Turks in Sumter County now than there was in the past, and Turks are reluctant to acknowledge the discrimination that does exist. Having seen light-skinned relatives avoid trouble by moving a few miles into the next county, they tend to say that the only people blindly committed to snubbing them are the whites who have always lived in the immediate vicinity—"that little ring around Dalzell." Local Negroes, in turn, sometimes single out the Turks as the area's most intransigent segregationists; Negroes making light of a Turk who used to be poorer than they were and is now intent on living the life of a middle-class-white segregationist sometimes sound like Turks sneering at the "poor crackers" who insist on sending their children to the Thomas Sumter Academy. "Some of 'em come into my house for coffee and I go to theirs," a Negro woman who grew up in the area told me. "But some of 'em actually thinks they're white." In the city of Sumter, a white person who has heard of the Turks may mention that they are generally upstanding and respectable people—and he may mention something about how some people think they're part colored but there might be nothing to it. In Dalzell, I met a woman who was much more direct—a stout woman in slacks who was sitting in the back of a small store drinking a Coke. "They're not Turks, you know," she told me. "I tell you what they are—they're part nigger. The whites wouldn't associate with 'em, so they had to marry with the colored." She took another swig of the Coke and smiled. "Oh, they got some of it in 'em, all right," she said.

The Turks still tend to stick together, and they still dread having attention called to them. But there are now a few non-Turk families from Shaw attending Long Branch Baptist. Local whites still don't marry Turks, but since the war an increasing number of the community's girls have married white airmen from Shaw. It is even possible that someday the Turks will no longer exist. Their existence as a group is now largely a function of family relationships and mutual protection; they have no special traditions to carry on except a love of hunting and an obsession about being white. I asked an elder of the Long Branch Baptist Church what he thought about the possibility of the Turks' gradually merging into the general population. A few minutes before, he had told me that he was, of course, proud of being a Turk but that many of his people were sort of timid about it. He thought for a while, and then he said, "I think maybe the majority'd be better off if it did play out."

Whatever untapped inclination toward race pride the Turks have should have been brought out in 1963, when, to everyone's surprise, Muhittin Güven, a Turkish Member of Parliament on a State Department tour of the United States, stopped in Sumter to pay them a goodwill visit. Kenan Taspinar, a New York businessman retained to serve as Güven's escort and interpreter, had read about the school case in *The New York Times* and suggested that Sumter be included on Güven's itinerary. "When the State Department called me, I tried to tell them it wasn't really relevant," Ira Kaye has recalled. "But they insisted." By the time Güven arrived in Sumter, it was not easy to tell that the presence of the Turks had

been the original reason for his visit. He went on the usual rounds
—receiving the key to the city, attending a dinner and reception the
mayor gave in his honor at the Holiday Inn, inspecting tobacco
markets and a furniture factory. Only one line, deep in the Sumter
*Item*'s account of the festivities, mentioned that he had also visited
"the Turkish-American community at Stateburg." A man from the
Sumter Chamber of Commerce was with him. "We had a real nice
covered-dish supper at the church," the Chamber of Commerce
man told me. "We took a picture of him with the old king out
there, and, you know, they could have passed for brothers—although the old king was darker." The local man in the picture was
Julius Benenhaley, who has never been a king but was for a long
time an elder at the Long Branch Baptist Church. A cheerful,
straightforward man in his seventies who looks like the patriarch of
some particularly robust Middle Eastern or Southern European
clan, he lives on a small farm not far from Hillcrest School. "I'm
proud of my Turkish blood," Benenhaley told me. "That's why I
was proud to meet that man who come all the way from Turkey."
It might be thought that all Turks would have been delighted to
have public confirmation of their Turkish origins, but a lot of
Turks don't like any talk about origins, and there was a strong
feeling that any outsider could bring only harm. Still, a number of
people turned out at the church, and Güven, by all accounts, had a
fine time. The Chamber of Commerce man says that Güven
thought the Turks might have originally been Maltese. Taspinar,
the interpreter, believes they could have been North Africans who
were part of the Ottoman Empire. Benenhaley remembers Güven
as a great fellow and treasures the picture of the two of them together. Some of the other Turks are still suspicious. "He *said* he
was a Turk," I was told by one woman. "I don't know what he
was, but he wasn't no Turk. He looked more like an Indian."

# G. T. Miller's Plan

Some time ago, a friend of mine who lives in Alabama told me that G. T. Miller, the proprietor of the G. T. Miller Feed & Grist Mill, in Luverne, had a plan to help Crenshaw County and the entire country. I've run into a lot of people at one time or another who have plans for helping the entire country—the plans usually have to do with something like going on the silver standard or signing up for Moral Re-Armament—but plans for Crenshaw County are rare. The problem is not that no one cares about Crenshaw County; it's that most people consider Crenshaw County beyond help. The one plan that most people who actually live in Crenshaw County have is a plan to get out. It's a rural county, about an hour south of Montgomery, and it has been notable in recent years almost entirely for its amazing rate of shrinkage. I figured that anybody who had a plan for Crenshaw County must be worth meeting. My friend admitted he didn't quite understand Miller's plan, but that didn't disturb me. I don't quite understand the silver standard or Moral Re-Armament.

According to my friend, G. T. Miller was a white man of about seventy who had done pretty well in business around Crenshaw County despite having had only three or four years of schooling. "He's not a racist," my friend said, "and he had some trouble with the Klan a few years ago. But he's not exactly a liberal, either. I'm not sure he'd know what you were talking about if you used that word. He might be more of a Populist, in a way, although he believes in business. And he's got a fallout shelter—a huge fallout shelter."

In rural Alabama, people who belong to organizations like the Ku Klux Klan often have a strong notion of general philosophy but get mixed up on details. It wouldn't surprise me to hear that someone in Crenshaw County might get in trouble with the Klan for, say, having a fallout shelter, or for not having one. But my friend said that the Klan had been pretty much on target when it threatened G. T. Miller and organized a boycott of his businesses. Miller had apparently refused to fire a Negro who had somehow interpreted the county's freedom-of-choice school-desegregation plan to mean that his son was free to choose the white school. Miller had even employed the son part time. Eventually, Miller had explained the issue on C.B.S. television news. "I couldn't see where I'd want to fire him because his young 'un was going to school," Miller said during the interview. "His young 'un's got a life to live, and he just as well have an education as my boy." After the program, a couple of thousand people from all over the country wrote Miller that they thought he was a hero. Some of them even sent money to help offset the losses he was suffering because of the boycott. A few of them said they thought it might be nicer if a man of Miller's courage and principles didn't use the word "nigger" quite so freely.

"We was doin' *extra* good till the Ku Klux got on us," G. T. Miller told me. He was showing me around his feed and grist mill—a roomy, remarkably neat place that smells slightly of the molasses that some farmers like to mix with corn when they grind their cattle feed. Miller is a husky man who doesn't look his age. He was wearing his usual outfit of bib overalls, a sports shirt, and a small felt hat. Before the boycott, Miller's mill was part of what amounted to a kind of one-man, rural, just-folks conglomerate. Only the feed mill remains open, but spread out along the highway, just inside the Luverne city limits, are buildings that once held a supermarket, a cotton gin, a trucking company, and a recreation center that included a dance hall, a bowling alley, and a skating rink. Once,

when Miller found himself with some time and space that weren't
being properly exploited, he started raising worms and crickets for
fish bait. Miller is proud that the Miller enterprises were built by a
poor, uneducated country boy—the businesses built up from
scratch, the buildings put together with cheap lumber from struc-
tures being torn down elsewhere—and he is quick to tell visitors of
the kind of youth that most respectable businessmen would not
choose to remember. He says that when he was a young man trying
to accumulate capital by barbering, a conviction for moonshining
gave him the opportunity to practice his trade for a while at the
federal penitentiary in Atlanta. He was a Klansman for a time himself as a young man, and he acknowledges that his arguments in
those days with the Klan and others included some beatings and
some shootings—a couple of which he lost painfully. "In them
times," he says, "a man fightin' the Klan around here had about as
much chance as a one-legged man at a tail-kickin'."

Having once been poor himself, Miller has always believed in
helping people by giving them jobs, but he believes he is helping
himself at the same time; it is obvious to him that businessmen get
back all the money they spend. "The workin' man don't keep his
money but three hours to three days," he told me. "Some of 'em
spends it in three hours; some keep it as long as three days. I did
me a survey on that once. Those folks on Wall Street oughtn't to be
scared to turn loose of that money, 'cause it'll be right back down
there in a little while anyhow."

A couple of hours after I met G. T. Miller, I began to sympathize with my friend's difficulty in trying to explain Miller's views.
Most of the people my friend and I come across—or at least the
people we talk to about plans to help the country—have a set pattern of beliefs. When people tell me what they think about disarma-
ment, I have a pretty good idea of what they are likely to think
about school integration. Not G. T. Miller. He believes in school
integration ("The niggers need an education, too; you can get
along with a fella when he's got a good education"), but he also
believes in his fallout shelter—the community's fallout shelter,
really, since he built it to hold sixty-four beds. As I understand his
views on the war, he's a hawk, but I'm not sure I understand his
views on the war. I know he's concerned about the country's being

torn apart by hatred and dissent, although I don't know whether he holds hatred or dissent to blame. "If we go on like we're goin', we're automatically whupped," he told me as we sat in his bomb shelter. "Russia's doin' nothin' but waitin'—like a buzzard on a tree a-waitin' for a mule to die."

Miller believes landowners have dealt unfairly with sharecroppers. He also believes that landowners are serving their country and helping to feed their fellow human beings when they figure out methods of more profitable hog production. When he approves of something, he often says, "Every time a man betters himself, he betters his country." When he disapproves, he often says, "That's no way to help your fellow-man or your country, either one." He has given a lot of people no-interest loans for down payments on houses, partly because he thinks they have a right to own something and partly because it's a Christian act and partly because he believes that people who own something themselves aren't likely to burn down other people's property. "Let it be his'n!" Miller says about housing for the poor man. "Have him pay a small down payment. If he gets into tight and can't pay it, wait on him till he catches up. When they get out demonstratin', he's not going to stick fire to that house."

Not being burdened with any notion of how he should feel about various issues, Miller arrives at some views that have a distinguished simplicity. He is opposed to foundations' not paying taxes, for instance, because foundations use the public roads just the way everybody else does. Being a practical man, he is not embarrassed when his Christian ventures and his business ventures overlap. He would be the last man to turn his neighbors away from his fallout shelter; he would be the first man to take his fallout shelter off his taxes. He lends people hospital beds, which he happened to get at a good price under civil-defense regulations, because he wants to be a good neighbor. He used to lend wagons to farmers, partly so they could haul their cotton to his gin, but he thought of that as a neighborly act, too. The plan he has for Crenshaw County seems to entail giving away his business.

A lot of Miller's ideas about Crenshaw County were formed from having spent ten years or so making a film on the area. It's actually split into two films—*What We Have* and *What We Need*. Miller showed them to me one day, in the living room of the modern house he and his wife live in—up the road from the feed mill, on top of the fallout shelter. He also got out his charts and his pointer and his American flags, so that I could see precisely what it had been like when he presented the films to church groups and service clubs in the area, before the trouble with the Klan started. "When we learn to love one another as the good Lord is trying to teach us to, we'll find out that our nation will move forward in a record speed," he said by way of introduction. "And at the same time we can help get poor people out of the gully, and help our nation, and accumulate a better world for all races of people." The charts—all hand-drawn—covered a great variety of subjects. One of them said, "We Need a Public Price Commission." One of them indicated the economic impact that one hundred new jobs had on a community. One of them said, "Slums Are Costly to All," and showed a kind of keyhole-shaped representation of an urban area, the round part of the keyhole being very crowded with tiny squares. "Down in the slums," Miller said, pointing to that part of the drawing, "a man becomes a kind of fanatic, due to the fact that he can't accumulate nothin'." The charts also had drawings of the recreation centers that Miller would like to see built. Not recreation centers like the one he used to run before the boycott. These recreation centers would be part of the plan to help Crenshaw County and the entire country. Miller has faith in the efficacy of training—he says, "I could take me a boy who don't know nothin' in the world except how to hitch up a mule, and wouldn't know that except the head's on one side and the tail's on another, and teach him to be a carpenter"—and his faith extends to the belief that people could be trained to get along with each other. "You'd have a hundred- or two-hundred-acre lot, and a good, nice tabernacle," he says. "You'd have different talks, twice a day." One architectural rendering—the one of the recreation center's dining hall—looked familiar to me. After a while, I realized that it was exactly the same as the keyhole-shaped representation of an urban area. The tiny squares that had been crowding the slums had become dining-hall tables.

As I watched the films, it occurred to me that white people in Crenshaw County had probably been more receptive to *What We*

*Have* than to *What We Need*—although, the entertainment opportunities being what they are in Crenshaw County, I can't imagine
that there would be a very large attrition rate in an audience even if
a film turned out to be a laudatory biography of H. Rap Brown.
The first film shows a lot of the modern farming methods in the
area, but the second shows some slums and some decrepit Negro
schools, and even some of the Negro sharecroppers near Selma
who were thrown off land for registering to vote and had to live in
tents. ("It throwed a hard burden on these people; at the same
time, it throwed a hard burden on our federal government that had
to give 'em welfare and support 'em.") Miller traces most of the
deficiencies shown in the film to one overwhelming problem—that
sharecroppers and small farmers and farmhands have had to move
to city slums because of mechanization or because a landowner has
found it more profitable to put the land into the federal soil bank
than to farm it. His plan is to get a lot of the area's small farmers—
black and white—to pool their resources and their energies and G.
T. Miller's enterprise and run an operation that will allow all of
them to remain.

There have never been many white people in Crenshaw County
who share Miller's views; there may be nobody anywhere who
shares Miller's views. But he was tolerated—and permitted to use
the courtroom of the county courthouse for his film lecture—until
he refused to fire the Negroes who had offended the Klan. At about
the same time, it was rumored around town—correctly—that he
had been guilty of overt kindness to some American Friends Service Committee volunteers who were in Luverne to work with the
community's Negroes. After one of the ghetto disturbances in the
North, someone circulated a paper saying that Miller's most recent
lecture had been sponsored by the American Friends Service Committee and that Miller had said he didn't blame slum dwellers for
rioting. The county commissioners decided that Miller could no
longer give his speech in the courthouse. The Klan, with the support of local businessmen, started a boycott of Miller's businesses
that was, by all accounts, pretty effective. Miller countered with a
broadsheet arguing that if he were forced out of business, which
seemed quite possible, the county would suffer economically. Eventually, the federal judge who had ordered the freedom-of-choice

plan into effect enjoined the Klan from harassing Miller and some other citizens. Gradually, some of the farmers who had formerly brought their feed to grind at Miller's started showing up again at the mill; Miller now estimates his mill business at about a third of what it was before the boycott.

Through it all, Miller says, if he saw a boycotter across the street he made it a point to cross over and say hello. The subjects of forgiveness and reconciliation are particularly moving to Miller; his eyes often fill with tears when he recalls his overtures to his enemies. "If a man is a Ku Kluxer and I know he hates me and I find out some of his folks are sick and need help, I call him, or I go to see him, either one," he told me one day. "I tell him I got a good hospital bed he can keep as long as he wants, and it won't cost him a penny in the world. You have to learn to forgive if you're askin' the good Lord to forgive *you*. So I never go to bed hating nobody. And that's the only way to win over enemies, too. You can fight 'em, but all you do is make 'em mad and worser. Our federal government needs to have a school for trainin' people on something on this same idea."

With business off, Miller spent a lot of time perfecting his plan for small farmers. He and Mrs. Miller gathered a lot of charts and documents and tables and had them run off in blueprint form, so they could make a set of scrapbooks on the plan. Tom Law, who works for an agency in Montgomery that gives technical assistance to projects applying for federal grants, sees Miller's plan as basically a marketing-and-production cooperative in poultry raising, differing from the normal co-op in that Miller's business would be included in the operation. But as described by Miller or the scrapbooks it doesn't sound that simple. The scrapbooks include Miller's ideas of what the county has and what it needs, prayers used by various denominations, and photographic layouts featuring pictures of cows with captions like "You take good care of me and I will produce you some good calves." The scrapbooks also contain detailed figures showing precisely how the co-op would work. The Office of Economic Opportunity has shown some interest in the project, and some of the people in Luverne—being in a position to welcome any kind of investment, even poverty-program investment —have decided that Miller is entitled to his ideas. One of the letters of recommendation in the scrapbooks is from the county commissioners of Crenshaw County.

Law is convinced of Miller's sincerity, but he has had some problems explaining to Miller exactly how things are done in the world of government grants—how meetings would have to be held and minutes recorded, how "checkpoint-procedure coordination forms" would have to be filed. Law told Miller that the blueprinted scrapbooks with talking cows were fine for internal distribution but might not be the best way to present the plan to Washington. Miller has some ideas of his own about how the bureaucracy of poverty ought to work. He believes, among other things, that poverty workers ought to be paid on a commission basis.

When I left Luverne, Miller loaded me down with blueprints and broadsheets and letters and files. While looking through the material in New York, I happened to come across the carbons of some letters Miller had written in 1967, a year before he appeared on C.B.S. to say why he couldn't fire the Negroes he had been ordered to fire. "Dear Sir," the letters said. "I finally had to do what you asked me to do. Stop helping the colored people and the poor people out in any way. Also had to lay off the ones you mentioned in our conversation. Yours truly, G. T. Miller. P.S. We appreciate your business in the past and hope to serve you in the future." The letters were addressed to some of the people who were later named in the injunction against the Klan. I telephoned Miller in Luverne.

"Well, we was finally forced to lay 'em off, being our business was off seventy-five per cent," he said. "We didn't lay 'em off cause we wanted to or cause they told us to."

"You mean as long as you had to lay them off anyway, you figured you might as well tell the boycotters about it?" I asked.

"Yeah. To see if the people boycottin' us would come back," he said, sounding pleased that I seemed to have caught on to the simple logic of it. "You understand how it works now?"

I told him I thought I did.

# The Black Womens of Wilcox County Is About To Do Somethin'

"Tis with Fingers of love that I pause here to request the honor of your present at the groundbreaking of the sewing center," Mrs. Estelle Witherspoon, the manager of the Freedom Quilting Bee, wrote the organization's friends and business acquaintances last month. "It will take place March 8 1969 at 10 A.M. We are so greatful and Thankful to the Lord that he have answered our prayers and ables us to by a piece of land through the help of our meny friends." Compared with most poor, uneducated Negro women living in the rural counties of the Alabama blackbelt—in fact, compared with just about anyone living in the rural counties of the Alabama blackbelt—the members of the Freedom Quilting Bee have a wide range of friends and business acquaintances. By the time the board of directors met on the Wednesday before the groundbreaking, several hundred invitations had been sent out—one of the quilting bee's advisers, a white Episcopal priest named Francis X. Walter, having had photo-offset copies of Mrs. Witherspoon's original made in Tuscaloosa. The board meeting was held in what the members call the quilt house—a two-room unpainted shack in Gees Bend that belongs to one of the members. In Gees Bend, a farming area in Wilcox County that is enclosed within an

elongated loop in the Alabama River, Negroes have lived almost
isolated from whites for years—first as squatters on the neglected
plantation their ancestors had developed as slaves, then as participants in a New Deal experiment in more or less cooperative farming, and then as small farmers or farm workers, and always as poor
people. Although some of the eighty-five or so women active in the
Freedom Quilting Bee live as far as sixty miles away, most of them
live in Gees Bend. Many of them work in their own homes. Some
work in the back of a dilapidated, sparsely stocked general store,
where some of the local men spend part of the day sitting on up-
ended soda cases around the stove, and where someone has
scrawled "Freedom Is Near" next to the door. Some work at the
quilt house. Some work at the Freedom Quilting Bee headquarters
—another shack, several miles closer to Alberta, where a few white
people live, but not close enough to be within reach of the telephone lines that end on the way from Alberta to Gees Bend.

A dozen board members, most of them heavyset women who
appeared to be in their fifties or sixties, gathered in the larger room
of the quilt house for the board meeting. The front window was
broken—the missing panes had been replaced with a flattened
pasteboard box that once held a turkey distributed by the Department of Agriculture surplus-food program—but a wood-burning
stove kept the room warm. There were three men present: Father
Walter, a serious, straightforward Alabamian in his thirties, who
was dressed non-clerically in a sports shirt and a tweed jacket; Ezra
Cunningham, a Negro farmer who is a field representative for the
Southern Cooperative Development Program; and Stanley Selengut, a New Yorker who was retained as the quilting bee's industrial-
development consultant last year with money from a grant and continued as a volunteer after the money was gone. Selengut, who has
a thick brush mustache and wears his sideburns somewhat longer
than is customary in Wilcox County, had arrived that morning
from New York. He had brought with him a revised plan for the
new sewing center (the board of directors had asked for an extra
bathroom with a bathtub, indoor bathrooms and bathtubs both
being in demand around the Gees Bend area) and some color
transparencies of pictures due to appear in *Life* this spring to advertise products of the Freedom Quilting Bee and the Poor

People's Corporation of Mississippi as the first test offering of a new *Life* merchandising project called Life's Treasures. Before the meeting, Selengut passed around the transparencies, and Mrs. Witherspoon passed around a magazine clipping that showed a picture of a quilted love seat in the summer house of Mrs. William Paley, a New York style setter who is regularly on the list of best-dressed women. In one of the major successes of Father Walter's early efforts to make Freedom Quilting Bee quilts fashionable, a Manhattan decorator named Mrs. Henry Parish II placed a large order for Mrs. Paley's summer house and for the nursery in the apartment of Mrs. Paley's daughter, another career dresser named Amanda Burden. Mrs. Callie Young, the quilting-bee president, held the *Life* transparencies up to the window, above the turkey box, where the light showed an icy-looking blond model and a blond little girl standing in front of a Freedom Quilting Bee rick-rack-pattern quilt and wearing the African dashiki-style mini-dresses now produced by the quilting bee. "Ain't that beautiful?" Mrs. Young said. "That's real pretty—that sure is."

The board meeting began with a hymn and a prayer. After Father Walter read through the program that he and Mrs. Carey of the entertainment committee had prepared for the groundbreaking, there was some discussion about who would introduce the special guests and who would register visitors, and there was a shorter discussion about whether to dedicate the sewing center to Martin Luther King, Jr., at the groundbreaking or to dedicate it to Martin Luther King, Jr., after it was up. Then Mrs. Young said, "Now we comin' down to new business"—and it was the business everyone had been waiting for. The sewing center had been scheduled to be built on an acre of land along the county highway that runs from Alberta to Gees Bend—an acre the quilting-bee members had acquired only after a long period during which it had seemed that no white landowner would sell—but in the week before the board meeting a white farmer named Lee Rose indicated to Mrs. Witherspoon his willingness to sell the quilting bee a much larger piece of property that included a house, a well, and twenty-three acres of land.

Mrs. Witherspoon related several conversations she had with Rose, introducing each of them with an exact rendition of how they had greeted each other—"He said 'Estelle?' I said 'Sir?' " (Mrs. Witherspoon has a local reputation as a mimic; she can imitate a couple of the whites in Alberta and a couple of the quilting-bee members, and she can reproduce both sides of the conversation the women had with the Wilcox County sheriff a few years ago when they went to the county courthouse to register for voting.) It sounded as if Rose's price went up with every conversation, until he was asking ten thousand dollars plus the acre the quilting bee already had. A couple of the board members shook their heads in wonderment at talk of that much money, but Father Walter reported that the American Friends Service Committee in Atlanta would be willing to make an interest-free loan if the board wanted to buy the land and thought that business was good enough to warrant it.

Business is getting better all the time. Father Walter first noticed some boldly designed quilts hanging on clotheslines at a place called Possum Bend in 1965; as director of the Selma Inter-Religious Project, which had been founded by clergymen who were on the Selma March, he was going through Wilcox County collecting depositions from Negroes who had been evicted because they registered to vote. Father Walter eventually organized the quilters into a co-op—marketing the quilts for fifteen dollars through his newsletter and some church mailings, and soliciting scraps from sympathetic white liberals. About a year ago, he came across Selengut, who sent someone to Wilcox County to work on design and quality control, invested in good fabric to replace the scraps, and decided that quilting, a difficult and time-consuming process, should be treated as a kind of expensive art form for the most talented quilters while more profitable lines were developed for the bulk of the quilting bee's business. The Freedom Quilting Bee, which did twenty-two thousand dollars' worth of business last year, already has twenty thousand dollars' worth of orders this year. Its problem is not whether it can sell what it produces but whether it can possibly produce enough to fill the orders it has sold. Mrs. Witherspoon reported to the meeting that a recent writeup in Woman's Day about the quilts had already resulted in more than a thousand letters; as the board members began smiling about that bonanza they were told that, considering large orders from Life and

Flamingo Park folk: Not all the youth were Mr. Nixon's sort

Wally McNamee—Newsweek

...ouse," the walkie-
...was due
...ime called
...eau Hotel
...startled to discover
...a giant peanut min-
...vd. Hasty inquiries
...alking peanut was
...bags on behalf of
...security agents ra-
...word to his part-
...eanut," he said.

**...ot Pre-Rehearsed'**

...', the elaborate security net-
...simply part of a larger master
...had been devised in advance
...that everything happened at
...(and in prime) time and that
...ned up in an improper place.
...for example, were given
...arked LIMITED ACCESS that
... no special access to any-
...e outer purlieus of Con-
...e extraordinary degree
...t (page 35) was ex-
...hen a messenger
...n the British
...a secret
...convention may yet cause prolonged
...the courts, and the makeup of the 1976

...e after-
...the courts, and the makeup of the 1976

...been arrested earlier). Among those
...jailed were poet Allen Ginsberg and the

about Pennsylvania and Ohio, plus Mayor Daley about Illinois (assuming Mayor Daley about Illinois (assuming) withholds his magic from McGovern'), upbeat about Missouri now that Sen. Thomas Eagleton is off the ticket.

## Six Democratic Soft Spots

The prospects for seizing control of both houses of Congress are also somewhat clouded. The Senate is a real possibility. If Mr. Nixon should get 55 per cent of the vote, predicts Colorado Sen. Peter Dominick, head of the GOP Senate Campaign Committee, that would be enough to pluck off the six most vulnerable Democratic seats—in Rhode Island, Oklahoma, New Mexico, Montana, North Carolina and Georgia—and give the Republicans command. But in the House, they would need to turn over 40 seats, and a NEWSWEEK state-by-state check last week indicated a probable net GOP gain of only sixteen.

And so the "new majority," if it materializes, may very well turn out to be only a Nixon majority—and not the dawn of a new era of Republican dominance or any of the other resplendent vistas that some convention goers were tempted to see last week. "This Nixon

AP

**Happy hands: A hug from Sammy . . .**

has spelled out some of his own proposals in such detail as to give the Administration what it sees as ample targets of its own. The President intends, for example, not to let the public forget McGovern's $1,000-per-citizen welfare scheme (even though McGovern himself has dropped it), the budgetary impact of the Democrats' platform proposals ("that would mean an increase of 50 per cent," he charged at Miami Beach, "in what the taxpayers of America pay") and particularly McGovern's proposals on Vietnam and defense spending (he himself, he told the legionnaires in a clear reference

fact. T  
had s  
sleeve,  
that his  
soon end  
breakthrough in  
gotiations. It deriv  
own reading of th  
tion in Vietnam.

The President v  
dow seat of a cu  
place to think and  
els on Air Force C  
up on a low table,  
roared on toward M.  
vention. It was an odd ac  
was in the cubbyhole with hi  
Mrs. Nixon had asked A  
velt Longworth (who describ  
as "Washington's perambula  
ment"), to go to the conven  
President's plane. Mrs. Lor  
cousin of mine and an old  
had volunteered to go a  
cort. When Mrs. Lon  
against the trip (no d  
is "pushing 90," as  
out), I remained  
guest list.  
When

Bloomingdale's and the fact that making dashikis or throw pillows. is so much more profitable than making quilts (Mrs. Witherspoon has conducted a time study), a lot of the inquiries would probably be sent along to a co-op in West Virginia.

Father Walter had been carefully neutral as he presented the alternatives the board had in considering whether to buy the farm, but after some talk about what might be done with twenty-three acres—a catfish farm or a pig-feeding program that could provide work for men in the community, a day-care center—he finally admitted, "I can almost taste that farm." The board members wanted to buy the farm as long as they didn't have to surrender their original acre, and someone put that in the form of a motion. Mrs. Young said, "All in favor say the word 'aye'—no, let me see you stand, that'll be better." All the board members stood.

There was a report from the cooking committee, name tags were handed out, and someone asked what the board members would wear for the ground-breaking. Ezra Cunningham, who had said little except during the discussion of potential agricultural projects, looked up and said, "I suggest they wear dashikis and miniskirts."

Father Walter and Selengut were, as usual, houseguests of the Witherspoons during their stay in Wilcox County. After Mrs. Witherspoon began drawing a steady salary (two thousand dollars a year) as the quilting-bee manager, the family moved into a relatively solid house that has indoor plumbing. Their property includes a yard for pigs and chickens, a patch of garden for growing greens, and, across from the garden, a tiny unpainted house that serves as a home for Mrs. Witherspoon's mother, a diminutive woman who always wears a man's felt hat and is known to everyone in the area as Ma Willie. Ma Willie did Amanda Burden's nursery. Among leaders of the Southern cooperative movement, which has assisted the Freedom Quilting Bee, pride in its accomplishments is sometimes coupled with resentment about its dependence on whites—one way to envision a Negro co-op is as a kind of black kibbutz that provides an alternative to white capitalism—but Father Walter and Selengut continue to feel comfortable among the quilting-bee members, who tend to be strong believers in Martin Luther King's teachings about love. The cynicism occasionally expressed in the co-op movement about white businesses that help themselves while helping the poor—about how much a decorator like Mrs. Parish charges for a yard of quilted material, for instance, or about how *Life,* which might expect to incur the displeasure of its advertisers by any step toward mail-order merchandising, can protect itself from criticism by making the first test with merchandise produced by poor people's co-ops—is never heard among members of the Freedom Quilting Bee. They are interested mainly in adding a few hundred dollars to a family income that is likely to be less than a thousand dollars a year.

On the evening of the board meeting, Father Walter and Selengut remained behind after dinner while Mr. and Mrs. Witherspoon, armed with a five-hundred-dollar check, went to see if Rose would accept a down payment to sell for ten thousand. (Mr. Witherspoon, a small, energetic, humorous man in his sixties, is unable to do farm work because of a hip injury and often helps out with quilting-bee business affairs.) Rose instantly accepted the offer. The following day, after Father Walter had driven to Alberta to phone the quilting bee's lawyer and the American Friends Service Committee, the Witherspoons and the Roses drove to the county courthouse to sign over the deed. That evening, Mrs. Witherspoon, unable to find an envelope around the house, wrapped a check for nine thousand five hundred dollars in a paper Christmas-party napkin, and her husband, after a few jokes about how much more money that was than Rose had ever held in his hand before, went with her to deliver the check.

It rained during most of Thursday and part of Friday. Father Walter, Witherspoon, and Selengut interviewed contractors; Witherspoon presided over the butchering of two hogs and the clearing of the section of Rose's cornfield that had been selected as the new site; Selengut staked out the building; and many members of the quilting bee stopped sewing and started cooking.

On Saturday, it was clear. At ten o'clock, two hundred or so people—about half of them whites from the university community in Tuscaloosa or from Atlanta or from New York—gathered a few hundred yards up the road from the new property. Father Walter had put on not only his clerical collar but an imposing liturgical hat and an elaborately brocaded cope. The board members wore hats and their Sunday coats—cloth coats with fur collars—but under their coats they wore dashiki-style dresses, a foot or so longer than miniskirts. The choral group from Tuskegee and the flute-and-drum trio from Memphis that were scheduled to perform had both encountered transportation difficulties, but there was a song from an Atlanta folk singer in West African dress and a hymn from the entire group. Then, led by a color guard carrying a cross flanked by an American flag and an Alabama flag, everyone marched down the county highway toward the building site, singing "I'm Going to Do What the Spirit Say Do." In Rose's muddy cornfield, Father Walter blessed the site and dedicated it to the memory of Martin Luther King, Jr. The board followed Father Walter and the color guard around the strings Selengut had placed to indicate where the building would be, and each of the board members turned over a shovelful of earth—all of them with the quick, efficient motion of people who are familiar with shovels. Lee Rose and his wife watched from the driveway. Rose told a visitor that he and his wife had been wanting to move closer to their children and had been happy to help out the colored folks by selling them the land. "We got a lot of good niggers around here and a lot of sorry ones," he said. "I guess it's that way everywhere with both races."

At the Pleasant Grove Baptist Church, a plain white structure in Gees Bend, there were several speeches, including one by Mrs. Young, the quilting-bee president, who said of the occasion, "It makes me feel like the black womens of Wilcox County is about to do somethin'." The special guests were introduced—representatives from the Federation of Southern Cooperatives, the manager of a co-op that was furnishing concrete bricks for the building, executives of a couple of foundations that are helping to pay for the building, a designer from Bloomingdale's who had color-styled some quilts and designed a line of throw pillows for the Bloomingdale's order, a man from Life's Treasures, a New York textile importer named Preston Schwarz, who had extended the Freedom Quilting Bee credit on the African dashiki panels he imports from a factory in Holland. Afterward, at the local school, everyone lined up for dinner—fried chicken, barbecued pork, collard greens, black-eyed peas, sweet-potato pie—and looked at a display of quilts and pillows and sunbonnets and pot holders and dashikis made by the Freedom Quilting Bee. Visitors were also encouraged to stop by the quilting bee's current headquarters—a rickety, unpainted, two-room shack that the Witherspoons used to live in. In one room, Mrs. Witherspoon and the assistant manager somehow handle the office work, hemmed in by a cutting table and bolts of fabric and finished quilts. In another room, of about the same size —a room in which all four walls and the ceiling are covered with faded flowered wallpaper—there is space for a small table and a quilting frame, around which a half-dozen members of the quilting bee usually work. The quilt on the frame was in the traditional Grandmother's Choice pattern of alternating squares of material. The squares were of black velvet, green velvet, and a Paisley print from Liberty of London. It will retail at Bloomingdale's for a hundred and forty dollars.

# MIDDLE-SIZED EVENTS

# Pollution at the Confluence

During the last New York World's Fair, I decided to begin reading the *Worker*—which I still prefer to call the *Daily Worker* since that sounds more ominous. I figured that any Communist newspaper presented with a target the size of the New York World's Fair deserved an audience. Imagine being an editor of the *Daily Worker* and being able to stroll over to an express subway that whisked you off to a hulking symbol of the sham and waste and cynicism and sheer physical ugliness produced by capitalism—all neatly laid out and outfitted with signs pointing the way to the various shameless examples. I looked forward to at least one biting editorial pointing out that only a society with a uniquely distorted view of the world could apply the term "world's fair" to what actually amounted to a collection of advertisements for American corporations. I also expected the *Daily Worker* to warn its readers that any workingman who was lured into the fairgrounds was really paying only for the privilege of paying more at every turn—a reaffirmation of the economic theory of Nate Eagle, the renowned carnival promoter and student of free enterprise, who said, "It's not how much it costs them to get in but how much it costs them to get out." The first reference to the Fair I saw in the *Daily Worker*—just below an advertisement for Puerto Rican Cabaret Night in honor of the People's Advocates Against the McCarran Act—was an advertisement that said, "We know you are going to the Fair. Why not buy your tickets from the *Worker* and help the paper financially?"

At the time, I was surprised at how easily the Communists had capitulated, but I have since decided that it was inevitable. A subtheme of American world's fairs is that radicals don't stand a chance in this country: if they're not disarmed by being offered a cut of the boodle, some other way to take them in can always be found. For instance, San Antonio's HemisFair seemed like another perfect target—a world's fair taking place in Texas, of all places, this summer, of all times, in a city whose Mexican-American population makes it a required stop on the tour of anybody studying poverty in America. But how can a symbol of American society be criticized while it is criticizing American society? HemisFair has a Hall of Issues, where marking pencils and paper are provided for anyone who wants to write a sign to tape on the wall—even a sign saying "How many Vietnamese fought in our Civil War?" or "HemisFair is a bad dream." Instead of the customary world's-fair shots of children skipping through fields, the film at the United States Pavilion shows spacious skies turned gray by air pollution, and impoverished old people staring vacantly at the walls of crumbling shacks. Water pollution is also popular. After a couple of days at HemisFair, the image of hideous substances being poured into rivers was so strong in my mind that I was barely able to restrain myself from sniffing suspiciously at the water coming out of the taps at the Hilton Palacio del Rio Hotel. The second act of the General Electric Pavilion's mixed-media musical on the joys of electric living is dominated by the problems of the day. At one point, the relentlessly cheery heroine sings, "When he goes to the city he should really have a ball/ Looking at the consequence of modern urban sprawl." If the girl from General Electric is singing about urban sprawl, where is a radical going to take his stand?

Although R.C.A. treats the fairgoer to some good shots of rioting in American cities, no one matches the United States Pavilion in pointing out just how dismal the country really is. In its film, the happy newlyweds who are speeding along America's highways waving euphorically at their smiling fellow citizens end up in a traffic jam; a pleasant, friendly American neighborhood turns silent and hostile when a Negro family arrives to move in. As the camera records a medley of American ugliness, a voice reads narration by W. H. Auden that goes, "Yes, we are free in our greed to let poisons/ Befoul the streams till the fish die,/ Discommodate cities, turn smiling fields/ Into junk graveyards and garbage dumps,/ Let noxious effluvia fill the air, polluting our lungs." Toward the end of the film, the narrator says, "The eyes of the world are upon us/ And wonder what we're worth,/ For much they see dishonors/ The richest country on earth." Naturally, the film is a big hit. A few citizens, it's true, have written to the local newspaper to complain that self-criticism is being carried a bit far, but an editorial in the San Antonio *Express* said proudly that the film "tells it like it is."

The exhibition section of the American Pavilion has the usual story of how "the men and women and children of this confluence came to our shores"—the theme of the fair is "The Confluence of Civilizations in the Americas," and the word "Confluence" is used as a synonym for practically anything—but there is also a display of assorted American problems entitled "The Confluence Road: Challenge for Group Action." After being treated to some more riots and a bit of pollution, the happy fairgoer walks down the exit ramp and sees himself on a television screen with a sign over it asking "Am I Part of the Problem?" At the next turn, he sees himself again, under a sign asking "Am I Part of the Solution?"—and then he is released to the bright colors and gay carnival music of the fairgrounds.

After a morning at the United States Pavilion, I went to the Hall of Issues, thinking I might write "Mea Culpa" in black marking pencil and hang it on the wall. The Hall of Issues is part of Project Y, a youth pavilion that also has a theater, a cabaret, an outdoor discussion pit, and, as the final badge of modernity, a Paraphernalia Boutique. Project Y presents people with "opportunities for involvement." The morning I was there, I joined about twenty other people—some Ys but mostly older people—in the theater for a film and discussion. A young man with a broad, constant smile got up and said that the film we were about to see had a story on one level—it was about a circus—but that "somehow or other something else is being told to you." The film was called *Parable*. The main character was a man in white robes who rode a donkey. He

went around the circus lightening the load of the humble, thus an-
tagonizing some of their oppressors. Finally, he helped three suffering players in a human marionette act out of their harnesses, got
into one of the harnesses himself, and, while spread-eagled in the
harness by the evil puppeteer, was killed by the people who had
been so angered by his acts of goodness.

"I don't get it," the lady on my left said to me. "Do you know
what the story was?"

"I don't know, Madam," I said. "It's a new one on me."

The international section of HemisFair, Las Plazas del Mundo, has
pavilions from two dozen foreign countries and the State of Arkansas. The average fairgoer might wonder what the Confluence a
pavilion from Arkansas is doing there. I guessed right away that it
might be the Parody Pavilion, a necessary feature at every world's
fair. At Expo 67, in Montreal, the Parody Pavilion was provided
by the Republic of Haiti. The Haitian Pavilion was a bar. I don't
mean it had a bar; it *was* a bar. Near the back door of the bar, there
was a small table with some plastic combs and some enamel kitch-
enware on it and sign above it saying something like "Commerce
and Industry." I suspected I had guessed right about Arkansas
when I entered the pavilion and heard a man behind me ask his
wife, "Do you think they'll have an exhibit on their prison system?"
I always try to visit the Parody Pavilion first; it gives proportion to
the rest of the fair. The Italian display on Columbus that says "Yet
westward did he set his prow on that August day of 1492" is more
meaningful after you have seen a display entitled "Hernando de
Soto Discovers Arkansas." The model of the world's largest ship in
the Japanese Pavilion can be measured against a model of the proposed extension of the Little Rock Municipal Airport, and the accounts of military victories by Latin-American patriots will recall a
scene entitled "The Battle of Pea Ridge, Arkansas."

Since I consider all descriptions of historical and engineering triumphs pretty much the same—equivalent to "La Salle Claiming
Arkansas for France" or "The Arkansas River Improvement Project"—I spend a lot of my time at a world's fair searching for a
good machine. The best machine I've ever found was a potato-

sorter in the Netherlands exhibit at Brussels—a marvellous instrument that bounced potatoes along a bed of crossed wires and, most of the time, dropped them into the section whose openings corresponded to their size, presenting an almost perfect betting device to anyone willing to wager on the size of a potato. At HemisFair, good machines are not easy to find—partly, I think, because most countries have confined themselves to the approximately fifty-by-sixty-foot pavilions assigned to them by the fair and don't have room for much more than a series of photographs and color slides and small manufactured objects in glass cases. I did discover one good machine—a piece of sculpture, really—hanging from the ceiling of the Swiss Pavilion. A large flying machine of pipe and cardboard and canvas, it had flapping wings, a beak opening and closing, and feet madly pedaling a bicycle—the first object I have ever seen that looked like a bird, a plane, and Superman. But the best machines at HemisFair are furnished by I.B.M., or what the public-relations men of the New York fair probably thought of as the Republic of I.B.M. At the I.B.M. Pavilion, a visitor can sit down at a machine that looks like a typewriter with a television screen on it, type out his date of birth when the machine asks him to, and learn from the screen how many years, how many months, how many days, how many minutes, and how many seconds he has been alive, what day of the week his birthday will fall on this year, and, if he happens to be seventeen, the fact that in 1951 Julius and Ethel Rosenberg were found guilty of giving atomic secrets to the Russians. During my turn, the machine asked me if I wanted to try my hand at a little quiz. I chose world geography. The machine asked me whether the longest river in the world was the Nile, the Amazon, or the Mississippi. I pressed No. 2—the Amazon. "You have made a good choice on a difficult question," the machine said. "The Amazon River has the greatest flow of any river in the world. It discharges up to 3.5 million cubic feet of water per second into the Atlantic." I beamed. I was only sorry I hadn't thrown in the fact that Lake Titicaca, in South America, is the highest, deepest lake in the world (other lakes are higher and other lakes are deeper, but no lake is both higher and deeper), as long as we were on the subject. "But," the machine continued, "the longest river is the Nile." It's no wonder that American capitalists had such an easy time taking in the *Daily Worker* at the New York fair. Who else would think of producing a discreet machine?

Looking over the products of the Republic of China at HemisFair one day, I suddenly thought I recognized a pair of shoes from the Chinese Pavilion at Montreal (a pavilion I considered one of the tackiest at Expo, by the way; when I read later that it had burned down, my first reaction was that the deed had been done by some visiting Chinese interior decorator, in one of those acts of excessive Oriental shame that we learned about from movies of the Second World War). I could be wrong about the shoes—the Chinese, after all, were not the only people in Montreal to demonstrate to the world their ability to turn out an ordinary pair of women's shoes— but many of the entertainment attractions of HemisFair do come from other fairs (Les Poupées de Paris from Seattle and New York, Kinoautomat from Montreal, Lanterna Magika from Brussels and Montreal). At HemisFair, a veteran fair-trotter sometimes gets the feeling he has traveled down that mini-rail before. Hemis-Fair has a first or two—notably, the first display of Alexander Girard's extraordinary collection of Latin-American toys and folk art, by far the best feature of the fair—but anyone familiar with world's fairs feels the need to glance up now and then to make sure that the architectural trademark looming over him is the Tower of the Americas rather than the Seattle Space Needle or New York's Unisphere, the great corpulent seal that I can still never recall without adding, "Reg., U.S. Steel Corp."

HemisFair does have one exhibit that nobody saw at Brussels— the Institute of Texas Cultures, a huge display dedicated to proving the proposition that its title should not strike people as a joke. Announcing that it would use solid history to correct the cliché that all Texans are boors, the Institute has arranged a tasteful and instructive exhibit dominated by historical artifacts of the various ethnic groups that have contributed to the state. Of course, nobody is fooled for a minute. Near the entrance, where it can't be missed, is a garish display of Texas products dominated by a green-and-white helicopter, a gigantic tire, and stacks of Pioneer Biscuit Mix and Texsun Grapefruit Juice—as if the designers felt compelled at the last minute to say, "Don't be put off. It's just us boors." The overall managers of HemisFair have tried to show more restraint. HemisFair has been publicized as a small, reasonably priced, almost dignified fair—a kind of scale-model synthesis of what people have enjoyed at other fairs. None of that flashy Texas stuff. So many people have responded to this pitch by staying home that HemisFair is already having its financial crisis, considerably ahead of the normal world's-fair schedule for financial crises. San Antonio is filled with complicated theories to account for the shortage of customers, but I find it hard to give up the notion that the poor Texans may have overcompensated and produced a spectacle so unspectacular that nobody is bothering to see it. Who, after all, wants to go to a dignified fair?

For those who do show up, the proprietors provide a lot of cheerful outdoor entertainment—a kind of reassurance that it's really all right to have a good time even if we have been poisoning the rivers and filling the air with noxious effluvia. There is a Mexican mariachi band, and a water-ski show, and a group of Indians who, under the sponsorship of Frito-Lay / Pepsi-Cola, climb a 114-foot pole every few hours and swing down on ropes, simulating the sacrifice of a virgin almost as an afterthought. On the day I saw the afternoon marching-band parade, a young man rode on a float in front of the band announcing periodically, "At six-thirty and nine this evening, Mr. Henri LaMothe will jump from a forty-foot platform into seventeen inches of water, at the Special Events Plaza." I was at the Special Events Plaza at five-forty-five, just in case. As long as I can remember, I have wanted to meet a performer of that particular feat of daring so I could ask him if it made any difference whether he dived into hard or soft water. In the plaza, a ladder with a small platform on it rose above a small, round pool—the sort people buy for their children to wade in.

At about six-thirty—after the Richardson High School Golden Eagle Band, which was scheduled to follow LaMothe's act, had warmed up for a while—a girl in a bikini came out to measure the depth of the water with a yardstick. It was exactly seventeen inches. Then an announcer introduced Mr. LaMothe—a distinguished-looking, somewhat bald man with a gray mustache. LaMothe stood poised on the platform for several minutes while the announcer spoke ominously of wind direction. Then he dived forward in a swan dive, landing perfectly on his stomach. The crowd cheered. I went to talk to him as he dried off. He told me right away that he had been able to do a belly flop without hurting himself ever since he was a boy in Chicago, and he started discussing his careers as a dancer, a water-show producer, and a commercial artist. I tried to figure out how I would ask my question about the water: "Uh, I guess this may sound a bit silly to you, Mr. LaMothe . . ." or maybe, "Speaking of water, Mr. LaMothe . . ." He was telling me about some of his appearances at shopping-center openings and sports shows. "Sometimes I think it'd be nice to have a little water softener in that water," he said, and he chuckled. There was nothing left to ask him about then except water pollution, so I chuckled, too, and headed toward the I.B.M. Pavilion, where I had been meaning to take up a machine's invitation to answer a few questions about wild animals of the world.

# Practice, Practice, Practice

A campaign for the presidency of the United States Jaycees, a service club for men between the ages of twenty-one and thirty-five ordinarily costs fifteen thousand dollars. It's a bargain. There is probably no way to come closer to the feeling of being nominated for the Presidency of the United States except to be nominated for the Presidency of the United States—and the only Jaycees that has ever happened to are Barry Goldwater and Richard M. Nixon. If there are more Nixon posters displayed at the Republican Convention in Miami than there were A. Bruce Coble posters at the Jaycee convention I have just attended in Phoenix, it will only mean that Miami, for some reason, offers more flat surfaces. In Phoenix, a presidential candidate like Roger R. Jenkins, a badge-and-trophy dealer from Seattle, could take it for granted that wherever he went he would be accompanied by a squad of aides who wore neat business suits, talked intently into walkie-talkies, and stood out among the Oklahoma Jaycee Indian costumes and the Mississippi Jaycee Confederate uniforms and the Indiana Jaycee basketball-referee shirts like Secret Service agents at a college reunion. Campaign workers in the headquarters suite of the candidate from Michigan answered the phone with "Smith for president," and everyone knew they were talking about Wendell E. Smith, a division zone manager for a grocery firm. At the annual conventions of the Jaycees (formerly called the Junior Chamber of Commerce but never officially connected to the senior chamber) demonstrators are dependable and uniformly enthusiastic. During the week of a convention, demonstrations wind through the hotels every evening on schedule, and after the candidate's name is finally placed in nomination he can be assured of a demonstration lasting the full twenty minutes allotted by convention regulations. In Phoenix, each candidate was wheeled through the convention hall on a kind of mobile speaker's platform —one hand on his wife's shoulder, one hand waving to the cheering thousands—followed by hundreds of supporters blowing whistles, beating drums, waving placards, and chanting a slogan like "We Back Mack" or "Align with Glines." During the polling of the delegations, if a state leader walked to a floor microphone and said something like "Mr. Chairman, the great state of Missouri, home of the world-champion St. Louis Cardinals, is proud to cast its seventy-five votes for that great little razorback from Arkansas, the next president of the United States Jaycees—MACK KOONCE!" Mack Koonce, an insurance man from Pine Bluff, Arkansas, could rest assured that every single member of every single delegation supporting him would stand up, wave a Mack Koonce placard, and make as much noise as possible.

All this is carried on with the knowledge that the winning candidate will give up his ordinary business for a year and move to the Jaycee White House, a ranch-style presidential residence in Tulsa, Oklahoma. His wife goes with him, of course; Jaycees sometimes refer to her as the First Lady. According to Jaycees, whoever does reach the Tulsa White House has "a lot of doors open for him" in the business world, and, according to the approved Jaycee history, a book entitled *Young Men Can Change the World,* he becomes the most lionized young man in the country ("He's an honored guest at the Indianapolis 500, the Phoenix Rodeo, and the Apple Blossom Festival in Virginia, to name just a few events he attends with bells on"). But "the experience of leading three hundred thousand young men" is usually mentioned by Jaycees as the most important plum of the presidency. In a chapter on the presidency, called "How to Make a Halfback Cry," the Jaycee history says, "If the Jaycee movement as a whole is a great college of practical experience, as many have described it, the intensive experience gained by the one top leader in the movement must be a valuable post-graduate course indeed."

At a time when there are warnings that the world is being taken over by the young, some people may find it comforting that so many thirty-three- and thirty-four-year-old men are still just practicing. Although Jaycee chapters are noted for running an unremitting stream of projects—holding Safe Driving Road-e-os, sponsoring beauty pageants, leading get-out-the-vote drives, building playgrounds—Jaycees consider a project less important for its own ends than for the opportunity it provides to amass experience and leadership training. The Jaycee presidential election seems to be an example of experience in pure form, since there are no issues. The impression made by the candidates themselves is considered only a minor factor, and the outcome is decided largely not by the demonstrating delegates but by a group of Jaycees known to all as "the politicians." A presidential candidate is almost always one of ten vice-presidents, and he automatically receives the support of those states he has been assigned to look after during his vice-presidency; other states are attracted by the politicians with reminders of past voting support and hints of future voting support. Jaycees appear to enjoy the political process for itself, no matter who the candidates are. It is a matter of some pride among them that the balloting in Phoenix lasted all night. Once a candidate withdrew, the delegates from states supporting him would merely switch placards and jump up with undiminished enthusiasm at every mention of their new favorite.

Jaycees believe officially in God and the free-enterprise system. Support for both is pledged in the Jaycee Creed. *Young Men Can Change the World* has a description that might be taken as the Jaycee ideal of a young man operating in a free-enterprise economy: "Tall, handsome, with a pleasing personality and a quiet but driving ambition, Tom worked his way up the ladder." The commercial-exhibit area at the convention included several ground-floor offers for young men interested in a free-enterprise opportunity. As I watched a lady demonstrate how Swipe could clean almost anything, I was approached by a man about selling some

Swipe myself. "You see, I sign you up and then I get a cut of what you sell, and then you sign people up and you get a cut of what they sell," he said. "That's free enterprise." In large cities, where Jaycee chapters have often not been as strong as they are in small towns, the Jaycees are just beginning to become involved in some ghetto projects, and a former president who addressed a convention meeting on urban problems explained that the key was to give those who live in the ghetto a chance to become "dynamic free enterprisers." The only time the welcoming speech by the mayor of Phoenix was interrupted by applause was when he said that property taxes had not been raised in Phoenix for eighteen years.

Jaycees also believe in a kind of constituency of young people. A Jaycee president once testified against the Medicare bill on the ground that Jaycees "and others like us must immediately begin payments to finance the cost of medical care for those over sixty-five currently receiving Social Security benefits who have not contributed a cent toward these medical costs." The Jaycees have always been a young man's crowd. When a member passes the age of thirty-five, he automatically becomes what Jaycees call "an exhausted rooster." Even professional staff members are not permitted to stay on in that condition. The most successful Jaycee public-relations project is its annual recognition of Ten Outstanding Young Men—an honor that in one year of uncharacteristically bad handicapping was awarded both to Douglas R. Stringfellow, the Utah congressman who later admitted to having invented most of his war record, and to Billie Sol Estes. Jaycees call everybody under thirty-five by his first name—a custom that, combined with their respect for the prerogatives of office, led them to refer to their national president in Phoenix speeches as President Jim.

In or out of presidential campaigns, Jaycees concentrate hard on youthful enthusiasm. On the first day of the convention, Paul J. Meyer—the president of Success Motivation Institute, Inc., of Waco, Texas, a Jaycee consultant, and a man introduced as the Master Motivator—lectured a Key Men luncheon on the value of enthusiasm. "Maybe the enthusiasts aren't the most cultured people in the world," Meyer told the Jaycees, "but they're the only ones who make history." It was like lecturing to a group of life insurance salesmen on the need for planning against unforeseen disasters. In their own public speaking—encouraged by a project called Speak-Up—Jaycees tend to inject enough enthusiasm to transform a speech into what used to be called a declamation. Both Speak-Up speakers and presidential candidates lean toward the inspirational—why a citizen shouldn't let the other fellow do it, or how one Jaycee "became on fire that he, Lewis Timberlake, could make Stamford, Texas, a better place in which to live." Jaycee speakers are apt to use a phrase like "the hallowed halls of our nation's capital" even when referring to the place where programs shouldn't come from. The national winner of the Speak-Up competition gave his speech at a general meeting of the convention. He told the history of the United States, speaking in the first person, as if he had personally seen it from the beginning. It was the first time I had ever heard anybody sound angry when discussing the behavior of the British during the period of the American Revolution. "They taxed our tea!" he shouted.

Jaycees seem to treasure an image of themselves as rowdy conventioners—being young, they are supposed to have more staying power than the Shriners or the American Legion—but at the end of the convention one of the Phoenix Jaycees in charge of local arrangements said that both the police department and the night-club owners had overestimated the impact that several thousand Jaycees would have on the city. One factor, he explained, was that there were seven candidates for the presidency, an unusually large number, and Jaycees from the candidates' assigned states had spent a lot of time demonstrating when they could have been in night clubs. Many Jaycees were accompanied by their wives (Jaycettes), wearing feminine versions of the appropriate state costumes, and some brought their children. The traditional convention debauchery seemed to be represented mostly by the dancing of two or three indefatigable go-go girls, who appeared, in one bikini or another, at convention social events in the evening and at the booth of Mr. Lucky's night club, among the free-enterprise opportunities and real estate offers of the commercial exhibits, from nine to five. At an event called the State Parties—two nights of more or less potluck dinners, with booths featuring the specialties of various states—a huge line formed for cherry pie being handed out by Michigan while at the next booth Tennessee Jaycees, dressed in coonskin hats and buckskin-style suits, were having trouble finding takers for free Jack Daniel's bourbon.

At Jaycee conventions, distinctions among the states are maintained with considerable enthusiasm. The annual convention parade is called the Parade of States, and states compete, mostly through membership figures, for their positions in the line of march. (This year, a state might have been better off finishing low enough in the competition to be left out completely. National Jaycee leaders disregarded the suggestion of the locals that parades in Phoenix during the summer should be held in the evening, if at all—the evening has always been reserved for state caucuses, President Jim later explained—and about a hundred and fifty paraders were overcome by the heat.) Jaycees can find something distinctive about any state, and a visitor may lose track of the fact that the delegates in referee shirts and the delegates in Indian costumes probably live in cities that are physically and culturally almost exactly alike. The Nebraska delegates wore white sailor uniforms, signifying the legendary Nebraska Navy. The Jaycees from Georgia had vests with a symbolic peach on the back, those from Oregon had shirts featuring pictures of lumberjacks, Kansans wore yellow vests with a sunflower design, and the delegates and wives from Idaho wore dun-colored outfits that succeeded in making some of them look like potatoes. Almost every state west of Ohio seemed to have some Western element in its costume. In Phoenix, where it is common for adults to own cowboy outfits, it was sometimes the presidential candidates in business suits rather than the delegates in cowboy shirts who looked out of place. One night, I passed two young men who were wearing Western hats, boots, gun belts, and tight Western-style shirts; I looked at their patches to see if they were Jaycees from Montana or Nevada or Michigan, and discovered that they were deputy sheriffs of Maricopa County, Arizona.

At the State Parties, Florida delegates, dressed in orange blazers, served orange juice, the Hawaiians served pineapple juice, and Kentucky colonels served mint juleps. At the New Mexico booth, small shots of tequila were given away, and New Mexico Jaycees, wearing tasseled Mexican hats, helpfully poured salt on the back of each guest's hand so that he could drink in the authentic manner.

Texas cowboys ladled out pinto beans and rattlesnake meat, and Wyoming cowboys gave away beef jerky. On the first night of the State Parties, immense crowds lined up for provisions like Illinois hot dogs and Wisconsin cheese. The hall became so hot that a number of people took what food they could get and went out on the lawn, where the temperature was one hundred and nine. The heat seemed to have little effect on the enthusiasm of the guests or the hosts at the Georgia booth, which featured Jesse Jewell's Portion Controlled Pre-Cooked Chicken Drumettes (wrapped in Delta Airline napkins), hard-boiled eggs from the Georgia Egg Commission, Coca-Cola, and, on two platforms behind the serving line, a rock band and a go-go dancer. A large crowd gathered in front of the booth to watch the go-go girl, and when the demand for chicken was finally satisfied, the Georgia servers gathered around the platform to stare up at her while clapping to the music. One Jaycee stood on a chair behind the dancer flicking water from a wet cloth in her direction to mitigate the heat. Jaycees in referee shirts blew whistles and Michigan Jaycees sounded auto horns. Arkansas delegates in red berets and several varieties of Jaycee cowboys came up to take pictures. At around eight o'clock, the closing time for the State Parties, the band began to play "Dixie," and a half-dozen Georgia Jaycees climbed up on the platform with the go-go girl to wave Georgia flags. Finally, one of them started throwing Jesse Jewell's Portion Controlled Pre-Cooked Chicken Drumettes to the crowd.

Local chapters also compete at Jaycee conventions, displaying their year's accomplishments in scrapbooks filled with documents known as R & R (Records and Recognition) Forms. R & R Forms are designed not only to provide a means of recognizing achievements but to train Jaycees in the organizational habits that might make them leaders. For every project a local chapter embarks on, the committee chairman fills out a Project Proposal Form, listing the Purpose and Benefits of the project, a Plan of Action ("This is an important administrative aid used by all good administrations"), a Budget, a Committee Organization Chart, a Committee Summary of Activities, and a Completed Project Report. With the help of these R & R Forms, Jaycees can gain leadership training from almost any activity; even organizing the District Three and

Four Crab Feed requires a systematic listing of what action is planned to gain the objective.

In the scrapbooks that prize-winning chapters from each state brought to Phoenix, there were R & R Forms on typical Jaycee community projects—sponsoring a junior olympics, holding a children's Christmas party—and there were also forms presenting the benefits and plan of action and organization chart for such activities as attending a state convention, electing chapter officers, and holding regular meetings. Many scrapbooks included completed R & R Forms on the completion of R & R Forms. Jaycees can assign a benefit to any activity. A party improves relations among the members, and a bowling team helps public relations. Actually, almost any project can be seen as a public relations benefit. "This project will benefit the city of Deer Park by having a flag in front of one of its buildings," the Deer Park, Texas, chapter wrote about a plan to buy a flag for a new civic center. "The chapter will benefit from the public relations for being civic-minded young men." Most of all, though, Jaycees find a local project—as well as a presidential campaign—beneficial in providing experience. The Minden, Louisiana, chapter wrote that its fund-raising candy sale would "help members develop the ability to sell themselves, the candy, and the Jaycees to the community." The Newton-Conover, North Carolina, Jaycees wrote that members would benefit from a peanut sale "by acquiring leadership training during their sale of peanuts to individuals." Leadership training, it says in *Young Men Can Change the World*, is the primary function of the United States Jaycees.

# Mardi Gras

Over the years, one of the Mardi Gras traditions observed by a few prominent Jewish families in New Orleans has been to leave town. Like a number of Mardi Gras customs, it is not practiced as widely as it once was, but traditionalists are confident that it is in no danger of extinction. According to most predictions, at least one or two of the Jewish families that occupy positions high in the social and philanthropic life of the city will continue to find it embarrassing to be present during the Mardi Gras season and not be invited to the balls of the most socially prestigious Carnival organizations —and the most socially prestigious Carnival organizations will never invite Jews to their balls. It might fit the Latin image of Mardi Gras if the exclusion were based on the religious implications of a pre-Lenten celebration, but, as a matter of fact, Mardi Gras in New Orleans was started by Anglo-Saxon Protestants and has never really had any religious significance. A stronger basis for the exclusion is that the most prominent of the Carnival organizations—the krewes of Comus, Momus, and Proteus—all have close connections, in some cases formal, with businessmen's luncheon clubs, and businessmen's luncheon clubs in New Orleans, like those in many American cities, are the last significant enclave of discrimination against Jews. It is impossible to separate the fact that no

New Orleans Jew is permitted to attend the Comus ball on Mardi Gras Night from the fact that no New Orleans Jew is permitted to enter the Boston club for a business lunch at any time—one of the peculiarly American features of Mardi Gras lending weight to the theory that underneath that gay Carnival costume beats the heart of Zenith, Ohio.

A visitor to Carnival in New Orleans this week finds no scarcity of reminders that he is within the continental and cultural limits of the United States. The most extravagant Mardi Gras parade— ruled over by Rex, that Monarch of Mirth and Lord of Misrule—is so relentlessly organized that about the only carefree Latin who would find it recognizable is a carefree Latin management consultant. Although the parades are staged by private Carnival krewes and have no advertising connection, they can occasionally reflect the American genius for creating fads that have promotional possibilities. In 1960, the maskers riding on the floats of the Rex parade added to the tradition of tossing beads and other trinkets to the crowd by dispensing aluminum souvenir coins called doubloons. Now souvenir doubloons are tossed from the floats of just about every krewe, coin dealers do a steady business in old (circa 1960) doubloons, and doubloons have been used for promotion by, among others, Labiche's department store, the Tharp-Sontheimer-Tharp funeral home, the New Orleans Saints football team, and Merrill Lynch, Pierce, Fenner & Smith. Over the past several years, the crowd watching the parades in the French Quarter or wandering up and down Bourbon Street during the general costuming on Shrove Tuesday has consisted increasingly of that band of all-purpose American event-attenders who seem to have emerged during the past decade from some gigantic incubator in Fort Lauderdale, carrying beer cans.

Although the layman may find the distinction between the Rex parade and the Tournament of Roses too subtle to discern, it is an article of faith in New Orleans that Mardi Gras has nothing whatever in common with other American civic celebrations—that it is not a spectacle staged by the city to promote its name and draw tourists but a spontaneous blowout by a citizenry justly famed for being wicked but charming. The fashion of saying that everybody would be just as happy if all the tourists stayed away is so widespread among New Orleans businessmen that it extends almost to hotelkeepers. As it happens, though, the city spends hundreds of thousands of dollars operating and promoting the Carnival, the Krewe of Rex (which has always had more civic than social significance) is precisely as independent of the city's business interests as the Chamber of Commerce is, and a number of businessmen would certainly not be just as happy if all the tourists stayed away. But it remains true that Mardi Gras is celebrated by the locals on a scale and in a style that set it apart from the American events with which it may share high-school bands and paper flowers and hot dogs. In some ways, its symbols are not at all American. The attitude toward the drinking and carousing and costuming in the streets is specifically anti-Puritanical; the Carnival balls that are buried in ersatz royal pomp and the parades that are based on maskers tossing trinkets to a begging crowd are specifically aristocratic rather than democratic. Students of Mardi Gras generally agree that the key to its unconscious symbolism is that on Mardi Gras Night, when the Rex ball is being held on one side of the Municipal Auditorium and the Comus ball on the other, Rex, who is publicly identified as King of Carnival and is receiving the greatest civic honor he can receive, takes his court to the Comus ball to pay his respects to the anonymous King of the exclusive Comus—acknowledging the primacy of the social over the civic.

The exclusion of the Jews, of course, is carried off in a style that is partly within the accepted traditions of American discrimination. In most American cities, social discrimination against Jews didn't begin until the latter part of the nineteenth century—it is not unheard of for Jews to be barred from clubs their ancestors helped found—and in New Orleans the first ruler of Rex, in 1872, was a Jew named Louis Salomon. (Since Rex permits Jews to attend its ball and even has a few Jewish members, a Jew could theoretically be King of Carnival today, except that the King is traditionally a member of the Boston Club, which does not offer membership to Jews, and a Jewish Rex could hardly follow the custom of taking his court to pay tribute to Comus, since he wouldn't be allowed in the Comus ball.)

In New Orleans, as in other American cities, club discrimination is the most awkward type of discrimination to fight—even after it is demonstrated that exclusion from businessmen's clubs means exclusion from most of the important decision-making in the city and is connected with the practice in some industries of excluding Jews from executive positions. Those discriminated against by businessmen's clubs are often the people least likely to get into a public fight on any issue, and this is certainly true in New Orleans, where the Jewish community is dominated by old German-Jewish families that have for years been almost indistinguishable from their gentile peers except at lunchtime and during Mardi Gras season. The local board of the Anti-Defamation League has refrained from raising the matter publicly—thereby making it easier for the local newspapers to maintain the respectful silence for which they are known. (This year, even the New Orleans *Times-Picayune* could not completely ignore a national dispute about a Navy memorandum permitting visiting officers to attend Carnival balls that excluded Jews, Negroes, and Italians; it carried an Associated Press story but inserted in parentheses the information that "Carnival balls are private and admission is by invitation only.") The accepted American way to deal with discrimination in businessmen's clubs is not to mention it, and if some newspaper insists on bringing it up (as happened in Kansas City last fall, the paper being, significantly, not the city's daily or the Jewish weekly but the *National Catholic Reporter*) the accepted American response of the confronted club president is that his club does not discriminate against people because of race, creed, or color, and may even have a Jewish member or two, although he can't think of one at the moment.

But in New Orleans everyone acknowledges that the discrimination against Jews by Carnival krewes and businessmen's clubs is specific and total, and people even seem to take a certain pride in how specific and total it is. Observers of the New Orleans social scene believe not only that a Jew will never be invited to join Comus but that a Jew will never be invited to attend the Comus ball as a guest—guests at Carnival balls being people who arrive in white tie and tails to watch the proceedings from the balcony of the Municipal Auditorium, like prom trotters who have somehow wandered into a basketball game by mistake. M. S. Edmonson, a Tulane anthropologist who has studied Mardi Gras, believes that the specificity of Jewish exclusion—like the pride New Orleans take in talking about internationally famous Mardi Gras visitors who couldn't get an invitation to the best balls—expresses one of the normal needs of "a stable provincial Society." Edmonson sees New Orleans society as one of the few in America that refuse to acknowledge the primacy of New York and jealously guard unique credentials—such as having a debutante daughter named Queen of Comus—that are meaningless on Park Avenue. In his view, if a Jew were invited to the Comus ball he would have to be invited not because of an unbroken line of forebears in the Comus court but because of the kind of credentials that would win him acceptance in any American city. Edmonson believes that the members of the Comus invitation committee know, unconsciously, that they cannot afford to recognize those credentials—that their claim to a society independent of and equal to New York's would be threatened by permitting one Jewish aristocrat to sit in the Municipal Auditorium balcony during the Comus ball.

"I'm not bothered by the Carnival balls at all," I was told by a prominent leader of the Jewish community. "I'm not concerned in the least. I regret only one thing about Mardi Gras—that so much money needed in other places doesn't get there." It is notoriously difficult to raise money in New Orleans for cultural or charitable purposes; in cultural institutions and city services—not to speak of median income and median years of completed schooling—New Orleans lags far behind most cities its size. One widely accepted (and almost never publicly expressed) explanation is that the people who should be the leaders in such matters are too busy deciding which debutantes are going to be in the Comus court, and that the people who should be the givers spend too much of their money on costumes and formal gowns and beads to throw from floats.

"I solicited for the Cultural Attraction Fund this year," I was told by a young businessman who has gradually come to resent Mardi Gras. "Guys my age couldn't give a hundred dollars, because they were pouring five or six hundred bucks into riding Proteus and going to the balls. The damn symphony doesn't play for two or three months because it can't get the Municipal Auditorium from the Carnival balls. The way the museums are in this city, about the only art I can take my kids to see is the paintings they sell to tourists in Jackson Square." Jews are extraordinarily prominent in providing what cultural life the city has, and a man who recently wanted to start a foundation in New Orleans having to do with music told me that the only people he could think of to sit on the board and contribute money were Jews—reflecting the possibility that Jews, who are excluded from Carnival krewes despite their prominence in the cultural and philanthropic life of the city, constantly become more prominent in the cultural and philanthropic life of the city partly because they are excluded from Carnival krewes.

Thousands of New Orleans residents who think of Comus only as a parade that doesn't throw enough beads also celebrate Mardi Gras, often in bizarre ways. Bands of Negroes still roam the streets of some neighborhoods in Indian tribes, as convinced of being real Indians as the dukes of Rex are convinced of being real dukes. Groups of working-class whites still lurch drunkenly behind Negro jazz bands in the parades of neighborhood marching societies. There are more parades than there ever were, and Carnival balls now seem to be given by any organization that can raise the price of a crown. But, all in all, a decreasing number of residents bother to wear costumes these days; many of those who do wear costumes ride on their own carefully organized float in the Elks parade and are rarely found roaming the streets. In the French Quarter, the traditional center of costuming, it is possible to watch hundreds of Mardi Gras celebrants pass down the middle of Bourbon Street without seeing anything more exotic than a Kappa Alpha sweat-shirt.

The newspapers regularly exhort people to mask on Mardi Gras, and a private campaign has been waged by Arthur P. Jacobs, a stout former policeman who, with his wife, runs a short-order grill on the corner of Bourbon and Dumaine. Like a number of other French Quarter residents, Jacobs has a theory to explain the decrease in costuming. "Conditions," he told me. "Conditions has ruined everything." This year, for the seventh Mardi Gras in a row, he closed his grill, strung up a public-address system on his balcony, erected a platform in the intersection, and assumed his Carnival role as president of the Bourbon Street Awards, a costume contest. "I've met a lot of people, and they've told me with their own mouths I'm the reason they're masking," he says. "Because of the prizes." Jacobs takes the sensible view that people ought to use Mardi Gras to dress and behave the way they cannot dress and behave the rest of the year, with no questions asked—"Live the Life You Love" is the motto of the Bourbon Street Awards—and his convictions are so strong that he prefers not to dwell on the fact that the beautifully gowned Female Costume Award contestants pictured in his grill are in fact males. Just before Mardi Gras this year, Jacobs was incensed at a local magazine that called his contest the "He-Sheba" contest—a misstatement of the type that he believes could discourage some people from wearing costumes at all. "This kind of criticism is out of line," he told me. "And that's the truth of it."

Among homosexuals, Mardi Gras is the Harvard-Yale game. A few years ago, *The New York Times* carried an item about a New York man who occasionally dressed as a woman and, using the sort of foresight employed by diabetes sufferers who carry instructions about insulin, always had in his purse a psychiatrist's note attesting to the fact that he was a transvestite. Except for such special cases, Mardi Gras offers about the only legal opportunity in the United States for people to walk around publicly in the clothing of the opposite sex. Homosexuals have never confined their Mardi Gras clothing to dresses; they have always provided some of the most extravagant costumes seen in the French Quarter. For a number of years, the most stunning costumes of the day could be seen at the corner of Bourbon and St. Peter, where Dixie Fasnacht—a former member of an all-girl band called the Southland Rhythm Girls and, even in recent years, a clarinettist on festive occasions—ran a bar called Dixie's Bar of Music. Dixie sold her bar and retired a few years ago, but even before that a change had come over the homosexual Mardi Gras. Homosexuals still arrive from every part of the country, and in the past seven years three krewes, each of which stages its own Carnival ball, have emerged in the local homosexual community. But a number of the local men who used to provide the most fantastic costumes no longer walk around the French Quarter in feathered sun-god outfits or gold body paint, being unwilling to face harassment from the ambulatory beer drinkers who now make up so much of the French Quarter crowd.

"It used to be that all the queens would go to Dixie's to show off costumes for a few hours and then everyone would go up Bourbon Street across Canal to the Sazerac Bar of the Roosevelt," I was told by a local antique dealer this week. "Now you couldn't make it as far as Canal Street without having beer cans thrown at you. A boy last year had his dress ripped off right on Bourbon Street. I used to paint my body and spend a lot of time on a costume, but I don't costume anymore, and I know sixty other people who stopped. It's too dangerous. That's why you don't see the fantastic kind of costumes you used to. These dopey straight people wear a pair of pajamas and they think they're hilarious." Most homosexuals now stick pretty close to the Bourbon Street Awards and the bar across the street (which helps pay for the trophies), or to the one or two other bars that have inherited some of Dixie's business. It is said that last year's winner of the grand-prize trophy at the Awards—a young man who was costumed, rather convincingly, as a chandelier—had not gone a block from the judging stand before some college kids were attempting to break his crystals with beer cans. It is the kind of story that convinces some citizens that Mardi Gras in the French Quarter, once the symbol of tolerance and individuality, has become just another American mob scene. "It's the lack of discipline you see all over the country," I was told by a leader of the New Orleans homosexual community. "That's what Mr. Freud has done."

# HOME FRONT

# The War in Kansas

PROTECTION

Protection is not the largest town in Comanche County. Coldwater, about fifteen miles to the east, has more than a thousand people to Protection's seven hundred, and there is no sign that Protection is closing the gap. Coldwater has the county seat—a factor that has decided which town survives in some rural counties. It also has the advantage of having a highway run through it, although not a terribly busy highway. There are two motels in Coldwater. The highway misses Protection by a half mile or so, and there are no motels. Although a traveler on the highway sees a couple of faded and peeling signs advertising the Hotel Brunswick in Protection, the Brunswick, a tiny old brick building that looks as if it had always considered the prospect of more than two or three stranded motorists at one time an excess of good fortune, has been closed for a year. Some people say that the Brunswick's problem was "uninterested ownership" in California, and some say the problem was the State of Kansas Health Department's standards. Protection is in southwestern Kansas, on flat, dry land about fifteen miles from the Oklahoma line; the wheat elevators of the Protection co-op can be seen from ten or twelve miles away. (Somewhat closer, a fragile-looking spire is visible next to the elevators: the tower for the Protection television cable.) The nearest big town is Dodge City, which is a sixty-mile drive, part of it on unpaved road. Most of the men seen in the Protection business district—a street that runs three blocks and then turns into a dirt lane—wear boots and Western hats, and when they go hunting it is often for coyotes. Many of them raise wheat or cattle, both of which have suffered from droughts for the past two seasons. Last year, Protection got six inches of rain instead of the normal twenty-two, and farmers say it has only rained twice in the past twelve months.

Even with rain, Protection has never hit it rich. There are a half-dozen empty storefronts along the main street, most of them empty for years. A dozen years ago, some of the businessmen in town thought they might be able to lure some tourists off the highway by developing Fort Protection, which lies a couple of miles to the northwest. Fort Protection is not the kind of fort most tourists are accustomed to—it is the area between a trench and a bluff where some of the townspeople are said to have gathered during an Indian scare once—but the businessmen thought it could be made attractive if the trench were dug out and a building erected. Charles Jones, the Protection pharmacist, had gone as far as to make a sign for the fort, but then a farmer refused to grant the necessary access to the old site. "It was quite a unique sign, too," Harris Powell, the owner of the town drygoods store, says. "The letters were burnt into the wood. That project just sort of fell through."

There has been some talk that one of the lakes due to be built as part of an Arkansas River development project will be near Protection and will draw vacationers into the area for fishing and boating, but some people in Protection believe that the lake is likely to be just a big mudhole, with no recreational facilities. Protection had its only experience with fame ten years ago, and that was brief. The National Foundation for Infantile Paralysis chose Protection to become the first town in the United States to have one hundred per cent of its citizens under forty inoculated with Salk vaccine for protection against polio, and the ceremonies were a matter for national television coverage. Local citizens are not certain how the town got the name that made this windfall possible; most people believe it had something to do with the town or the fort being a protection against the elements or the Indians, but others think it had something to do with the protective tariff. The National Foundation presented Protection with a bronze plaque to commemorate the mass inoculation, and Harris Powell, who was mayor at the time, built a squat concrete water fountain on the sidewalk in front of the town library, next door to his store, and put the plaque on it. Not long ago, it occurred to Powell that the National Foundation might be interested in returning to Protection to mark the anniversary of the inoculation, but he has not got around to writing a letter on the subject.

About the only economic break that Protection has ever had was having Lane Myers born there. Myers, now in his sixties, went to Wichita to work after high school—as a good part of the Protection High School graduating class has done ever since—but he came back to Protection after the Second World War to start his own plant. For a while, he made grain augers, and then he manufactured steel posts for the government. Finally, in 1953, he was awarded a Defense Department contract for the manufacture of concertina barbed wire — particularly heavy barbed wire that pulls out from a reel to form a fifty-foot maze in the pattern of an outsize, misshapen, vicious-looking concertina. Myers has a way with machines that is often remarked on in Protection. He designed and built all of the machines he needed to produce concertina, and began production with twenty or so workers in a dreary-looking cinder-block building at the end of Protection's main street, just before the railroad tracks.

The plant has a strangely homemade quality, as if a few neighborhood friends were carrying on a weekend manufacturing project in somebody's abandoned garage. Aside from company offices, it is almost entirely one large room, filled with an overpowering clacking noise. The barbed wire is produced by a machine that joins two wires—tying one around the other to produce barbs—and then it is fed onto openwork drums, where workers attach clips in various places so that it will open up into a tangled concertina pattern. A machine that includes an old tire as a base presses down the wire for shipping. An oven that looks like part of a homemade cookout stove heats another type of wire so that it can be flattened and cut into the clips and into carrying handles.

For a dozen years—except for one year when he did not win a

government contract—Myers continued to turn out concertina wire
in his original plant. At one point, Protection was the nation's only
source of concertina barbed wire. Then, two or three years ago, the
demand for concertina increased drastically. It is normally used as
what the military calls "anti-personnel wire entanglements," and
American troops in Vietnam often stack three reels of it together to
construct thorny pyramids in front of their emplacements. In August of 1965, after two sons-in-law had joined Myers in the business, he more than doubled his operation. He leased a second
cinder-block building—situated just on the other side of the railroad tracks and labeled by a Pepsi-Cola sign "Lane Myers Plant
2." The Lane Myers Company began to work a double shift five
days a week and a single shift on Saturdays and Sundays, employ-
ing sixty-five production workers. The expansion meant that Lane
Myers was providing jobs for thirty-five men who had grown up in
Protection and was drawing workers from all over Comanche
County and even from Oklahoma. Some of the extra workers com-
muted from nearby towns, but about a dozen of them moved to
Protection to be near the plant. Soon after Lane Myers Plant 2
opened, there were no more houses available for rent in town.
Businessmen along the main street found that business improved a
bit in 1966 despite the drought—although they were still faced
with the trend toward driving into Dodge City for shopping—and
that the population remained stable. With both plants in operation,
the Lane Myers Company provided a payroll of a thousand dollars
a day and spent almost that much locally for supplies. "In a little
town like this," Charles Jones says, "two or three extra people
help."

The dramatic expansion of Lane Myers production did not bring
a dramatic expansion of Protection's feeling of involvement with
the war in Vietnam. The "Welcome to Protection" sign that lists
the virtues of the town for the benefit of those traveling on the
nearby highway—a sign that the Jaycees have been meaning to
repaint—does not mention Protection's part in the war effort. Occasionally, someone has expressed mild regret that the town's good
fortunes came from war—particularly a war that many find hard to
understand—but it is not easy to feel like a war profiteer in Protection; after all, even with a double-shift concertina-wire factory, Pro-

tection has never done much more than hold its own. Because the plant has been making wire for years, it has never been looked upon as completely a creature of the war, and the management has always insisted that it would be producing concertina wire for the government even if there were no war. In most parts of Kansas, about the only people who cannot avoid an involvement with the war are those who have relatives in it—or relatives threatened with the possibility of being in it—and there are probably fewer of those people in Protection than in comparable Kansas towns. Workers at the plant, most of whom are young men, are deferred from the draft. They are engaged in what is considered an essential industry, and it is thought that attaching the clips to concertina wire requires a digital dexterity found only in the young.

Last month, a year and a half after the expansion, the Lane Myers Company finally fell into the traditional pattern of Protection economic life: it laid off about as many workers as it had added in 1965. The government had "redeployed" the Myers concertina contract from thirty-five thousand reels a month to ten thousand reels a month. There has been talk in Protection that the cutback may be only temporary, and that the problem was apparently just a matter of the government's difficulty in financing contracts toward the end of a fiscal year. (The people at the Construction Supply Center, the government agency in charge of the contracts, agree that the cutback could be only temporary, although they seem to think that the problem is that there may finally be enough concertina barbed wire.)

Several families have left town, but a number of the laid-off workers have remained, hoping that the government will increase its order after the new fiscal year begins, or that Lane Myers will figure out a machine to manufacture something besides concertina entanglement wire. "It's made a change in business," J. D. Rowland, who is Protection's real-estate agent, insurance man, tax accountant, and utility-bill agent, said after the layoff. "We can feel the pinch of it—along with our drouth." Protection businessmen are aware of the role the plant plays in deciding the question that always hangs over towns like Protection—the question of continued existence—but they have sent no delegations to Washington to argue for a return to full production. People in Protection have no feeling of being able to influence the concertina wire boom, any more than they have a feeling of being able to influence the plans for the Arkansas River development project, or the publicity campaigns of the National Foundation for Infantile Paralysis, or the rain. J. D. Rowland says, "The town did nothing to get the plant, and it never built any apartments or anything to promote the influx of workers, or anything like that. It just happened Lane Myers was born here."

NEWTON

There is good reason for Mennonites to be well thought of in Kansas. For one thing, they brought the wheat. They had originally left Germany for Russia, lured by Catherine the Great's promise of immunity from taxes and conscription. When they resettled in south-central Kansas, they brought with them a strain of wheat called Turkey Red. Wheat had not been grown in Kansas with great success until then, but the strain developed by the Mennonites for the dry Ukrainian steppes turned out to be ideal for the soil and climate of the Kansas plains. It became the basis of a winter-wheat crop that now accounts for a seventh of the wheat grown in the world. Also, the Mennonites are good neighbors. People in Topeka say that after a tornado wrecked part of their city last year, the Mennonites suddenly appeared and began the job of cleaning up, as if they had some sort of contract. In Reno County, just south of Hutchinson, there is a small colony of Amish Mennonites, migrants from Pennsylvania, who still wear beards and drive horse-and-buggies, but the vast majority of the Mennonites in Kansas long ago adopted American customs. Many of them have branched out from farming to business. Some have married outside the church and raised their children as Methodists or Presbyterians.

One American custom that most Mennonites have not adopted is fighting wars. If a boy from a small Mennonite town in south-central Kansas decides to go into the Army, the decision becomes, in the words of one Mennonite student, "the talk of the Ladies' Aid." Mennonites, more than any other religious group in the country, tend to fulfill their military obligation through a program of "alternative service"—working for two years in some place like an Army hospital or a relief center. The Kansas Selective Service people speak highly of the Mennonites. The Selective Service System has been having trouble with the Jehovah's Witnesses in Kansas for at least twenty years; Witnesses who are denied ministerial exemption and accept alternative service sometimes do not show up for it and have to be jailed. The Mennonites, on the other hand, arrange their own alternative service with such dependability that the draft board hardly needs to become involved.

Accepting the Mennonites' conscientious objection as routine has been easier for the state draft-board officials in Topeka than it has been for the Mennonites' neighbors in Newton. A trading town of some sixteen thousand people, thirty miles north of Wichita, Newton is the headquarters of the General Conference Mennonite Church (the religion's most progressive branch); about fifteen per cent of the people are Mennonites. "We don't deny them this choice of not going in," says Mrs. Patti Burnette, a non-Mennonite, who is the city treasurer and the only female American Legion post commander in Kansas. "But it is a little hard to live around." Another non-Mennonite citizen of Newton says, "People here get along all right until a war gets near. The conscientious-objection business has always stirred up animosity, and when it gets closer to wartime the animosity always comes out. Someone might send their son and he gets the hell shot out of him, and the boy next door didn't go." Mennonites have a long memory for the animosity brought to Newton by war; they still tell stories of the First World War, when they were accused of being not only slackers but German slackers.

The hostility was not brought on by any public opposition to the war on the part of the Mennonites. Traditionally, their pacifism has taken the form not of actively opposing the government's participation in war but of separating themselves from it. In the last couple of years, there have been some signs of a subtle change in this tradition. In the past, traveling ministers of the General Conference Mennonites' Peace and Social Concerns Committee have spoken to congregations about peace and conscientious objection in general religious terms; the ministers now include references to the history and background of the Vietnam war—although, the head of the committee says, "there is still some suspicion of this in the churches." The *Mennonite,* a weekly magazine published by the General Conference, put out a special issue on Vietnam. The cover picture was of a weeping Vietnamese mother clutching her baby as South Vietnamese soldiers casually walked through a village; the lead article, written by a Mennonite pastor, was called "The Moral Bankruptcy of America's Vietnam Policy" and was a strong attack on the American involvement in Vietnam in historical and political terms. Maynard Shelly, the editor of the *Mennonite,* believes that a number of Mennonites object to the war in Vietnam specifically as well as to war in general, but he thinks a factor of at least equal importance is that the Vietnam war has come at a time when some Mennonites have begun to question the traditional Mennonite reluctance to become involved in political action. This has been particularly true at Bethel College. Bethel is in North Newton, a virtually all-Mennonite community separated from Newton proper by a line that is invisible to all but the Newton or North Newton eye. In the last few years, Bethel students have gone to Selma to participate in the civil-rights march and to Washington to demonstrate for a nuclear-test ban. Involved Mennonite students now scorn the idea of taking alternative service in a convenient American hospital, and they arrange to spend their two years working someplace that is at least uncomfortable and preferably dangerous. Some of them work in Vietnam.

Most of the twenty or thirty students who belong to the Peace Club at Bethel are the kind of young Mennonites who believe that social and peace concerns must be demonstrated. "I think some young people begin to feel that it's a fine Christian witness to go to Vietnam and bind up the wounds, but perhaps it would be better if we could keep them from being wounded," Shelly says. There is some reason to believe that the Peace Club members would feel a need to bear witness against any war that came up at this point in the history of the Mennonites, but there is no doubt that they believe the war in Vietnam to be particularly immoral. Last fall, after some discussion about Vietnam, the students in the Peace Club decided to stage what they called a Repentance Walk and Mail—a walk to the post office in downtown Newton, where they planned to mail protests against the war to Washington. They were repenting —they later said in an advertisement in the Newton paper—"as individuals who have stood by in apathy while our country became increasingly involved in an unnecessary and unjust war." They chose November 11th, Veterans Day, as an appropriate time to walk to Newton.

Newton war veterans, among others, were outraged. "The torch has been flung," Patti Burnette, the American Legion commander, informed the membership in a newsletter. The Legion and the V.F.W. decided to stage a Veterans Day parade on November 11th. It would be the first time in a number of years that the veterans' patriotism had manifested itself in such a display, and the commander told her men, "It is regrettable that it must take such action to get us 'off our chairs' and 'on our feet.' " The membership was informed that the Legion and the V.F.W. had worked diligently "toward the final accomplishment of having the Protest March called off."

There were many people not in the Legion who believed that the relations built up between Newton and North Newton since the last war were fragile enough without flaunting the one Mennonite position that Newton people had always found "a little hard to live around." Some Mennonites began to see the old signs of wartime in Newton. "They started calling Bethel 'K.U.'—'Kraut University,' " a member of the Peace Club said later. "And somebody put a sign on the North Newton line saying 'Entering Red Zone.' " There was talk of the peace walkers' being met in downtown Newton by young men bearing baseball bats.

In an editorial that accompanied the *Mennonite*'s thorough history of the events surrounding the walk, Shelly wrote, "The cost of the peace walk . . . was being tallied in terms of baseball bats, yellow paint, canceled pledges, loss of future students, possible dissension in the church, and ill-will of the community. One financial adviser to the college placed the possible loss at a half-million dollars. Others worried openly about the future existence of the school. Was the price too high for a one-hour walk to Newton?" The student paper carried an editorial opposing the walk, on the ground that it would do more harm than good, and the editorial was immediately reprinted in the Newton paper. There is a very small group of students at Bethel who actually favor the present American involvement in Vietnam, but the real pressure against the march came from a much larger group of students who are firmly pacifist but believe that Mennonites should take no part in secular protest—particularly in Newton. "They kept coming into my room," one of the organizers of the peace walk recalls. "They'd say, 'What are you going to do to our college? Who's going to wash the yellow paint off our cars?' The majority of the students were against it."

According to the *Mennonite*'s account, the president of Bethel, asserting the right of the students to make the walk if they wanted to, spoke during a Peace Club meeting on some of the disadvantages entailed, and later admitted that he had hoped his words would lead the students to call off the walk. A few days later, he asked directly that the walk be canceled, and finally he put his request in writing. After some discussion, the Peace Club members agreed to compromise by limiting the walk to North Newton and mailing their letters from the North Newton post office. On Veterans Day, about ninety people, including the dean and a number of student leaders, walked from the campus to the tiny North Newton post office, a few blocks away. Three hours later, the shops in downtown Newton closed and the veterans' parade began. It included color guards from the National Guard, the American Legion, the Gold Star Mothers, the Daughters of Union Veterans, and the V.F.W. Auxiliary; four Vietnam veterans; a Spanish-American War veteran; the Newton Blue Angels; the Scarlet Lancers of Wichita; three Air National Guard airplanes flying overhead; and a .50-caliber machine gun firing blanks from the bed of a truck. The veterans felt they had won the day. "Choosing November 11th was a direct insult to every veteran," Commander Burnette said later. "We weren't denying them their right to march. But on that day! Downtown! We had spent twenty years building up this feeling, and we didn't want a stigma on the community."

Readers of the *Mennonite* had mixed reactions to the events reported by Shelly. Some wrote that they were proud of the students for translating the church's beliefs into action and disappointed at the failure of the church and the college administration to give them more support. Others took the traditional view: "Does world peace not have to stem from individual peace? Can peace in Vietnam be achieved by starting a small-scale war in Newton because of a proposed peace walk? Is our message to the world one of peace marches and demonstrations or is it the message of the saving knowledge of Christ as Saviour and Lord of our lives?" Although the *Mennonite*'s account of the walk was carefully objective, the accompanying editorial left no doubt where the magazine stood. "In its action on the Peace Walk the Bethel College administration has passed judgment on the Mennonite church," the editorial said. "When the chips are down, the Mennonite church will not put its money and its middle-class reputation where its preaching is. . . . We're not angry. We're brokenhearted. . . . Perhaps it is the better part of valor to retreat today to save our lives and institutions for tomorrow when we can rise up and serve God again. But what if there is no tomorrow? What if the dirty little war becomes a dirty big war? And what if that war begins and ends with a big bang? Will we be guilty of saving that which we cannot keep?"

Some people in Newton think that relations with North Newton have been damaged slightly by the controversy surrounding Veterans Day—a banker who has been trying to raise money in the community for a fine-arts building at Bethel says some potential donors have used the controversy as an excuse not to contribute— but it is thought that the town has avoided the kind of bitterness that was predicted if the peace walk went downtown. The Peace Club has invited the American Legion to come to Bethel for a discussion on the Vietnam war, and the American Legion leaders have agreed that such a discussion would be a good idea, although so far they have not managed to find a convenient time. A week or so before Veterans Day, the Newton paper reported that the Bethel director of development, Merle L. Bender, had appeared before the city commission to notify it officially that the peace walk into Newton had been canceled. "Bender told the commissioners that the college had not stood in favor of the march," the item reported. "He said 606 students had enrolled at Bethel College this year, and that only 10 to 12 were members of the Peace Club." Visitors to Newton are often reminded that the march was indeed the work of a minority, and that relations between Newton and North Newton are now pretty good, though not as good as in peacetime.

# No, Sir, I Can't Go

The class of 1955 entered college during a war that was questioned by practically nobody—certainly not by the members of the class of 1955, who were, by and large, not in the habit of questioning anything—and graduated at a time when it was taken for granted that the United States would have to maintain a large military force to defend itself and other people from overt aggression. Taking R.O.T.C. was considered sensible; the most widely voiced concern about being commissioned in the Air Force was that any area flat and desolate enough to be an ideal place for an airbase was likely to be less than an ideal place to live. Nobody talked about the damage bombs could do to women and children. Speeches about aggression did not include the possibility that the United States could ever be considered the aggressor. The leading student in the Air Force R.O.T.C. program at Washington State University in 1955 was a young man from Wenatchee, Washington, named Dale Noyd. He accepted the regular (as opposed to reserve) commission offered by the Air Force to Distinguished Military Graduates, learned to fly a jet fighter, and eventually spent three years in England as a member of a NATO fighter squadron. He won commendation for landing a badly crippled plane instead of bailing out; his efficiency reports glowed with praise for his intelligence and his perfectionism. He remained in the Air Force after his first five-year commitment was over—a patriotic, articulate, extraordinarily conscientious young man who believed that flying a jet for NATO had served "a useful deterrent purpose." His military career ended this month, at an airbase in flat, desolate land not far from the Texas state line, by the verdict of a general court-martial.

Both Dale Noyd and the country had changed a lot since the fifties. At the close of his tour in England, in 1960, Noyd applied for a program under which he could attend graduate school in psychology as an Air Force officer. Noyd, as the phrase went in the decade before college graduates began to say there was nothing worth doing, wasn't sure what he really wanted to do. When the early decisions to increase American military advisers in Vietnam were being made in Washington, Noyd was at the University of Michigan, working hard in his courses, having long discussions about world affairs with other graduate students in the Psychology Department's coffee lounge, developing an intense interest in writers like Tillich and Camus. After 1963, when Noyd began teaching psychology at the Air Force Academy, he followed the debate about the American presence in Vietnam with a political awareness greatly broadened by his years at Michigan—and the American presence changed from military advisers to supporting combat troops to chief participants.

By going to school at Air Force expense, Noyd had incurred a service commitment until June, 1969, and he was almost certain to be reassigned as a fighter pilot before then. Late in 1966, stating that he could not participate in a war he considered immoral, he asked that he be allowed to resign his commission or that he be classified as a conscientious objector and assigned to duties that did not conflict with his conscience. He applied as a humanist—eligible for consideration as a conscientious objector under the Supreme Court decision that the religion required does not have to include a belief in the God recognized by conventional faiths. His application was turned down, on the ground that a non-pacifist who objected only to a particular war could not qualify as a conscientious objector. Before the application became public, Noyd and his lawyers tried to persuade Air Force officials that they could avoid an embarrassing test case by simply sending Noyd anywhere to perform any duties that did not contribute directly to the war in Vietnam; it remains a matter of conjecture why Captain Noyd is not at this moment a base housing officer in Thule, Greenland. Instead, he was transferred to Cannon Air Force Base, outside of Clovis, New Mexico; the federal courts eventually decided they did not have jurisdiction to hear an appeal of the Air Force ruling until Noyd had been through the military courts; a second conscientious-objection application was denied (although the Cannon base commander recommended approval); and, last December, Noyd was ordered to train fighter pilots who would almost certainly be going to Vietnam. He respectfully declined, as he had said he would—the fifties way of handling such a situation is not "Hell, no! We won't go!" but more like "No, sir, I can't go"—and he was charged with willful disobedience of a lawful order.

Although Noyd had changed and what the country was asking of its officers had changed, the Air Force had remained the same. On the first day of the court-martial, Marvin M. Karpatkin, who served as Noyd's chief defense counsel on behalf of the American Civil Liberties Union, spent hours inquiring into the beliefs and experiences of the ten Air Force officers who sat on the court, in order to decide how to use his one peremptory challenge. When Karpatkin asked the officers if they had any bias against the American Civil Liberties Union—which Noyd was connected with not only as a client but as a dues-paying member—it turned out that only two of them had ever heard of the American Civil Liberties Union. None of them was aware of the Air Force regulation that permits those already in the service to apply for conscientious-objector status, and only two or three were aware of the fact that conscientious objectors serve in the Army as medics. None of them knew any conscientious objectors personally, or knew anybody who knew any: None of them had ever had any discussions about conscientious objection. None of them belonged to any organizations that had taken a stand on the subject one way or the other (although one lieutenant colonel wasn't certain of that; he said he belonged to the National Rifle Association and the Blue Lodge Masons). About the only articles dealing with conscientious objection any of them could remember reading dealt with Cassius Clay.

"Do you think it's wrong for the Air Force to set up procedures for those who have become conscientious objectors since they joined the service?" Karpatkin asked the president of the court, a thin colonel who, like a couple of other senior officers on the court, had a crew cut and spoke with a drawl.

"Anyone in the Air Force should be required to do whatever is required by his job or mission," the colonel said. "If it's to go overseas, he should go overseas."

"I suppose what I'm asking is: Is it a good or bad regulation?" Karpatkin said.

"Well, let me answer like this," the colonel said. "Congress and the Department of Defense made such a law, and the Air Force wrote a regulation."

"Have you ever heard of the doctrine, stated by St. Thomas Aquinas, of just wars and unjust wars?" Karpatkin asked a few moments later.

"No, sir," the colonel replied. "I don't recall it."

Nobody ever had any doubt that Noyd would be found guilty. Noyd himself—like the Southern Negro college professors who used to demonstrate against segregation, and the Eastern intellectuals who now demonstrate against the war—is one of that class of modern Americans who are sufficiently educated to view their own imprisonment with some of the detachment they would bring to any other minor historical event. Before the trial began, he explained calmly to friends that an officer who has fought in Vietnam would find it psychologically difficult to acknowledge the possibility that the cause he fought for is unjust—another interesting demonstration, Noyd thought, of the "cognitive-dissonance" phenomenon explored by Professor Festinger, at Stanford. The only question relevant to Noyd's immediate future was how severe the sentence would be—a rather important question, since the military has no provisions for granting bail during appeal. Noyd's lawyers made it clear from the start that, unlike Captain Howard Levy, the Army doctor who was sentenced to three years in prison last June after refusing to give medical training to Special Forces troops, Noyd would not use the trial to claim that the war is, in addition to being unjust, illegal. The one issue that Noyd's lawyers hoped to bring up for purposes of appeal could be stated in terms of religious freedom: Must a man—a man whose decision is based on legitimate religious convictions—be conscientiously opposed to all wars in order to be conscientiously opposed to one?

Even in citing the Thomist principle of unjust wars, the defense avoided getting into the matter of what had led Noyd to believe that the war in Vietnam is unjust. The court never heard Noyd's views on the state of democracy in South Vietnam or on anti-Communism as a basis for foreign policy or on the Geneva accords. In fact, at times during the five days of the trial it was possible for a spectator to forget about the war in Vietnam altogether. The testimony was occasionally drowned out by the roar of F-100 jets in which pilots were training for Southeast Asia, but the rambling old wooden base hospital in which the tiny courtroom was situated created the impression that any unfriendly aircraft the pilots faced would probably be Japanese. When it was testified that Captain Noyd had refrained from indoctrinating cadets with his views, the views referred to were on conscientious objection; the possibility that Noyd might try to convert any troops to his views on the war, as Levy was accused of doing, was never brought up. Vietnam intruded only in such isolated incidents as the appearance of Lieutenant Matthew Husson—the specific pilot Captain Noyd had refused to train—when, for a few minutes, Noyd was accused not of some symbolic gesture but of refusing to prepare for the war in Vietnam one blond, impossibly young lieutenant who began his answer to any question with "Sir," like an underclassman in a military school. "Lieutenant Husson, who sat on this stand, was going to Vietnam," Noyd testified later. "The skills that I would impart to him would be used in tasks that I thought were wrong, and, in addition to that, I may be training a young man who would forfeit his life in a cause in which I cannot believe."

It is conceivable that the principle of selective conscientious objection could be tested during the appeal of Noyd's case, but the officers of the court-martial panel heard little more about it than they did about Vietnam. Although the refusal of the federal courts to interfere had left Noyd with no way to contest the legality of the Air Force's decision except to disobey an order that conflicted with his conscience, the law officer (judge) ruled on the second day of the court-martial that testimony on the legality of the Air Force's

decision was not relevant to whether or not Noyd disobeyed the
order—an encounter with civil and military justice that Karpatkin
compared to being used as a Ping-Pong ball. The defense had expert witnesses prepared to testify on the validity of humanism as a
religion and the validity of selective conscientious objection as a
religious principle, but, despite hours of maneuvering by the defense, their testimony to the court before the verdict was limited to
little more than the character testimony by one professor of theology that he personally knew Dale Noyd to be a religious man.

With the trial narrowed almost to a question of Dale Noyd's
character, Karpatkin produced a parade of Air Force officers, some
of them wearing the same wings and combat ribbons worn by most
members of the court, to testify that although they did not approve
of Captain Noyd's actions, they had absolutely no doubt about his
sincerity and integrity. It was agreed that he was incapable of acting out of hypocrisy or cowardice. It was agreed that he had performed flawlessly in every task the Air Force had ever assigned him
except training Lieutenant Husson in an F-100. The president of
last year's Air Force Academy graduating class testified that Captain Noyd was about the finest man he had ever met. Noyd remained an impressive Air Force officer throughout the trial—mod-
estly narrowing Karpatkin's implications about the excellence of
his record as a teacher and flier, precisely answering the technical
flying questions asked at one point by members of the court, reaffirming his willingness to fly in Europe or Korea, smiling reassur-
ingly at his wife, talking convincingly of the depths of his beliefs.
"Do you consider Captain Noyd a religious man?" Karpatkin kept
asking the witnesses. Everybody did.

In certain matters of civil liberty in America, of course, any co-
herent body of beliefs has to be called a religion in order to give its
adherent equal protection with people whose religion requires
church on Sunday and a vivid image of the hereafter, but the atmosphere of religiosity at Noyd's court-martial became at times
almost medieval. The witnesses prepared to testify on the nature of
Noyd's conscientious objection were sometimes referred to as "the
theologians"—conjuring up visions of St. Augustine and John Calvin waiting to come on base and have their say. In one attempt to
get such testimony before the court, the defense contended that

Captain Noyd had acted out of religious compulsion—as opposed to the mental compulsion sometimes claimed in insanity pleas—and suggested that the compulsion be attested to by theologians rather than psychiatrists. Jeremiah and Martin Luther were alluded to regularly, and at the close of a day's testimony no one was surprised to see one of the theologians being interviewed on the philosophy of Paul Tillich by a man from the Amarillo *Globe-Times*. Part of the defense's closing argument in the extenuation and mitigation hearing before sentencing was given by a priest from Georgetown University—a priest with a law degree who had originally been scheduled to testify as a theologian.

Karpatkin established the atmosphere on the first day by asking each court member about his church affiliation, and in his opening statement he referred to Noyd's reaction to Tillich and other thinkers as "that which in an earlier stage of the world, perhaps, might have been considered a religious experience." As it happens, Noyd, with the seriousness often found among those who revere intellectual matters while living in nonintellectual environments, can speak about the lessons of, say, Camus more or less religiously. ("If the definition of 'Supreme Being' is limited to include only the traditional Christian concept of a personalistic, anthropomorphic, and omnipotent supernatural-creator-object-being whom I worship and upon whom I depend for salvation or a meaning for my life, then I do not believe in such an object-being," he wrote in his conscientious-objection application. "If, however, the definition is to include the 'God beyond God' or the 'ground of Being' of Paul Tillich, the 'existential Being' of Martin Buber, or 'the perfect pattern, envisioned by faith, of humanity as it should be' of David Muzzey, then I believe in a Supreme Being.") But, by the law officer's ruling, the officers on the court, all of whom had told Karpatkin that they had never heard of humanism, could not be given an explanation of what Noyd meant by it; since they also lacked an explanation of why he considered the war in Vietnam unjust, it is not altogether inconceivable that some of them rendered a verdict under the impression that Noyd belongs to some small Christian sect that prohibits its members from killing Asians during certain seasons of the year. It sometimes seemed that at any moment the trial counsel (prosecutor) would object to the entire proceeding and explain to the court that the defendant was not some kind of religious eccentric but a man who had rationally, without any interference from Yahweh or Jesus Christ, come to the decision that the acts they and their fellow-officers had been committing in Vietnam were immoral; instead, the trial counsel, in his summation, acknowledged that Captain Noyd was a sincerely religious man and said that the question was what would happen to the Air Force if every man could put his religion above his sworn duty of obedience. As in many ceremonies carried out in the presence of clergy, everyone was elaborately polite; the Air Force and Noyd never acted angry at each other.

Although the trial counsel's restraint was a matter of legal strategy, the military seemed comfortable with the image of Captain Noyd as a man of religion. How else could he be explained? He was not some misfit draftee but a regular officer. What except some quirk of religion would make such a man refuse to participate in the Air Force mission of prosecuting the Vietnam war? When, in the testimony before sentencing, a theology professor explained that according to Tillich's definition "a man's ultimate concern is God for him," the lieutenant colonel from the Blue Lodge Masons ascertained that the Air Force could also be a religion, and that the court-martial was thus not a matter of religious persecution against Noyd but of two religions coming in conflict—an image later adopted by the trial counsel ("Each of you must decide which of these religions should fall away and leave the other standing").

The maximum sentence for willful disobedience is dismissal and five years at hard labor. The prosecution asked for dismissal and two years. The finding of the court was dismissal and one year. When the sentence was announced, Noyd saluted the president of the court properly and, a short time later, drove his own car to his own home, to remain temporarily under house arrest. Contrary to pre-trial predictions, the court had not insisted on the Air Force's bureaucratic due; with time off for good behavior, Noyd could be a free civilian several months before he had paid the Air Force the time he owed it. For a while, when the court seemed to be taking a long time bringing in the verdict, some of Noyd's friends even allowed themselves to think that perhaps religion and propriety had managed to melt completely the disagreement between Noyd and the Air Force. But, as the law officer had observed while discussing legal definitions with opposing counsel, "a man may be guilty of willful disobedience even if he says 'No, sir.' "

*Mount Vernon, Iowa, April, 1968*

# The Last Peaceful Place

When the students of Cornell College reported for classes last September, most of them would have described themselves as supporters of the American presence in Vietnam. By March 31st, the day Lyndon Johnson announced that he was withdrawing from the Presidential race and taking steps to initiate peace talks, there were few supporters of the war (or of the President) left at Cornell. The entire process had taken just six months.

Last year, parents who were searching for a place where their son or daughter was likely to receive a respectable education unaccompanied by placard carrying, beard growing, and pot smoking might well have settled on Cornell, a small, peaceful liberal-arts college in eastern Iowa. "When the Cornell recruiter comes to your school," a senior recalled recently, "he kind of talks past the kid to the parents." Of the institutions allied with Cornell in the Associated Colleges of the Midwest, a few are rather undemanding academically, and at least one—Carleton—has academic standards that are considered too rigorous for most students. Grinnell, in the eyes of some Midwesterners, has gone hippie.

Cornell remains the kind of place that many middle-class and upper-middle-class parents associate with the idyllic college life—a small college with a good faculty and a relatively homogeneous student body, a tree-shaded campus on a hilltop in a quiet town, with rolling cornfields visible from the huge stone chapel that looms over the other buildings. Quite a few of Cornell's thousand students come from the Chicago suburbs, two hundred miles away —there are slightly more students from Illinois than from Iowa— and there are delegations from the suburbs of Minneapolis and St. Louis and Denver. All but a few students live in red brick dormitories, and those who pledge "social groups" stencil Greek letters on the sidewalk. The students talk about how middle-class they are and joke about the overprotectiveness of "Mother Cornell" and berate themselves, mildly, for apathy. Cornell is too idyllic for some —junior-year attrition is a serious problem—but most of its students seem comfortable in a peaceful place where they can spend four years among friends, protected from the world's problems. When *Look* did an article on "The Case for the Small College," it used Cornell as a prototype.

The Campus Chest drive at Cornell began to drift away from direct supervision by the Student Council two or three years ago, for no particular reason. It became accepted that the drive's co-chairmen would plan money-raising activities, find some worthy beneficiary for the money collected, and select successors to repeat the process the following year. Last spring, the money from the Campus Chest went to a leper colony in Pusan, Korea. An obvious choice for co-chairman of this year's drive was Doug Peterson, a straightforward young man from Moline, Illinois, who was a member of the swimming team and the president of the junior class. Last fall, he and the other co-chairman, a young lady from Nebraska named Mary Luschen, began collections in the usual manner. Pictures of candidates from dormitories and social groups were placed above jars in the Commons, a modern brick building that serves as a student union and central dining hall, and students were informed that the candidates who drew the most money would be named Mister and Miss Campus Chest. At a Student Council meeting, Peterson reported that he and Miss Luschen had decided on a beneficiary for this year's drive. The money would go for medical supplies for Vietnamese civilians—half to South Vietnam and half to North Vietnam. Most of the people whose pictures were above the jars decided that they did not want to be Mister or Miss Campus Chest after all; they took down their pictures. The Student Council decided to look into its right to supervise the Campus Chest drive.

Cornell had never had a controversy about the war before. There had been one small anti-war demonstration the previous school year—some students and faculty members held a silent vigil in the spring—but about the only people who paid much attention to it were those who threw water bombs or played the Green Beret song as loudly as possible through the open windows of nearby dormitories. Cornell was known, in fact, for an absence of controversy of any kind—except, perhaps, some mild disagreements about mild extensions of dormitory-visitation privileges. "Last year," a Cornell coed said recently, "Cornell College didn't recognize the existence of the war in Vietnam." When Doug Peterson revealed what he planned to do with the Campus Chest money, the campus newspaper took a poll that showed at least seventy-five per cent of the students opposed to the idea. The president of the Student Council —Joe Gebhardt, an athletic young man from the Chicago suburbs —expressed opposition as someone who might very well be in Vietnam himself before long. "I could rationalize protest rallies back home on the basis of free speech," he was quoted as saying, "but it would be hard to stomach the knowledge that there were soldiers shooting at me who had been healed by contributions from the United States." At a special meeting, the Student Council reasserted its authority over the Campus Chest, and when Peterson and Miss Luschen declined to change their plans for disposition of the money they were replaced. The campus newspaper headlined its coverage of the confrontation "G.I. JOE BOMBS CAMPUS CHEST." Charged with finding a more suitable beneficiary, the new co-chairmen selected MEDICO, the Asian relief agency founded by Dr. Tom Dooley.

Peterson and his supporters, emphasizing that their concern was humanitarian rather than political, decided to continue their project independently of the official Campus Chest. When a professor suggested that they adopt some symbol, they took to wearing maple leaves—the most readily accessible symbol on the Cornell campus in the fall. The loose organization that evolved—the Maple Leaves —eventually had thirty or thirty-five members, a number of them

students who had at one time or another left Cornell for a semester
on such programs as the Experiment in International Living. The
Maple Leaves were not precisely identical with those on campus
who might grow beards, or with the twenty or thirty Cornell students who began to attend anti-war demonstrations at the University of Iowa, twenty miles away, but the overlap was close enough
for the organization to be identified with the small amount of anti-
war protest that existed at Cornell—run by what Joe Gebhardt
called "the radical element." There were members of the Maple
Leaves—Doug Peterson, for instance—who retained their standing in the respectable Cornell community, but it was clear last fall
that most students, like most of their parents, believed that the only
proper position of an American during a war is support of his government.

The Campus Chest controversy began the first widespread discussion of the war at Cornell. The war was also coming closer in
other ways. The assumption that student deferments would be extended through graduate school was shattered by an announcement
from the Selective Service System. There were anti-war demonstrations at the University of Iowa that involved hundreds of students
and, during a protest against Dow recruiting in December, involved
the use of riot clubs and Mace by the police. Some state legislators
called for the dismissal of a University of Northern Iowa English
instructor who had counseled his students to resist the draft. The
Des Moines *Register* reported the death of an Iowan in Vietnam
almost daily; eighty were killed in the first three months of this
year. Some Cornell students who had begun to follow the war in
the newspapers grew suspicious of the Administration's optimism,
particularly after the Tet offensive.

In February, some members of the Maple Leaves passed up dinner so that their rebates from the dining hall could go toward the
collection for medical supplies, and they spent the dinner hour sitting silently in an open lounge of the Commons. There were a few
dinner rolls thrown at them, but it was thought that those who did
the heckling were the few people on campus who would heckle
anybody, regardless of the politics involved, and that the hawkish
atmosphere that had made the demonstration last spring an easy
target for ridicule was no longer apparent.

Partly to prove that it was not trying to shut off campus debate on the war by canceling Peterson's project, the Student Council had decided to sponsor a week of Vietnam speeches called "Challenge '68." In the fall, nobody had anticipated any problems in arranging a balanced program, but by the time "Challenge '68" was held, during the first week in March, articulate supporters of the Johnson Administration's Vietnam policies were difficult to find in eastern Iowa. Everyone agrees that the speeches had an extraordinary effect on both the students and the local citizens—particularly a speech by David Schoenbrun, an anti-war television commentator, whose appearance in a college-sponsored lecture series had been incorporated into the Vietnam series. Some members of the local Republican organization had previously attended discussions about the war with Cornell professors; the day after the Schoenbrun speech, the Mount Vernon Republican caucus passed a resolution calling for a halt in the bombing of North Vietnam. At the close of "Challenge '68," a poll of the students showed that sixty-five per cent favored de-escalation and cessation of the bombing of the North, and eleven per cent favored immediate withdrawal. One and nine-tenths per cent favored continuation of present policies. By the time of the New Hampshire primary, a week later, most students at Cornell—including Joe Gebhardt—considered themselves opponents of the war and supporters of Eugene McCarthy.

A few of those who changed their minds had been deeply committed supporters of the war. But it is generally agreed at Cornell that last fall most of the students were, in the words of one coed, "hawkish by habit." Relatively untouched by the war, they had not yet given it any serious consideration. What gave them the appearance of hawks—even to themselves—was habitual patriotism and confidence in established authority. Judging from the rate at which their support melted away with exposure to information and personal involvement, it appears that, beginning in the fall, most Cornell students began to think about the war and began to oppose the war at the same time. When they returned from spring vacation, they learned that a straw vote in the local Democratic caucus the previous week had given McCarthy sixty-five votes and Johnson one. In fact, McCarthy had overwhelmed Johnson in Democratic caucuses around the state. On the night the students returned, President Johnson announced a partial halt in bombing and his own withdrawal from politics, and there was joy at Cornell.

Scott Suneson—a bright, youthful-looking junior who is married and lives off campus—had been planning to turn in his draft card the following Wednesday night at an Iowa City rally that was being held as part of a national collection of draft cards and statements of complicity with those who resist the draft. The President's speech caused him some hesitation. Also on Wednesday, a Cornell faculty meeting was scheduled to begin discussion of a resolution that would favor banning military recruiters at Cornell as long as the draft was being used as a punishment against demonstrators, and after the speech one of the resolution's sponsors suggested to his colleagues that it might be worth considering whether a battle over recruiting remained relevant.

For the average student at Cornell, though, the Johnson announcement seemed almost a logical extension of the process that had begun with their own change of position. About the time most Cornell students decided that Vietnam policies had to be changed, the McCarthy candidacy, the New Hampshire primary, and the Johnson withdrawal reassured them that the political system was responsive to the need for change. After Johnson's speech, a group of Cornell students who had spent their spring vacation working for McCarthy in Wisconsin gathered at a professor's house and began to talk about likely Vice-Presidential nominees. (The next night, McCarthy workers in Wisconsin, fearing a Johnson sympathy vote in the primary, phoned the professor for some last-minute election-day volunteers, and within a couple of hours he was able to round up fifty-two students for an all-night ride to Racine.)

Most Cornell students had never thought of taking part in demonstrations—and thereby becoming identified with what Joe Gebhardt still calls "the radical element." ("Before McCarthy," a Cornell senior said last week, "those of us who opposed the war had no way to show it.") Although the Maple Leaves controversy had receded—Doug Peterson was unopposed when he ran for president of next year's Student Council, and nobody thought much about it—most Cornell students would probably still oppose a project that in any way aided North Vietnam as long as American troops were in the field. There are perhaps a half-dozen people at Cornell who are seriously considering jail or Canada as alternatives to the draft if the war does not end. The others would be happy to find a way to become deferred or at least a way to avoid the infantry, but there has never been any doubt that they would go if called, whether they opposed the war or not. Perhaps if there had been no McCarthy candidacy and no Johnson announcement there might have come a time when the mainstream of Cornell students would have begun to question the system itself and to change their minds about the propriety of protesting in the streets, but from all indications that time was still a long way off. It is possible that parents who considered Cornell the last place their children were likely to be caught up in anti-war activities were right.

For Scott Suneson and a few others, the President's change of heart turned out not to have been in time. At a press conference in Iowa City on Monday—a press conference devoted almost entirely to statements of why the President's speech did not mean the end of the peace movement—Suneson announced that he would be among those turning in draft cards Wednesday night. Suneson had not thought much about the war until Christmas vacation, but once he began reading books about it he became sufficiently outraged to consider his possession of a draft card immoral. On the day after the press conference, the University of Iowa paper reported that one student who had been scheduled to participate had decided after hearing Johnson's speech not to turn in his card. But Suneson had decided that the speech did not affect the morality of his cooperation with the system, and he resisted pressure from his father and his neighbors and one of his philosophy professors to reconsider his decision. Working with Mike Hill—an amiable young man who, because of a shaggy red beard and a fondness for wearing a peace pendant and buttons, is generally considered the closest thing Cornell has to a hippie—Suneson went on trying to persuade people to attend the rally or to sign complicity statements.

On Wednesday morning, Suneson and Hill took some time off from helping to organize the rally to help organize a demonstration for the faculty meeting that afternoon. The sponsors of the recruiting-ban resolution had decided to go ahead, and one of them had told Suneson that one argument being used against the resolution was that the students were opposed to it. (Another was that it would mar Cornell's image as a peaceful, protected place.) That afternoon, fifty or sixty students gathered to stand on the sidewalk and hold pro-resolution placards as faculty members filed in to the meeting. As the demonstration broke up, Suneson became involved in a long conversation with one of the other participants—Gary Barnard, who had been his roommate when they were both freshmen. A blond, gangling young man, Barnard, unlike most Cornell students, had been brought up in a tough urban neighborhood before moving to a suburb just outside the Chicago city limits, where he went to high school. His interest in the war was also recent, but he was considering turning in his draft card at the rally. Suneson seemed to argue for the moral necessity of the act and warn of its legal consequences at the same time. Barnard could think of a lot of reasons against it himself, including the Johnson announcement. Suneson said the only difference the announcement made was that another President would run the war, or run another war. "Maybe it would be better to wait until they try to induct me," Barnard said. "I want it to be effective. Also, I guess I'm scared."

About twenty students, several of them wearing McCarthy buttons, met at the Commons at seven-thirty that evening for the drive to Iowa City. Barnard had decided to turn in his card. At Iowa City, he and Suneson sat on the stage, both of them looking ill at ease. About four hundred people, a smaller crowd than had been hoped for, were in the audience. When Barnard was called on, he walked to the lectern and said, in a strong Chicago accent, "Cornell College is twenty miles that way, in the middle of nowhere. It's straight. You don't see the beards, you don't see the beads. I'm straight. I'm wearing the uniform: the button-down shirt, the V-neck, the stay-presseds, the penny-loafers, the whole bit. That's the point I want to make: I *am* straight. And there are a lot of straight people who are moving. What I'm doing now wasn't easy. I'm scared out of my mind. Most of you people probably sympathize with what I'm doing and with the peace movement. But it's for the outside people I want to make the point. Last year at this time, I probably wanted to kill all those little gooks in Vietnam. Tonight, I'm turning in my draft card. And, like I said, I'm scared. But I thought about it. I think this is a message to the outside people, the straight people who don't think. All the kooks with their beards and their beads—all they're asking you to do is think about it. Read. Listen. Get it the way it is. And if you get it the way it is, maybe you'll change your mind. They're not saying, 'If you don't go our way, we'll draft you.' "

Barnard got the only standing ovation of the evening. After the last speeches, a crowd gathered around him, shaking his hand, congratulating him on his speech.

"I never thought you'd do it," a red-haired girl from Cornell said to him.

"I never thought I'd do it, either," Barnard said. "I never would have thought it two months ago, or a year ago." He paused. "A year ago!" he said, and he shook his head in amazement at the thought.

At the end of the rally, two hundred and twenty-three statements of complicity were turned in, thirty-five of them from students and members of the faculty at Cornell. Since the Iowa University students who were likely to turn in their draft cards had turned them in long ago, the only draft-age student on the platform with Suneson and Barnard had come from Iowa State. Eleven documents of one kind or another were turned in—including a draft-delinquency notice and a Wave's discharge card. Suneson and Barnard had become the first Cornell students to turn in draft cards publicly. It was a few hours after the United States and North Vietnam had finally established contact for peace talks.

*Nassau County, Long Island, November, 1968*

# The Kids Against the Grown-ups

In discussing the awesome level of political activity maintained by Allard K. Lowenstein as a student, those who knew him at Yale Law School sometimes insist that when people called New Haven information to ask for his telephone number they got an instantaneous reply, as if they had asked for the number of the New York, New Haven & Hartford Railroad. Several years after that, in the late fifties and early sixties, Lowenstein's friends and acquaintances —a group that, according to some calculations, is large enough to be expressed as a percentage of the American population—often joked about his being the oldest living student politician in the United States. In those years, Lowenstein appeared to be about the only adult in America who believed that the college student of the American Dream—healthy, exuberant, basically right-thinking— was either politically interested or politically interesting. Whether Lowenstein was officially working as a dean at Stanford or as a foreign-policy adviser in Washington, he continued to spend a lot of nights sprawled in the second-hand armchairs of college-dormitory rooms, arguing with equal intensity about the evils of South Africa or the role of the fraternity system. Even in New York or Washington, Lowenstein always seemed to be accompanied by a couple of clean-cut young men who would be introduced as, say, a recently returned Rhodes Scholar and the president of the University of North Carolina student government—a pair of Wasp outriders, ready at any hint of trouble to shake hands hard and talk about commitment to the democratic process.

The events that caused other adults to take such students seriously came about largely because of Lowenstein's efforts. The participation of hundreds of Northern white college students in the Mississippi voter-registration project of 1964 was the outgrowth of Lowenstein's having induced a number of Stanford and Yale undergraduates to go to Mississippi the previous year to hold a mock election; the students who went to New Hampshire last winter to work for Eugene McCarthy and the Impossible Dream were, like McCarthy himself, present partly in response to the urgings of Lowenstein, who was once almost alone in believing that the Vietnam-war policy could somehow be changed by the electoral process. It was not surprising that when Lowenstein himself decided to run for Congress this year in the Fifth District of New York—a collection of middle-class bedroom communities that extends into Nassau County from New York City along the South Shore of Long Island—he attracted hundreds of weekend volunteers from colleges like Yale and Harvard and Smith, and put together a full-time staff so young that his official campaign manager, a middle-aged man named Horace Kramer, sometimes seemed to be playing the role of token grown-up. Although some of the weekend volunteers had worked in the McCarthy or Kennedy campaigns, most of them appeared to be students who had never been involved in politics before; a large number of the Yale volunteers were freshmen. When staff members were asked one day how they had been able to persuade so many students to devote autumn weekends to the house-to-house canvassing of Nassau County, they suggested that some of the more politically involved students might have wanted to make one last attempt at working for social change through the electoral process, and that some of the girls might have decided to settle for the Saturday-night canvassers' party in Lawrence or Long Beach because they hadn't been invited to New Haven for the Dartmouth game. "To tell the truth," one young man said, smiling, "I think most of the kids who came think they're personal friends of Al's."

Many Nassau County citizens who saw Lowenstein on television as a leader of those opposing Mayor Daley's regulars at the Chicago Convention identified him not just with the respectable campaign volunteers who have always formed the core of his following but with the Yippies in Grant Park and the S.D.S. occupation forces at Columbia and the depraved acid-heads who threaten to offend grown-ups in the street—or, for all a grown-up knows, might be living under his own roof, cleverly disguised as his children. American voters have never been scrupulous about precise identifications; Lowenstein is a leader of kids, and the campaign in the Fifth District eventually concerned the suspicions harbored by adults about all kids. Speaking one day before a Lions luncheon in Long Beach, Lowenstein offered an eyewitness account of how young people who had gone to Chicago to work for McCarthy's candidacy had been beaten by the police while they were sitting quietly in the McCarthy campaign suite. When asked what seventeen-year-old girls were doing in a Chicago hotel in the first place, Lowenstein said that adults ought to be grateful for the young people who were willing to participate in the political process, and that the channeling of young people's dissent into such activities was the only way to avoid the disruptive politics of confrontation that he, along with most other Americans, deplores. "They went there for trouble," a man down the luncheon table muttered. "That's what—for trouble."

Lowenstein's opponent—Mason Hampton, Jr., a conservative lawyer—is thirty-seven, two years younger than Lowenstein, but he made it clear from the start that he was on the side of the grown-ups. He spoke of the breakdown of law and order as having been caused by "the permissive view gone wild." Because Lowenstein is a vice-chairman of Americans for Democratic Action, Hampton could have confronted him with any number of A.D.A. resolutions that Nassau County voters might consider at least unwise and perhaps treasonous; the one Hampton chose was a resolution against treating the use of marijuana as a crime. Lowenstein kept repeating that he was opposed to the legalization of marijuana, but that still left him far less militantly grown-up on the issue than Hampton, who for a while seemed to be proposing capital punishment for marijuana sellers—a position that prompted one of the jollier members of Lowenstein's staff to put up a sign in the office reading "Mason Hampton is a junkie." The Hampton forces occasionally claimed to have their own influence with the young. ("We have students, too, only ours don't use obscene language," a Hampton campaign worker told me.) But a week or so before the election Hampton predicted that he would win because his polls showed that he was getting the support of sixty-five per cent of the voters over forty-five. One of the Hampton campaign pictures that appeared in local papers showed him flanked by four or five middle-aged women who were dressed completely in white—white tennis shoes, white skirts, white sweatshirts with Mason Hampton bumper stickers stuck on them—and were waving what looked like cheerleaders' pompons. The caption identified them as "Mothers for Hampton."

One of Lowenstein's primary-campaign posters described him as the man who had "helped bring America's young people home," and his general-election campaign was based partly on the premise that there are some American young people worth having at home. In high schools of Republican towns like Rockville Centre and Freeport and Baldwin, straw votes showed that even students who favored Richard Nixon supported Lowenstein—as if they realized that their reputation was on the line. The visits of polite young men and women to the residents of the South Shore were designed not merely to bring word of Lowenstein's candidacy but to demonstrate to the citizenry that polite young men and women actually still exist. Senior-citizens clubs that invited Lowenstein to speak were delighted to find him accompanied by a courteous young friend named Franklin Delano Roosevelt III; in the last weekend of the campaign Lowenstein was joined by Wendell Willkie II. During that final weekend, in the West End of Long Beach—a lower-middle-class neighborhood, where Hampton is treasured as a man who first came to public notice as the lawyer for some Long Island parents who were opposing a plan to integrate schools by busing students—Irish Catholics who had almost shouted Lowenstein off the platform a couple of nights before were astonished to open their doors and be handed some Lowenstein literature by earnest young men who had come in for the weekend from Notre Dame.

"Regardless of the preparations you've made for a dialogue, you'll find that most of these people don't want to talk," a Lowenstein staff member said to a group of students from Boston while briefing them for a Saturday of canvassing. A congressional race in Nassau County is not a crusade for peace. A year or so ago, Lowenstein, as the leader of a movement that set out to end the war by replacing the President, might have been considered a bit of a traitor by the residents of Nassau County, but almost everyone is against the war now in one way or another. For weeks after the Chicago Convention, Lowenstein resisted the demands of local Democrats that he support Hubert Humphrey, going no further than to say, after mid-October, that he had decided to vote for Humphrey himself. But the long weeks of campaigning gradually submerged Lowenstein's role as a lone dissident to the extent that the issue stressed by his campaign workers in the final days was that Hampton was not a regular—being a founder of the Conservative Party who had managed to get Republican endorsement, rather than a proper Republican—and that Lowenstein was therefore the only candidate in the mainstream of the two great political parties. Most people visited by the canvassers didn't want to talk about any issue—even the burden of taxation on middle-income families. Many of them didn't know who was running. Except that someone seems to have persuaded a particularly large number of residents that there is something classy about having house numbers written out in script, the South Shore looks like any other collection of suburbs. An area known as the Five Towns is largely well-off, Jewish, and liberal; the communities that are strung along the Long Island Rail Road a bit farther from the city are mainly middle-income, Republican, and Catholic. Except for that rough division, the towns seem to have no more distinct identities than the district has. People read a jumble of New York and suburban newspapers. A political candidate who wants to buy television time can buy only the ruinously expensive time on New York metropolitan channels. Canvassing door to door is about the only reliable method of campaigning. In a sense, the student volunteers—energetic, articulate, delighting in producing computer print-outs that indicated precisely when each of the hundred Yale volunteers would arrive and leave during the weekend—served merely as the only available bearers of campaign propaganda to the Fifth District's close-mouthed residents. Usually, volunteers didn't need preparation for a dialogue in order to hand out campaign brochures—any more than Lowenstein needed a Vietnam policy in order to shake hands with housewives at the Big Apple supermarket in Freeport. "They're just bodies," Hampton said of the students. He claimed that in a district with a four-to-three Republican edge in registration, a strong Republican organization, and a Democratic organization hostile to Lowenstein, he could outnumber the students easily with the grown-up bodies of Republican committeemen.

At first glance, Lowenstein's full-time staff seemed to differ from the weekend volunteers only in being, on the average, two or three years older. They were mostly intelligent, good-natured young people from colleges like Yale and Stanford—the same kind of young people who had followed Lowenstein to Mississippi and to New Hampshire. (Lowenstein has always maintained that stories of students in New Hampshire shaving beards to be Clean for Gene were exaggerated, since almost all the students were clean-cut types to begin with.) Many staff members had worked against the Vietnam war in the Presidential primaries or in Chicago, and they could have viewed the President's announcement of a bombing halt and new negotiations as a tribute to their efforts and a personal triumph for Lowenstein. But on the night of the announcement there was an air of dejection around Lowenstein headquarters. The members of the staff had felt Lowenstein moving closer to an endorsement of Humphrey all week, and although they agreed that few weekend volunteers would care much one way or the other, they were less certain of their own feelings.

A few staff members were more or less non-ideological people whose concern about an endorsement was based on whether or not it seemed to be good politics. In general, though, the staff members were dismayed at the prospect of the endorsement because they have a harsher view of the American political process than the view held by Lowenstein or by the weekend volunteers. "I think we have much less faith in America than Al does," one of them had told me a couple of days before. "And it's not just one or two issues that bother us—it's the whole stupid framework of thinking in this country." When Lowenstein did announce his decision to endorse Humphrey, he had to defend it in a long emotional staff meeting; a few people said that only personal affection for Lowenstein kept them from leaving the campaign. Lowenstein insisted that the important fact about the President's announcement was that, no matter what kind of face-saving rhetoric it was couched in, it meant a reversal of the war policy and an end to the bloodshed. Some of the staff members were not persuaded that the announcement really did herald a significant change in policy; the attacks on Laos caused some of them to refer to the new policy as "a relocation of bombing." More important, they thought that the tone of Johnson's announcement—his inability to acknowledge that the government had been wrong and that the protesters who had been called traitors for so long were in fact right—was another indication that those in control of the country had learned nothing from Vietnam. To these staff members, the attitudes of the leaders of both political parties meant that even if the war in Vietnam ended, a war someplace else would take its place. "Al argued that the American people have shown that they won't stand for another Vietnam," one girl said later. "But we just don't believe that's the way things work. We might as well get new signs ready and just leave the name of the next country blank."

The following day, volunteers began to arrive for the final weekend of canvassing, and, as had been predicted, none of them seemed particularly concerned about the Humphrey endorsement. On Saturday night, Lowenstein spoke to a gathering of hundreds of high-school and college volunteers, devoting some time to an explanation of why he believed that he had been committed to endorse Humphrey as soon as a bombing halt was announced. The students listened respectfully, and after the speech only one person came forward to state his objections and announce that under the circumstances he could not continue to work in the campaign.

A few nights later, even more students jammed a ballroom in Baldwin to await the election results. As the returns were phoned in from Lowenstein headquarters, where the candidate and a number of his young campaign workers were manning telephones and adding machines, Horace Kramer, the campaign manager, read them out to the huge crowd—occasionally accompanying the figures with a request to hold down the noise a bit or an admonition about standing in chairs or a reminder that if he didn't love them all quite so much he might find them somewhat exasperating. Lowenstein seemed to run slightly ahead all night; about midnight, the band began to play "Mrs. Robinson," and everyone joined in. Finally, about one in the morning, with a narrow victory assured, Lowenstein arrived—to almost hysterical cheering from the kids, and chorus after chorus of "The Impossible Dream" from the band. "Part of our constituency," he said, "has to be that the point of view of young America has to be heard in Congress as it hasn't been heard before."

"I think the main thing it'll prove if we win is that we've run a good campaign," one of the staff had told me earlier in the evening. It was a point of pride with the Lowenstein staff that in sheer technique—in organization and mechanics—the kids could outclass the grown-ups. The extraordinary amount of time and energy that the staff had put into the campaign may have accounted for some of the emotion in their response to Lowenstein's endorsement of Humphrey, but the difference in attitude between the staff and the part-time volunteers was too deep to be explained by strain or fatigue. Lowenstein's recruiters had found that many college students who had worked for McCarthy wanted nothing to do with a campaign in Nassau County or anywhere else. Quite a few Lowenstein staff members were people who had stayed with electoral politics long enough to see a change in the policy they opposed, but after the primaries and the Chicago Convention and the dreary realities of a congressional campaign, some of them no longer had enough faith in the system to believe that the change made any difference. Lowenstein's critics on the New Left have argued that he prevents students from recognizing the kind of revolutionary changes really needed in America by channeling their dissent into attempts at minor reforms within the established political system. But it's possible that the reaction of a lot of intelligent young people to any sustained exposure to the American political system is to turn against it—and that the weekend volunteers retained their relatively hopeful view only through lack of experience. After all, some of Lowenstein's New Left critics—now among those who have come to believe that the established political system is hopelessly fraudulent and corrupt—were themselves, only a few years ago, the healthy, exuberant, basically right-thinking young men from colleges like Yale and Stanford who went to Mississippi with Allard K. Lowenstein.

# Targets

During a year I once spent in Atlanta, those permanent residents who enjoyed entertaining me with lists of civic attributes always seemed to include the boast that Atlanta was "the fourth target on the Kremlin's map of nuclear destruction." Exactly the same phrase was used every time—"the fourth target on the Kremlin's map of nuclear destruction"—and it was always expressed in a prideful tone, the same tone used to tell me the number of national firms that were represented in Atlanta, or to inform me that Atlanta was the second-highest major city in the United States. I was always at a loss for a decently appreciative reply. "I see" or "That's interesting" seemed a pedestrian way to respond to the possibility of a nationally ranked apocalypse. Once, in a confused effort to be a good guest, I burst out with "I think it ought to be *first!*" My informant for a moment looked gratified—then uncertain, and then offended. The Bomb, which has been blamed for juvenile delinquency and for an increase in tornadoes and for a decrease in humorists and for general despair, has even made civic pride confusing.

The citizens who live around Chicago were informed last fall that the Sentinel Anti-Ballistic Missile System would include a site in the area, because Chicago was such an eminent target for nuclear destruction. Practically none of the citizens took the selection as a point of pride. In fact, some of them objected to having the site on the theory that it might *make* Chicago an eminent target. Chicago is presumably important enough to be a target already (of just what rank I don't know; the people in Atlanta knew only which city was No. 4), and it might be thought that having some defense against nuclear destruction would make everyone feel more secure. But the only known defense against a nuclear missile is another nuclear missile, in this case a Spartan missile with a multi-megaton warhead, and a lot of people in Chicago, musing on the multi-megaton warheads that a Spartan site would have to keep at the ready, have come to believe that the possibility of their own defense accidentally destroying them is no more remote than the possibility of an enemy nuclear power maliciously attacking them— and is much harder to put out of their thoughts. Chicagoans tend to believe that if Chicago has to be defended it could be defended very nicely from South Dakota, although they also speak highly of northern Iowa.

The Chicago *Sun-Times* phoned a few Dakota mayors to ask, more or less, how they would feel about the gift of a Spartan-missile site from the people of Chicago. The mayors said they would be delighted. From my experience in Atlanta, I would guess that some cities in the United States might welcome a site as a way to assure themselves of the importance that is implied by a place in the hypothetical holocaust. Also, there are some areas so poor or so obsessed with economic development that they would probably welcome the Federal Typhoid and Scrofula Center if the government guaranteed a large payroll and promised to contract for the construction locally. Fifteen cities have been chosen for Sentinel sites, and practically no protest has been heard from the smaller ones (or from New York—raising the possibility that New Yorkers have resigned themselves to living in a state of permanent disaster that could not be affected by an accidental nuclear blast or two). The Defense Department's announcement on February 6 that the Sentinel program would be held up until it had been reviewed—an announcement celebrated by Chicago anti-ABM protesters as a Pentagon retreat brought about partly by their efforts—presumably threw such proposed Sentinel hosts as Great Falls, Montana, and

Grand Forks, North Dakota, into civic gloom. "They love us in Albany, Georgia," the Army colonel in charge of Sentinel "site activation" told me.

The colonel has had less than romantic experiences with citizens in Seattle, Boston, Detroit, Los Angeles, and, particularly, Chicago. In Glenview, one of five suburbs that were under consideration for the Chicago site, the village board passed a resolution against having a site anywhere near Chicago and sent the resolution to eighty other towns and villages in the area, suggesting that they pass it as well. After the Army announced that it had decided on an abandoned Nike base in Lake County, four miles south of Libertyville and about thirty miles north of the Loop, some people from a group called Northern Illinois Citizens Against ABM obtained a court order temporarily blocking any construction. At public meetings, the Army has shown Lake County citizens color slides of the computer-operated nuclear-defense system designed to protect them and their loved ones from what are commonly referred to as "primitive Chinese missiles" (conjuring up visions of thousands of Chinese peasants laboriously carting the mud of the Yangtze to crude molds, creating out of the baked earth something that roughly resembles an intercontinental ballistic missile, straining together to pull it back on some enormous catapult, and launching it seven thousand miles over the Pole in an attempt to obliterate Chicago). But the same meetings have almost always included a scientist from the Argonne National Laboratory, a center for nonmilitary nuclear research just west of Chicago; explaining that he is speaking not as an official representative of the laboratory but as a private citizen who happens to be a nuclear physicist, he reminds everyone that an unauthorized explosion is possible, even though extremely unlikely, and that such an explosion would destroy from a hundred and fifty thousand to two million citizens, "depending on which way the wind is blowing."

A citizen who looks into the abstract arguments about the wisdom of a defensive-missile system is likely to find them confusing enough to encourage his retreat to the sports pages. Sentinel is, among other things, an anti-ballistic-missile shield that everyone agrees could not stop a concentrated missile attack, a strictly defensive system that its critics consider more belligerent than our current policy of keeping enough offensive missiles to make any attack suicidal, a five- or ten-billion-dollar "thin" shield against the Chinese (who have no missiles) which many people believe will grow into a fifty- or hundred-billion-dollar "thick" shield against the Russians (who have too many to be affected by a thick shield), a boondoggle according to Dwight Eisenhower, a sensible compromise according to Robert McNamara, a "pile of junk" according to the prevailing view among scientists, and a functioning national program by act of Congress. Although the protest movement in Chicago has had the effect of providing a constituency for anti-ABM senators who may be interested in the abstract arguments about the wisdom of defensive-missile systems, it has made its appeal to people interested mainly in not being blown up. The diagram most often used by ABM opponents for posters and leaflets demonstrates the consequences of a nuclear explosion near Libertyville by superimposing a series of concentric circles on a map of the Chicago suburbs—showing which towns would be in the Blast Area, which in the Fire Area, which in the Body Burn Area, and which would be far enough away to permit some hope that the wind would not carry too much fallout in their direction. There has been no attempt to compose a battle cry about how Sentinel could hinder efforts to control nuclear arms; the poster announcing the first meeting in the suburbs north of Chicago to protest the selection of Libertyville was headlined "A Bomb in Your Backyard?"

A way to misunderstand the problems of local protest in the United States is to assume that if Karl Marx were reincarnated in, say, Muncie, Indiana, as a decently dressed jobholder with revolutionary ideas he would be barred from speaking at the luncheons of the local Lions Club and Rotary Club and Kiwanis Club. Service-club program chairmen fear the absence of a speaker more than they fear the revolution. Chances are he would be invited to speak, he would call for the workers of the world to throw off their chains, he would be asked three or four courteous questions from the floor (none of them dealing precisely with workers' throwing off their chains), and then the chairman would glance at his watch, remind the membership of the rule about breaking up at one-fifteen sharp, and say, "Karl, it was real nice of you to come, and I'm sure you've given us all a lot to think about." Although the Argonne nuclear physicists who began the anti-ABM protest in Chicago last fall have, strictly speaking, been criticizing one of the government's attempts to defend its people from the Communist threat, the emphasis on safety has avoided identification with appeasement, and they have remained well within the political tolerance of local service clubs. In the evenings, the scientists have often appeared with Army spokesmen at public meetings held in high-school auditoriums—the soldiers and the scientists traveling around Lake County like old prizefighters staging exhibitions, or like William F. Buckley, Jr., and Arthur Schlesinger, Jr., touring the Ivy League debating circuit.

The Army team ordinarily consists of two full colonels (one of whom introduces the other), a lieutenant colonel working the slide projector, and a civilian public relations man with a pipe, a Sentinel tie clasp, and an elaborate tape recorder. One of the colonels, using a retractable pointer to gesture at the slides, carefully goes through the components of the Sentinel system—the long-range Spartan, the shorter-range Sprint, to catch those missiles that manage to elude the Spartan, the two types of radar—and assures everyone that chances of an accident are "essentially nil." Then the Argonne scientist explains what an accident could mean, and argues that if the Army is planning only the thin area-defense system approved by Congress there is no reason to build Spartan sites within a hundred miles of heavily populated areas. One evening, somebody asked one of the colonels why a missile designed to intercept the enemy hundreds of miles away had to be so close to the city. The colonel mentioned something about an increasing Chinese threat and the parameters that had been calculated, and finally said, "It just does." The Army spokesmen have been accused of using security restrictions to avoid answering legitimate questions—or to hide the fact that their answers might not be particularly persuasive. The colonels usually manage to give the impression that they could demolish the opposition's argument if only they were the type of men who were willing to break their sworn oath of secrecy instead of exerting the awesome will power necessary to restrain themselves. Sometimes when a citizen asks a question the colonel will start to form the words, pause, and then say, "I'm sorry, I just can't

tell you that." Then the physicist, announcing first that he is privy
to no confidential information, will answer the question from what
he has read in the newspapers.

When a garbage dump in a suburb west of Chicago was being
considered for the Spartan site, the Argonne scientists found themselves allied with residents who were concerned that a military
takeover of the dump would mean increased garbage-hauling
charges. But, for the most part, the leaders of the protest against
the Libertyville site—including the physicists themselves—oppose
the entire ABM system and see the argument about where the site
should be mainly as a way to dramatize the issue of whether Sentinel should exist at all. One of them pointed out the sources of
protest to me on a map of the Chicago area one day, like a guerrilla
leader with a degree in sociology pointing out places where his men
might expect to find pockets of local support: Highland Park,
where there are said to be battalions of indefatigable liberal Jewish
housewives who can be counted on to organize letter-writing campaigns to Congress from lists of Women for Peace members and to
organize people all over the area into local anti-ABM lobbies; Lake
Forest College, where the president of Northern Illinois Citizens
Against ABM teaches; a Quaker meetinghouse not far from Lake
Forest. The centers of protest are not in the circle designated
"Blast Area." In Evanston, a suburb so far from the proposed site
that it has nothing more than deadly fallout to fear, I attended a
meeting at which almost a thousand people donated a dollar apiece
to hear Senator Philip Hart, of Michigan, and Jerome Wiesner, the
former science adviser to President Kennedy, attack the ABM. The
meeting was sponsored by the Thirteenth Congressional District
Politics for Peace, with the cooperation of groups like Skokie
Valley SANE and the Niles North High School Students for Peace,
Human Rights, and Democracy. A table in the hall held literature
on the ABM, Vietnam, and China, along with McCarthy shopping
bags to carry it all away in. "We stopped nuclear testing, we stopped fallout shelters, we are in the process of stopping the war in
Vietnam," a speaker from the North Shore Committee of Clergy
and Laymen Concerned about Vietnam said. "And we will stop the
ABM."

A few days before the Pentagon announced that it was suspending Sentinel construction, I visited Libertyville and Mundelein— Mundelein being the town that would, according to the calculations, disappear along with Libertyville in case of a nuclear accident at the proposed site. At a public meeting in the Mundelein High School auditorium, I found myself in the presence of precisely fifty-two concerned citizens. The Libertyville-Mundelein ministerial association has issued a statement against the ABM system, but that is about the extent of protest in the two towns closest to the site. Libertyville and Mundelein are farther from Chicago than towns like Glenview and Highland Park—in an area where subdivisions are still separated by cornfields and by a few well-manicured horse farms. Mundelein, which had less than three thousand people after the war, grew to sixteen thousand so quickly that there was apparently no time to build a center of town. A lot of the postwar arrivals live in subdivisions with names like Clearbrook Park ("A new experience in friendly suburban living") and Hawthorne Hills ("Luxury homes—$19,900") and Loch Lomond (which got its name from the fact that the developer had the foresight to precede construction with the installation of a man-made loch). Some of the people who moved to Mundelein from Chicago to acquire a yard or to get away from the Negroes now commute only as far as nearby industrial parks, and a number of people have moved in specifically because of expanding local industry. Libertyville looks down a bit on Mundelein—Libertyville houses tend to be somewhat more expensive, it has fewer renters and more middle-rank executives, and it has been established long enough to have a conventional downtown—but the residents of both of them are, in general, not as rich or as sophisticated as the people who live in the bedroom communities closer to Chicago.

A Women for Peace mailing list would be hard to find in the Libertyville-Mundelein area. Some of the stores on Libertyville's main street have stickers, furnished by the local V.F.W., that say, "America—Love It or Leave It." In Mundelein, a sign on the flagpole in front of the village hall says, "By order of the Village Council, Old Glory will fly perpetually from this mast until the hostilities in Vietnam are ended. In tribute to the gallant fighting Americans who daily are giving so much for so many." There have been anti-ABM protests in politically conservative areas around Chicago—in fact, some businessmen are opposed not only to having a local site but to spending billions of dollars of tax money for another weapons system that sounds as if it could become obsolete before it is operational—but the residents of Libertyville and Mundelein seem to have not only conservative politics but a conservative approach to political action. "This just isn't an activist sort of town," one of the Libertyville ministers told me. I had lunch with the Libertyville Rotarians, and the men I talked with agreed that most residents of the town would just as soon have the missile site somewhere else. But even though it was widely believed around Chicago that such towns as Westchester and Glenview were passed up by the Army partly because of local protest, people in Libertyville tended to think that not much can be done about a government decision once it is made.

"A payroll like that can't hurt any town," I was told by Wilbur Livingston, the sales manager for a Chicago hardware company and a Mundelein village trustee. "Most of the opposition is from the peace-at-any-price people in upper-income places like Glencoe and Winnetka. My particular feeling is that the government didn't just come here on a Saturday and say it was going to build on a Sunday. There had to be a lot of thinking in it, a lot of thinking."

For some people in Libertyville and Mundelein, the easiest way to deal with the confusion brought on by the Bomb is to assume that the powers-that-be must be making the proper decisions. "The almost miraculous technology of our world today has far surpassed our meager ability to comprehend," Mayor Charles Brown, of Libertyville, said when the village council gave its mild approval for the missile site. "Under these circumstances, it would certainly seem more prudent to place our confidence and our security in the hands of those whose lives are dedicated to the profession of defending and protecting our lives, our loved ones, and our properties than to try to accumulate sufficient knowledge to make an independent decision."

Wilbur Livingston showed me around Mundelein with a civic pride that reminded me of some of my guides in Atlanta. He pointed out the new schools and the new factories and the block where some old houses were going to be torn down for a new shopping district. Then we drove out to the proposed Sentinel site. Before it was an abandoned Nike base it had been an abandoned Navy air-training field. The paint is flaking off the Nike-base buildings, and grass is growing through the runway of the Navy airfield. There are a lot of broken windows and a couple of abandoned cars; the local teen-agers use the site as a place to drink beer and stage drag races. The area around the site is mostly farmland, although across the road a huge marquee identifies a place called the Tally Ho Country Club, and not far down the road from the Tally Ho there is a small residential district that looks like the result of a developer's somehow building a lot of houses in an isolated cornfield by mistake. "I don't know why they call this the Libertyville site," Livingston said, in a tone of mild irritation, as we drove out through the broken gate. "Libertyville is at least four miles from here, and right now we're only an eighth of a mile from the Mundelein village line."

# The Folks at Home

A lot of Midwesterners who live in the East are careful to preserve their Midwestern identity, the great crime for a Midwesterner being not to leave the Midwest but to leave the Midwest and forget where he came from. When I read recently in one of those Daily Almanac columns Midwestern newspapers often run that exactly ten years ago the governor of Missouri went to New York to talk with sixty former Missourians in "key industrial positions" about bringing more industry into the state, the scene in New York appeared before my eyes—the former Missourians in key industrial positions acting vaguely embarrassed at being comfortable in some plush Eastern boardroom, kicking at some imaginary dust on the carpet now and then, tugging at whatever was left of their forelocks, and asking the governor what the folks back in Joplin and Moberly had in mind in the way of industrial tax incentives. Thomas F. Eagleton, the junior senator from Missouri, doesn't face an election until 1974, but last year he went back to Missouri forty-one times to see the folks. I made it back twice myself last year, and I'm not running for anything.

My Midwestern credentials come from having been born and raised in Kansas City, Missouri, a city that is known as the Heart of America. It was also known as the Gateway to the West until St.

Louis, by spending forty-nine million dollars on a Gateway Arch
and an undisclosed amount on press agents, wrested that title
away, leaving my home town to be described in a Missouri tourist
booklet as, of all things, the City of Fountains. (Justice came to St.
Louis when, in celebration of a Spanish heritage that had previously been well disguised, it imported both the Spanish Pavilion
from the New York World's Fair and a replica of the Santa María.
The Spanish Pavilion operation went broke at about the speed of a
New York World's Fair, and the Santa María sank to the bottom
of the Mississippi, not far from the Gateway Arch.) I suppose if I
were asked to name my United States senator by one of those poll-
sters who go around periodically to demonstrate that the American
public has never heard of the Secretary of State, I would say
Thomas F. Eagleton, despite the legal technicality of my New York
registration. The alternative would be Stuart Symington, and although he has lived in St. Louis much longer than I lived in Kansas
City, he didn't grow up there, and I have always thought of him as
an Easterner. (One thing I learned in high school in Kansas City is
that Midwesternism cannot be created or destroyed, only changed
in form.) During the past several congressional primaries in the
Nineteenth District of New York, I have been berated by friends
for not taking more interest in which Reform Democrat should
have the right to be defeated by a congressman named Leonard
Farbstein, and I have tried, in vain, to explain to them that I am
represented in Congress by Richard Bolling, of the Fifth District of
Missouri. Even so, I took in all the recent publicity about Middle
Americans with a certain amount of detachment until last month,
when I read a Toronto newspaper's series on the subject dateline
Kansas City, Missouri, and realized that the Middle American everyone has been talking about is, in a manner of speaking, me.

That doesn't mean I know much about my part of the Midwest.
A characteristic of displaced Midwesterners is that their vision of
their home towns remains pretty much the same as it was when
they left. Despite an abundance of evidence every day, I still find it
hard to believe that some aspects of American life considered perfectly ordinary on the coasts could possibly exist in Kansas City—
psychiatrists, homosexuals, radical politics, marijuana except in the
suitcases of transient jazz musicians. When I decided to take a trip

to Missouri with Senator Eagleton to see what the folks at home
were thinking, I had no more idea of what to expect than would the
members of the Eastern Communications Conspiracy, many of
whom are, of course, from the Midwest themselves. In the week
before we started around the state, my home town—the Heart of
America—had eight bombings in three days.

When I worked as a reporter in Atlanta, the bankers I called to ask
about, say, the state of the prime interest rate or the workings of
the Federal Reserve System would often begin by saying something
like "Shoot, it ain't nothin' very complicated"—the double negative being, in the minds of Atlanta bankers, the great leveler. Eagleton manages to get along easily with small-town folks without
affecting the double negative, despite the fact that he is a city boy
from St. Louis and went to the St. Louis Country Day School and
Amherst and the Harvard Law School. (Which turns out to be the
type of background that is currently standard for senators from
Missouri. Symington went to Yale and married the daughter of a
senator from New York. John Danforth, the young man who has
just filed as Symington's Republican opponent in November, went
to the St. Louis Country Day School and Princeton and belongs to
a family that has established a foundation with assets of a hundred
and forty-five million dollars. Upon investigation, I found, to my
embarrassment, that my home-town congressman, Richard Bolling, attended Exeter—raising the possibility that Leonard Farbstein and all his sophisticated opponents are, as congressmen go,
just folks after all.)
    In small Missouri towns, Eagleton has the advantage of a friend-
liness and informality that make it seem natural for people who
have just met him to call him by his first name (the Midwestern
way to address any other human being) even if he *is* a senator. He
also has to his advantage a Midwestern, non-senatorial way of not
taking himself completely seriously—so that he can tell a group of
college students that he is always available to deliver his "superbly
emotional commencement address," or can arrive at a library-
groundbreaking ceremony held outdoors in a driving rain and announce to the committee that the only library-groundbreaking
speech he knows takes forty minutes.

Eagleton started his swing around the state by speaking at two St. Louis high-school programs on the environment. Lindbergh, a public high school in the southern St. Louis County suburbs, looked like part of the Midwest I remember. It's a modern, clean-looking school of the kind whose particular rung on the middle-class ladder I usually try to judge by the number of Mustangs in the parking lot. The dense cloud of smoke in the boys' room had the innocent and nostalgic aroma of Lucky Strikes. The students, all of them white, were neatly dressed and carefully combed, with only enough longhairs among them to make up a small rock group or two. They greeted Eagleton enthusiastically, and asked polite questions about how anti-pollution laws could be made stronger and whether or not Americans would be willing to decrease their standard of living in order to improve the environment.

A couple of hours later, Eagleton spoke at John Burroughs, a private day school similar to St. Louis Country Day, at the invitation of a student named Sidney Symington, the senior senator's grandson. At Burroughs, there were several black students, wearing Afro haircuts and dashikis. A lot of the white students had long hair, a lot of the girls were in blue jeans or bell-bottomed slacks, and some of them weren't wearing any shoes. Eagleton is generally popular among students—he is only forty and he doesn't sound patronizing and he works in the Senate against defense spending he considers excessive or judicial nominations he considers mediocre —but the questions at Burroughs were much more pointed than the ones at Lindbergh. The students asked Eagleton whether concern about environment was a cop-out from more controversial problems like race and the war. They asked why people wouldn't be better off working to change the entire system than just arguing about its symptoms. The small-town folks in Missouri can take comfort in the fact that, comes the revolution, it will just be a matter of one gang of private-school boys trying to overthrow another gang of private-school boys.

Eagleton asked for questions just about everywhere he went in the state—at a Kiwanis luncheon in Jefferson City, at a new college in St. Joseph, at a covered-dish supper sponsored by Democrats in Mexico, Missouri—but the folks didn't seem to have any one particular subject on their minds. After we left St. Louis, I didn't hear any questioner who sounded angry or excited. At a breakfast sponsored by the rural electric co-op of Grundy County, in the northwest section of the state—an area that is Republican more or less the way a farm county in Iowa is Republican—it didn't take long for the breakfast guests to run out of questions. Although Eagleton's trip took place at a time when the press was beginning to talk about the possibility of American military involvement in Cambodia and Laos, there were several question periods at which no one asked the Senator anything about the war. In Jefferson City, which is known as a particularly conservative town, Eagleton's remarks about the ramifications of the coup deposing Sihanouk and about his own opposition to sending American troops into Cambodia drew only one or two questions about the war from the Kiwanians. (During that discussion, I couldn't help wondering whether the British, when they were the ones with the empire, expected merchants in middle-sized Yorkshire cities to ask Members of Parliament probing questions about the various political factions important to the stability of Gujarat.) In some places, a subject like crime or inflation wasn't even brought up. During the entire trip, nobody asked about the bombings that have occurred in cities as close as the Heart of America; nobody asked about campus unrest. In three or four places, someone asked about the country's being more divided or troubled than in the past, but in the atmosphere of the occasion the question sounded as if it might be about some other country.

Midwesterners are, of course, known for becoming less excited than people on the coasts about issues, unless the issue affects them directly. (In Mexico, which is part of an area in central Missouri that was settled by people from the upper South and is still known as Little Dixie, Eagleton finished third and last, in the 1968 Democratic senatorial primary—a showing his local backers blame partly on his support of strong gun-control legislation.) In Missouri, politics still means party politics, and which party it is still depends a lot on who settled in what section of the state in the early nineteenth century. The southwestern counties of Missouri vote Republican because they were settled by Tennessee hill people who were loyal to the Union. As a Democrat, Eagleton was supported not only by working-class wards in St. Louis but by conservative Southern Democrats in the Boot Heel—the counties in the southeast corner of Missouri, which became part of the antebellum South rather suddenly, in 1910, when swamps along the Mississippi River were drained to create rich cotton plantations. In the general election, he also carried Mexico, traditionally a Democratic town, against a conservative Republican opponent whose views on government were presumably much closer to those of the voters—Little Dixie being an area so conservative that, in the opinion of one local citizen, some people are philosophically opposed to parking meters.

Eagleton thought that one explanation for the mild and unfocused nature of the questioning was that people in Missouri who are bothered about one thing or another may still not want to start an argument about it at a covered-dish supper. It also occurred to me during the trip that Midwesterners, particularly compared to Easterners, have a way of underestimating, rather than overestimating, how well they understand national issues—as if understanding exactly what the politicians in Washington are talking about would be putting on airs. It's a characteristic that, along with their routine support of their country in foreign affairs, made them appear to be in favor of the war in Vietnam until their boys started getting killed in great numbers and it began to become obvious that the deaths would not result in a military victory. It is also a characteristic that made them happy to hand the complicated problem of the Vietnam war back to the people in Washington as soon as President Nixon assured them he would withdraw troops until it was all over. By the time President Nixon went on television to announce that American troops had moved into Cambodia, Eagleton was back in Washington, and he got two hundred letters about the decision from the folks at home—running twenty to one against it. But I still can't imagine Missouri taking on the kind of crisis atmosphere that seemed to develop in the East after the President's speech. It's easier to imagine one of the citizens of Grundy County hearing about the latest developments in Southeast Asia from the Eastern Communications Conspiracy on television, shaking his head, and saying that the situation over there is just about too complicated for the average person to understand.

On Eagleton's last day in Missouri, he went to Drexel, a town of about seven hundred and fifty people, to dedicate a park. Drexel is only an hour or so south of Kansas City, and Clyde Thomas, the editor of the Drexel *Star,* came up to Kansas City to escort the Senator's party to the ceremonies, having prevailed upon the local funeral director to provide transportation with his nine-passenger limousine. Drexel prides itself on being a progressive town—a town that has increased its population at a time when a lot of small farm towns are dying. Just before we came to the city limits, Thomas pointed to a field on one side of the road that was scheduled to be an industrial park someday and a field on the other side that he said would make a perfect airport.

The park being dedicated had been named in honor of H. T. Smith, known locally as Shorty, a farm-implement dealer who, during his tenure as mayor, pushed through such improvements as modern water and sewer systems. But the ceremonies seemed to be part of the Midwest that existed before towns began worrying about modern water and sewer systems and bond issues and industrial parks. The Drexel High School band performed. Boy Scouts directed traffic. The stage was lined with red-white-and-blue bunting. H. T. Smith and his entire family sat on the stage, the women of the family wearing orchid corsages. The local American Legion chapter sold refreshments in a pavilion built by the local Lions Club.

It occurred to me that the bombings in my home town might have at least stirred a bit of outrage in Drexel, a peaceful community only an hour from the targets.

"Got any crime in the streets here?" I asked Thomas as the nine-passenger limousine rolled past comfortable-looking frame houses that were displaying the American flag.

"Hell," Thomas said, "we don't hardly have any tire marks in the streets."

I asked Thomas what he thought of the bombings in Kansas City.

"Looks like it's pretty good for us," he said, with a smile. "Folks get scared up there, a lot of them are going to move down to Drexel."

# Two Army Stories

For Armed Forces Day this year, Fort Dix had plans that included an authentic hand-to-hand combat demonstration on the baseball field by members of the Green Berets, a scout-dog demonstration, and free jeep rides for the kids. Anti-war demonstrators had plans that included marching past the new signs that say "Unauthorized Demonstrations Prohibited" into Fort Dix. By the morning of Armed Forces Day, the Army had canceled its own plans and was putting final touches on its preparations for thwarting the plans of the unauthorized demonstrators. At the public information office, a captain was testing a field-telephone system by repeating, "Round Robin, this is Bulky Elbows. Round Robin, this is Bulky Elbows." At the base's main entrance, two spools of concertina barbed wire had been placed where they could be pulled quickly across the highway leading into the base. By noon, a few thousand demonstrators had gathered on the shoulders of the highway, just across a road that runs in front of the base. Virtually all of them were young. A lot of them wore motorcycle helmets. A lot of them wore neckerchiefs that could be pulled up around their faces in case of tear gas. Some of them wore hospital masks made of gauze, and some of them wore conventional gas masks. They displayed placards and buttons and headbands and droopy mustaches and blue jeans and, in some cases, war paint. At about twelve-thirty, the concertina wire was pulled across the highway, and, inside the base, soldiers in battle dress dismounted from two trucks that had been brought to within a few hundred feet of the entrance. A reconnaissance helicopter circled overhead.

*As part of the Armed Forces Day celebration in 1959, twenty other soldiers and I landed in a helicopter on Governors Island, in New York Harbor, swept down the airfield, and captured an incinerator from about twelve I.B.M. clerks. We were all in full battle dress. It was the only action I saw in the Army. I was stationed on Governors Island, then the headquarters for the First United States Army, which includes Fort Dix, and ordinarily I worked in an office. The way we took the incinerator used to be my only war story— the truth and the embellishments fused beyond distinction, the way they are in most war stories. But when I read about this year's Armed Forces Day, I realized that for the last few years I haven't heard any of those peacetime war stories, even my own. Yet we did take that incinerator from those I.B.M. clerks.*

Shortly after the concertina wire was pulled into place, the crowd began to move toward the entrance, led by banners representing Youth Against War and Fascism and the American Servicemen's Union. The demonstrators stopped at the wire and began chanting, "Big Firms Get Rich—G.I.s Die." Then a couple of the demonstrators moved the concertina wire off the highway, and the crowd began to advance slowly into the base. Soldiers wearing gas masks and carrying rifles with fixed bayonets formed a line across the highway and moved toward the entrance in a rhythmic two-step, their rifles at "on-guard" position. The crowd retreated, and the soldiers stood in a line in front of them at the entrance. The bayonets were a few inches from the demonstrators' faces. A team of soldiers with tanks of gas stood behind the line. Some of the demonstrators impaled their leaflets on the bayonets. A lot of them began to talk to the soldiers, none of whom talked back. They argued that the soldiers' real enemies were the brass and the lifers— the officers and the career Army men—who could order G.I.s to do anything, including killing women and children in Vietnam. "The enemy's behind you!" the demonstrators shouted. "Turn your guns around!"

*The officer in charge of the assault on the incinerator—a young infantry lieutenant I'll call Steven Fox—was what we referred to at that time as "R.A. All the Way," meaning he was a career Army officer and took his career seriously. He always stood rigidly straight, and he was suspected of shaving only at night so he would look tough all the next day. We were always careful to give brisk, military salutes to Lieutenant Fox, although we occasionally saluted him left-handed. The left-handed salute was possible if you were walking in a group and everyone else saluted right-handed. Lieutenant Fox always returned the salutes properly, but after a step or two he would slow his pace momentarily and a puzzled look would come over his face as he tried to reconstruct the picture of that thicket of upraised arms. At the first meeting attended by those in our company chosen for the assault group, he spoke to us as if we were the only people there, although the room also held about a dozen members of the company that was stationed on the island to run a battery of I.B.M. computers. The I.B.M. clerks were to be the defenders of the incinerator, but since the enemy in an Army maneuver is always called the Aggressor, even if he is defending, they wore cardboard "A"s pinned to their fatigue caps.*

State troopers formed a line of defense across the road that runs in front of the base—civilian property, but a route that could be used to outflank the military defenders. The state troopers carried long batons. At one end of the line, two troopers warmed the engine of a machine that is capable of emitting great billows of gas. The main part of the crowd turned from the soldiers to face the state troopers. "If you know what the struggle's about, move up front," a girl said over a loudspeaker. But the front ranks of the demonstrators remained thin as the crowd slowly advanced toward the police line. A state police lieutenant with a bullhorn told them to disperse. They continued to advance. A couple of bottles shattered on the highway near the line of police. War whoops came from the woods at the side of the road, where some of the demonstrators were trying to move around the troopers. Finally, the troopers charged, clearing the road mainly with the use of the gas machine. The people in the woods were chased out by troopers swinging batons. One demonstrator racing through the woods seemed to slow down for a moment, and the state trooper chasing him brought a baton crashing down on his head. The demonstrator ran a couple of feet farther, and then staggered and fell to his knees. The trooper hit him a couple of more times and ran off. The demonstrator crawled a few feet, and then someone came and helped him to a first-aid station.

*At the first meeting, the Lieutenant explained that one of our men would be wounded, just after he threw a smoke bomb in the direction of the incinerator. He would be evacuated by a second helicopter. The rest of the men would continue crawling down the grassy airfield, supported by a machine gun firing blanks, that would be set up near the attack helicopter and would be replanted at the end of the assigned crawling distance to cover the final standup charge. I was arbitrarily named machine gunner, a selection I began to appreciate that day at rehearsal when most of the moving seemed to be done by the riflemen. After we had all pretended that we had descended from a helicopter, the riflemen had to move slowly toward the incinerator, half of the line crawling while the other half covered them with rifle fire. Accompanied by my assistant machine gunner—a huge, muscular, uncannily stupid private I'll call Hiram Parker—I lay comfortably on the grass while Lieutenant Fox walked up and down the line of riflemen instructing them on how to crawl properly. We were all told by Lieutenant Fox to simulate noise, since the blanks would be saved for the actual attack. The riflemen simulated noise by pulling the bolts of their rifles back and forth, but we didn't have a noise-making bolt on our machine gun, so Lieutenant Fox told us to simulate noise verbally. We said "Rat-y-tat-y-tat-tat-tat."*

After the first advance had been broken up by the state police, the speeches that were to have preceded the march began, and a Black Panther, one of perhaps a dozen black people in the crowd, told the demonstrators that it was foolish for people armed with sticks and stones to attack an Army base. (The Army press officer had made it clear that live ammunition had been issued only to a select group of marksmen, who were allowed to shoot only at a specific human being at the specific order of the commanding general.) Some of the demonstrators had picked up heavy sticks and tested them for balance, but nobody organized a second assault toward the police, who had re-formed a line across the road. A line of demonstrators stood facing the soldiers at the entrance, and another line moved over to face soldiers who had come to protect a grassy hill that led from a short fence on Fort Dix property to the road guarded by state troopers. But a lot of demonstrators found a space on the grassy areas around the intersection and sat down. Despite the gas masks and helmets, part of the demonstration took on the picnic atmosphere that no demonstration in the spring can quite escape, unless someone is actually being shot.

*Lying on the grass of the airfield, saying "Rat-y-tat-y-tat-tat-tat," I began to take great pleasure in the lulling sound of my own voice. The spring sun warmed the grass and glistened on the harbor, which was visible on the other side of the incinerator. Two or three times during the afternoon, an ocean liner floated past, looking almost close enough to touch. Occasionally, I would turn my eyes from the incinerator and watch construction workers slowly swing beams into place on the Chase Manhattan Bank building being built near Wall Street. Several times, I discovered myself falling asleep, only to be brought back by the sound of Lieutenant Fox's shouts to some errant crawler. Parker was equally mesmerized.*

*"Let's hear some noise from that machine gun!" Lieutenant Fox shouted from across the field.*

*We had both allowed our simulated noise to drop to a murmur, and we said loudly, "Rat-y-tat-y-tat-tat-tat."*

*"I can't hear you!" the Lieutenant shouted. "These men need machine-gun support."*

*"RAT-Y-TAT-Y-TAT-TAT-TAT!" Parker and I screamed.*

"Do you want your son to die when he's eighteen?" one of the demonstrators screamed at the state police. "Is that what you want?" Some of the demonstrators shouted "Pig!" at the Army officers or at the United States marshals who stood in civilian clothes behind the soldiers, but only occasionally was someone rude to the soldiers themselves. The soldiers stood silent, hard to tell apart in their gas masks and helmets and flak jackets. Not getting any argument from the soldiers, the demonstrators occasionally argued among themselves. "We *must* organize the working class!" a collegiately dressed young man with short hair shouted at a bearded man who had been making fun of an M.P. "The working class displayed its interest last week on Wall Street by beating up demonstrators," the bearded man said. When a soldier was relieved on the line, he would immediately peel off his gas mask and go over to sit on the grass and have a cigarette. A couple of soldiers were interviewed by a radio-news reporter. No, they said, they didn't mind the taunts, but the gas masks were uncomfortable and it was hard to hold a rifle in that position for that long.

*Parker had to carry the machine gun, and all I had to carry was the tripod, but on the second day of rehearsals I learned that the tripod was almost too much for me. The difficulty was that the riflemen covered perhaps three hundred yards in fifteen minutes of alternate crawling and resting but, in order to provide firepower for the final charge, Parker and I were expected to cover the distance in an all-out dash. As we started the run, I began to worry that I would arrive behind Parker. About halfway through the run, I quit worrying about that and began to worry about whether I would arrive at all. My breath was coming in painful gasps, and the lumbering figure of Parker became blurred as the distance between us increased. When I finally reached our assigned position and fell to the ground with the tripod, Parker had been standing there for some time, holding a machine gun with no place to put it.*

*The next day, while the Lieutenant was watching us say "Rat-y-tat-y-tat-tat-tat" from our first position, I brought up the subject of the run. "I was thinking, sir," I said. "Maybe it might be more effective if Private Parker and I take a few short hops down the field ourselves, so as to stay closer to the attack line and provide better firepower."*

*"You'd be cut down before you got six steps, soldier," Lieutenant Fox said.*

*"I'd keep very low, sir,"* I replied. *"I'd keep very, very low, and also zigzag."*

*"You'd be an open target,"* he said.

I straightened up and said, *"Private Parker and I are not afraid, sir."*

*"You're my responsibility, soldier,"* Lieutenant Fox said. *"I can't let you do it."*

When the Lieutenant had left, I suggested to Parker the possibility that he might run a little more slowly so I could keep up. *"Are you kidding?"* he said. *"Those bastards might cut me down."*

"Those pig lieutenants don't care about you," the demonstrators kept saying to the soldiers. "They don't care if you go to Vietnam and get mowed down. You don't see them standing out here all day wearing gas masks." None of the officers, in fact, were wearing gas masks, but the soldiers didn't turn around to see. After a couple of hours, the demonstrators brought a loudspeaker up to the line, and someone spoke to the soldiers over it about joining the American Servicemen's Union. When the loudspeaker was withdrawn, the conversation along the line eventually gave way to one or two demonstrators at a time holding the floor to make speeches to the soldiers or to make fun of the marshals and officers standing behind them. A couple of the marshals stood just behind the soldiers, staring at the demonstrators with smirks frozen on their faces. "Look at them like they stink," one of the marshals said to the other. On a hill inside the base, what looked like several families had gathered to watch the proceedings. "Don't you know that G.M. is making five hundred million a year off this war?" the speaker said. "Man, can't you relate to that?" The soldiers remained silent.

*We boarded our attack helicopter on Staten Island and then sat silently staring at each other, our helmets pulled down low over our eyes and our weapons clutched in our hands. As we hit the airfield and rushed out, screaming our assigned yells, I saw that we were a good fifteen yards farther downfield than we had been in rehearsal. I figured I could make the run with that head start, but making it wouldn't satisfy Lieutenant Fox if Parker had to stand around with the machine gun waiting for me. As Parker was clicking the machine gun into place at our first position, I glanced up and discovered that we were only about ten feet from the crowd of spectators that extended down the side of the airfield. I fired my first burst, and I was delighted at the improvement real blanks made over "Rat-y-tat-y-tat-tat-tat." Some Boy Scouts in the crowd near us shouted encouragement. I gave the enemy six or eight more bursts. I could see some of the riflemen starting their crawl on schedule. I fired three more bursts, and suddenly screamed, "Take that, you Commie thug-punks! Take that one for the old Gipper!" Or words to that effect. The Boy Scouts cheered. Parker gave me a puzzled look.*

*"Shell Quemoy and Matsu, will you!" I shouted. "Frame Shoeless Joe Jackson, will you!" I fired again.*

*Then Parker stopped feeding the ammunition belt and started staring at me. "They're only the I.B.M. guys," he said.*

*I nodded thoughtfully—convinced. "You're right, Parker," I said. "So why should we hurry down the field?"*

*Parker ran at a half trot—I kept my hand in his belt just to remind him—and, with me at full speed, we managed to make it down the field at the same time. I don't think Lieutenant Fox noticed us anyway. The I.B.M. clerks fled before our firepower in disorganized retreat.*

At four o'clock, almost four hours after the lines had formed, the remaining demonstrators were about ready to leave the entrance of the base. "It had no organization," a girl holding one end of a "Free Bobby Seale" banner said to her companion. "Of course, I don't know what we could have done even with organization." The crowd at the entrance left, and only a few demonstrators remained facing the troops along the grass between the fence and the road. "You see, every time we come they have to put you out here in front of us," a demonstrator was explaining to a soldier. "And every time they put you out here, we get to talk to you. One of these days, you'll be out and you'll be on this side of the line." Then a major said over a bullhorn that the remaining demonstrators were going to be moved out. He sent in a fresh line of troops—about a hundred soldiers—and ordered them to put their rifles at "on-guard" position. "You must be out of your goddam mind!" one of the demonstrators shouted. "You're going to send them against all six of us?" The major, seeing that he had much more power than he needed, replaced the line of troops with a small group of M.P.s who were wearing khakis and no gas masks and were carrying only billy clubs. The demonstrators left. "Peace and freedom, guys!" one of them called over his shoulder. "Happy Armed Forces Day!"

# BUYING AND SELLING

# Buying and Selling Along Route 1

### I WAS A PIG AT GREENWOOD DAIRIES

An ice-cream cone at the Greenwood Dairies has half a pound of ice cream on it—making it so top-heavy that it is ordinarily presented to the customer upside down, resting on a piece of waxed paper. That's the single-dip cone. The double-dip cone has an even pound, or about a quart of ice cream—the same amount that Greenwood serves in a locally famous sundae called a Pig's Dinner. A Pig's Dinner has four scoops of ice cream resting on a bed of sliced bananas, covered with a choice of topping, and served in an eight-inch plastic trough. The customer also gets a yellow button that says "I Was a Pig at Greenwood Dairies." The buttons are a particularly popular item.

In the thirties, when Paul Sauerbry, a former 4-H champion from Oelwein, Iowa, came to Lower Bucks County, the area between Philadelphia and Trenton, it was almost as rural as Iowa—despite the impression Sauerbry had received at a Washington 4-H convention that "lots more was going on in the East than in Iowa, and where things are going on there must be money." Sauerbry bought Greenwood Dairies, a small, two-route milk business, and moved it to Route 1, then the main route up the East Coast and the only direct road between Philadelphia and New York. There was plenty of milk available from farmers right across the highway—at least until the early fifties, when all of that farmland became Levittown, Pennsylvania, a community of seventeen thousand houses. Even before Levittown, Sauerbry had steadily expanded his operation. He now has a fleet of green-and-white trucks that deliver ten to twelve thousand quarts of milk a day. The store that he began in the early forties to sell his own ice cream now looks more like a restaurant than a store and does a few hundred thousand dollars' worth of business a year in bulk ice cream, ice-cream cones, Pig's Dinners, light lunches, a small line of groceries, souvenirs, and stuffed animals.

Sauerbry still thinks of himself as a dairyman. The store has a modest sign, decorated with a sundae not much larger than the ones served inside. The store accounts for less than a third of Greenwood's annual sales—although, as the *Milk Plant Monthly* has pointed out in an admiring article on Sauerbry, it brings in not only money but prospective customers for milk delivery. Sauerbry and his son, who also works in the business, are proud that their ice cream is made of freshly condensed milk rather than dried milk, that the mint chocolate chip has the same kind of authentic chocolate found in a chocolate bar, and that the vanilla is made with real vanilla beans. But they realize that the size of the portions is what brings many people into the store.

Sauerbry is also aware that a lot of people can't finish the portions, causing a certain amount of waste. The trash bin in front of the dairy always contains a number of half-eaten half-pound ice-cream cones. Sauerbry has thought of cutting down portions rather than steadily raising prices; in fact, the Pig's Dinner used to have five scoops of ice cream rather than four. But he doesn't think his customers will stand for further reductions. The most common complaint at Greenwood is not that helpings are too big but that the customer did not receive his fair share. Sometimes people return a sundae complaining of niggardliness, and the Sauerbrys have to put the sundae on the scale to demonstrate that it does indeed weigh a pound. The Sauerbrys do not seem to be the kind of people who might spend a lot of time musing on why a dairy that makes its vanilla from real vanilla beans finds it necessary to sell it by serving more than most people can eat—and throwing in a pig button.

"When we started dipping cones, in them days there were quite a few dairy stores," Sauerbry says. "We all gave big portions." If the younger Sauerbry is asked why Greenwood Dairies customers are so fond of large portions, he just shrugs and says, "Everybody wants quantity."

WORKING OUT A DEAL

The merchandising method of Reedman's, the world's largest car dealer, seems to be based on the theory that a lot of Americans have bought so many new cars that they consider themselves experts at the art. Respecting the fact that a man of experience will have gone beyond loyalty to any one make of car, Reedman salesmen are equally helpful about selling him a new Chevrolet or a new Plymouth or a new almost anything else; Reedman's has fourteen new-car franchises. Reedman salesmen will reassure a customer that the small Plymouth station wagon and the small Dodge station wagon, both of which Reedman's handles, are virtually the same car—the slight difference in headlights and the different names being merely a way to make one car do for two different dealers. Good hard shoptalk is expected among experts. Included in the Reedman display of the Plymouth Duster and the American Motors' Hornet is the competing car not handled by Reedman's, the Ford Maverick—its roof decorated with a sign drawing attention to the relative puniness of its wheelbase, its trunk open to reveal a sign that says "The Exposed Gas Tank Is in the Trunk Floor." Since the customer will be sophisticated enough to know precisely what he wants in a car—whether, for example, he can do without air-conditioning but must have vinyl bucket seats—Reedman's has an inventory of some five thousand cars, and a computer that will instantly find out if a particular model is available and will then type out a precise description of it before the customer's eyes. An enormous selection being a great advantage in dealing with expert car purchasers, some people in the trade say that Reedman's sells so many cars because it has so many to sell—a merchandising adaptation of Mies van der Rohe's "Less is More" dictum that comes out "More is More."

The Reedman newspaper advertisement invites customers to a

hundred-and-fifty-acre, one-stop car center that has a ten-million-dollar selection of cars—and then, adding the note of exclusivity that is considered necessary in advertising even the world's largest, it says, "Private Sale Now Going On." The premises on which the private sale is held look like the average citizen's vision of the supply depot at Cam Ranh Bay. Behind a series of showrooms on Route 1, just down the road from the Greenwood Dairies, the five thousand cars are lined up on acres and acres of asphalt—the neat rows interrupted by occasional watchtowers and the entire area surrounded by a heavy, iron, electronically monitored fence. On a busy Saturday, attendants direct streams of traffic in and out of the customers' parking lot. Hostesses with the dress and manner of airline stewardesses circulate in the showrooms offering to call a salesman for anybody who feels the need of one. Muzak, which reaches the most remote line of hardtops, is interrupted every two or three bars by calls for salesmen.

The opportunity to perfect a veteran car buyer's style is so great at Reedman's—the opportunity to shrug off a computer's offer of a Dodge Coronet with fourteen extras, to exchange jargon about engines and wheelbases, to take a new model for a few spins around the Reedman test track and make some observations to the family about how she handles on the curves—that some people seem to make Saturday at Reedman's a kind of outing. A lot of them, of course, find themselves buying a car, with vinyl bucket seats and air-conditioning. The route back to the customers' parking lot leads through a small building where the customer is greeted by a man even more helpful than the hostesses. "How'd you make out, sir?" the man asks. "What kind of car were you looking at? What was your trade-in? Who was your salesman? Of course you want to think about it, but why wait?" There is no reason for an experienced car buyer to concern himself with the fact that his most recent experience was so recent that he has yet to pay for the car he has; the first sign on the Reedman lot begins, "If you still have payments on your present car, truck, etc., we will pay off the balance and work out a deal."

Although selling at Reedman's is based on working out a deal rather than on glamour or showmanship, a car dealer cannot afford to create an atmosphere of pure, unglamorous functionalism. If anyone is going to be totally practical, why should he spend his money on an overlarge, gas-eating, non-functional, instantly depreciating new car? Although the Chevrolet section of the Reedman showrooms is crowded with as many models as can be crammed in, the decor includes huge crystal chandeliers and wallpaper of raised-velvet fleur-de-lis patterns on ersatz gold leaf. On one wall of the showroom, a picture display of Reedman service facilities describes one of the three waiting rooms available for service customers as having "fifteen stereophonic speakers mounted in the acoustical ceiling," as well as "embossed vinyl covered walls, plus carpeting, velvet draperies, a crystal chandelier, and living-room type furniture." Any car buyer of experience recognizes that as a description of something that, with the addition of some heavy-duty whitewall tires, could provide great transportation until next year's models come out.

DON'T SIT DOWN

Only a few small, arrow-shaped signs lead customers a mile or so off Route 1, near Reedman's, to the farm outlet of Styer's Orchards. Styer's advertises in a local shopping paper, but Walter Styer believes that, basically, satisfied customers bring business and dissatisfied customers keep it away. "It's important never to have anybody griping on you," he says. Styer's will usually replace a jug of spoiled apple cider even if the customer himself let it spoil by leaving it unrefrigerated—as if it contained preservatives, like the processed cider that Styer cannot mention without a slight grimace. Walter Styer is a small, almost bald man in his seventies. His family came to Lower Bucks County in 1910 to start a tree-nursery business, which gradually changed into a fruit business. In the forties, people in the area used to come down the narrow lane to the Styers' farmhouse to buy apples, and eventually the Styers started using the barn as a store and the neighbors started coming in to help with the selling. After the building of Levittown and the opening of a United States Steel plant in Fairless Hills, the Styers finally opened a store out on the road. Styer says the business has now grown to the point of having an overhead of three hundred and fifty thousand dollars a year.

Styer believes in salesmanship. "I used to sell at the Farmer's Market in Trenton, and we almost took over that market," he has said. "It got so the other farmers didn't like us. For one thing, I never sat down. I was always ready to help the customer. Some of the farmers would turn over a box and sit down and just stare at people, but I would always get people talking—ask them what kind of apples they liked, or something like that. Once, I was selling strawberries at fifteen cents a box, and next to me a fellow was selling the identical strawberries at two boxes for a quarter. Pretty soon, I sold all my strawberries, and he hadn't sold any. And he asked me why. I looked at his strawberries and I said, 'First of all, look how you've got them arranged. The stems are sticking up. People don't eat stems. Rearrange them with the stems down. Then you ought to get paid for your time for doing that, so charge fifteen cents a box like I did.' Then I stayed to watch, and I told him, 'Don't sit down.' Pretty soon, he sold all his strawberries."

The Styers are not in the position of having to think up sales pitches to justify changes made in this year's model by somebody they don't even know. Almost everything sold at the farm outlet is from their own farm. A lot of the salesmanship is merely a matter of presenting well what they are confident is good merchandise. The store is immaculate. All of the apples are washed and displayed in neat rows of clean half-bushel baskets. There is always a bin of free apples near the door. The apple pies and pumpkin pies are baked in stainless-steel ovens before the customers' eyes. The walls are decorated with Indian corn. There are a few standard signs for Pennsylvania apples ("Nature's Toothbrush"), but most of the signs are done in crayon—giving them a nice, neat homemade look, as if they had been commissioned to the best drawer in the sixth grade.

Styer is proud of the store, although he laments the failure of most of the clerks to lead customers into conversation. "You *got* to be a salesman," he says. When Styer greeted an out-of-town visitor at the farmhouse recently, he had just returned from a business meeting (the family has other interests in Lower Bucks County, including some of the real estate on Route 1), and he looked like a banker who had been home only long enough to take his jacket off.

Before taking his visitor to see the store, he excused himself for a few minutes and returned wearing an old pair of corduroy pants and a dark cardigan sweater very much like one Paul Sauerbry wears around the dairy. "That's a farm outlet, and people don't want to see a business executive out there," he said. "You got to look the part."

MOSTLY SELL

The Two Guys Discount Department Store in the Levittown Country Club Shopping Center, across Route 1 from Reedman's, is small by the standards of Two Guys stores but large by the standards of, say, football fields. It is a hundred and five thousand square feet, and, like all Two Guys stores, it is what people in the Two Guys chain call "mostly sell"—that is, most of its space is space in which customers actually buy merchandise. In a Two Guys store, the stockrooms and the sales space are virtually identical; one step in the supply process is saved by having customers help themselves from merchandise that is brought in by Two Guys trucks from a central warehouse and stored right on the selling floor. The Two Guys store in Levittown has a kind of warehouse look—one huge room containing massive stacks of every type of merchandise, with the merchandise on the lower part of some stacks still in packing cartons. In the toy department, the customer sees not just one or two Talk 'n' Do Choo-Choos but twenty Talk 'n' Do Choo-Choos. In the hardware department, a dozen or so examples of each type of hammer extend from racks on the wall. The art department has three-dimensional "Last Supper"s fifteen deep. In Boutique Shoes, one shelf includes thirty-five identical pairs of black pumps.

Displaying merchandise in mass contributes to the efficiency of the Two Guys central-warehouse operation, and it also makes people buy more. Since the advent of the supermarket, retailers have known that seeing, say, twenty cartons of avocado-colored Tahiti tumblers in a mass creates an impulse to buy some avocado-colored Tahiti tumblers. A lot of shoppers who might pass up a display demonstrating the virtues of a hair dryer find a six-foot stack of hair dryers irresistible. Two Guys has even discovered that if all the red coats are hung together rather than scattered among the other coats on the rack, they sell faster. More is More.

## COME FLY WITH US

Jim Flannery's Constellation Lounge is a Constellation. It originally belonged to Cubana Airlines. Flannery bought it two years ago from an airline based in Delaware and had it placed over his restaurant, on Route 1, not far down the road from Two Guys. Motorists approaching from the south come around a curve just before Flannery's and find the Constellation suddenly in front of them—coming in low over the Esso station, as if some desperate T.W.A. pilot who had been on a holding pattern over LaGuardia since before the jets came in finally decided to land on Route 1.

Except for having a Constellation on top of it, Jim Flannery's looks like a lot of suburban restaurants—a windowless building with the owner's name written on the side in plastic script. It has leatherette booths as well as tables, a menu specializing in steaks and seafood, a bar, and a piano player who was once with Arthur Godfrey. The walls are lined with the paintings of local artists— many of the local artists in this case being Levittown housewives who specialize in still lifes and matadors and sad-faced clowns. The Constellation provides a second bar, entered from the main restaurant by a stairway decorated with a mural called "A History of Flight."

Flannery says that a lot of men whose wives have been reluctant to take their first flight bring them to the Constellation Lounge as a kind of transition step. The waitresses have found that the reaction of most people to being in a lounge that is also an airplane is to make a joke about hijacking. As part of his effort to give a feeling of actual flight, Flannery covered the windows with color transparencies of aerial views of places like Miami and New York, and some customers complain about not being able to see the actual view out the window although the actual view happens to be a section of Route 1 lined with four or five filling stations, a furniture store, a Kiddie City discount toy store, a used-car lot, and an enterprise called the Skyline Diner and Carwash. Flannery, who considers the Constellation a "functional sign," serves drinks in the kind of throwaway glasses used in airplanes and uses "Come Fly with Us" as his motto for billboards and radio ads and napkins. He gives away souvenir pins and tie clasps that are in the shape of Constellations but do not mention the name of the restaurant. "It's subtle," he says. "Very subtle."

On a week night recently, the downstairs bar was crowded—a jolly group was singing "Happy Birthday" to somebody named Arthur—but there were few diners, and the Constellation Lounge looked like a ghost ship. Flannery said business had been slow all week. He thought it might have had something to do with the President's asking people not to spend so much. "Have you seen those TV ads they're running where the guy keeps buying things and pretty soon he turns into a pig?" he asked a guest. Flannery shook his head in wonderment over the ways of government, and said, "A few years ago they were encouraging people to buy."

# Sno

Walking from the Oval Track to the Endurance Track at the Fifth Annual Paul Bunyan Snowmobile Derby, I happened on a man in a parka who was trying to peddle a Chevroletful of canvas snowmobile covers. Since I judged the temperature to be four or five degrees short of the temperature necessary to sustain human life, it was possible that his constant patter was only an attempt to keep his mouth from freezing shut, but, all in all, he struck me as an aggressive salesman—a man quick with persuasive explanations of why it would be pound foolish not to invest twenty-five dollars to protect a thousand-dollar machine. He was experiencing unrelieved failure. It suddenly occurred to me that I had stumbled across what may have been the only example of unsuccessful merchandising in the short, awesomely profitable history of snowmobiling. I immediately took the salesman in hand. "You should be wearing a snowmobile suit!" I shouted to him. It was necessary to shout, because the way a lot of snowmobilers enjoy a derby most is to bring their own machines on trailers and spend most of the day buzzing around the grounds, stopping at the track occasionally to watch the contestants in the two-and-a-half-hour Grand Prix race zip by. "Nobody at a snowmobile derby is going to pay any attention to anybody who isn't wearing a snowmobile suit," I explained. I spoke from some experience, being dressed at the time in a sheep-skin coat that I had considered quite fashionable until I realized that everyone at the derby assumed I was there to replace the hot-dog supply at the refreshment tent or repair the loudspeaker system.

A snowmobile suit is ordinarily a one-piece coverall of quilted material—the kind of thing an airplane mechanic might wear if he happened to work at a very cold airport. Like mechanics, a lot of snowmobile owners wear patches identifying the make of machine they tinker with, but the color of a snowmobile suit alone is usually enough to indicate whether the wearer drives an Arctic Cat or a Polaris or a Scorpion. The snowmobile industry is color-keyed. The owner of a Ski-Doo—a black-and-yellow machine that has the largest share of the market—ordinarily wears a suit that is black with yellow piping, plus black snowmobile boots with Ski-Doo patches on them. A snowmobiler who is particularly fashion-conscious—most often a female snowmobiler—may wear under the Ski-Doo suit yellow wool tights and a yellow sweater with black piping. The inner clothing can be used as what is known as an après-snowmobile outfit, making the wearer a merchandiser's dream—brand identification almost down to the skin.

The cover salesman happened to have a red deer-hunting outfit in his car that we decided might pass for a snowmobile suit, al-though the patch sewn on it said "National Rifle Association" in-stead of "Sno-Pony" or "Ski-Daddler" or "Sno*Jet." When I couldn't find him later in the afternoon, I assumed that my market-ing advice had enabled him to sell all his covers and go home to watch some game on television—the way he had wanted to spend his Saturday afternoon in the first place. I wanted to tell him about meeting a couple wearing black-and-white snowmobile suits with patches that said "Snow Goer." When I asked if they knew why whoever had named their make was the only person in the field who felt it necessary to spell out "snow" to the very end, they told me that Snow Goer was not a machine but a magazine—a publica-tion that happened to consider it good business to have its own snowmobile suits. I did find the salesman again at the end of the day, and he reported, with restrained gratitude, that he had sold three covers. Brainerd, like all the other places that call themselves the Snowmobile Capital of the World, is a small town, and the salesman thought his problem might be that not many people in a small town walk around on a Saturday with twenty-five dollars extra in their pockets. That was not the problem. "Get a proper patch!" I shouted. It was obvious that all he needed was a patch on his hunting suit saying something like "Sno-Cougar Covers." I didn't see him Sunday, but if he followed my instructions he is now a very rich snowmobile-cover salesman.

None of the people representing snowmobile manufacturers at the derby seemed in need of my marketing advice. They all had snowmobile suits on, all bepatched with their brand names, and the fact that a state like Minnesota, which ten years ago had no snowmobiles, now has a hundred thousand seemed to be an indication that the snowmobile industry had been getting good advice from somewhere. Also, I couldn't think of any promotional possibilities in a snowmobile derby that they hadn't exhausted. Although the Brainerd derby is considered only a middle-sized event on the snowmobile-racing circuit, several of the manufacturers had brought their factory racing teams, the results of certain races having too great an impact on sales to be left to amateurs.

"People are kind of silly about racing," the representative of one manufacturer told me. "They know that the machines that race are not the same ones they get in the showroom, and very few people actually buy snowmobiles to race them anyway. But they don't like the thought of being left behind on the trail. They want a machine just a little faster than their neighbor's. Not much; just a little."

Johnson Motors, which makes a snowmobile called a Skee-Horse, sponsored a Skeeburger Fest on Friday night at the Brainerd Armory, where the Exchange Club served the skeeburgers and Miss Brainerd welcomed everyone to town ("Have a good time, eat a whole bunch, and have a ball"). On Saturday, a few hundred snowmobilers went on a Snowmobile Moonlight Cruise—driving their machines twelve miles to a cookout and back, with guides, mechanics, trailmarkings, hot dogs, and souvenir patches furnished by Evinrude, the producer of the Evinrude Skeeter. A couple of the companies that make snowmobile oil offered extra prize money for drivers who won races while displaying the company decals, and another oil company towed its banner above the derby grounds by plane Saturday afternoon and furnished place-mats and matches for the Awards Banquet at the Elks Lodge that night. The local race officials, sanctioned by the United States Snowmobile Association, wore bright-orange snowmobile suits with a patch that said "Miller High Life Snowmobiler."

At a Friday evening parade through the streets of Brainerd, and during the day at the derby, the public relations man from the largest distributor of Ski-Doos hauled behind his snowmobile a yellow sleigh that held Miss Minnesota, accompanied, for good measure, by Miss North Dakota—both of whom would alight occasionally to hand out Ski-Doo "Think Snow" buttons or Ski-Doo safety booklets. Miss Minnesota is retained for such duties through the Miss Minnesota Pageant at a straight hundred dollars a day (with special rates for appearances under two hours), and both she and Miss North Dakota appear at snowmobile functions exclusively for Ski-Doo—leaving Arctic Cat, a Minnesota company, to make do with Miss Wisconsin and Miss Michigan. At the Skeeburger Fest, the Johnson representative, in a friendly mood, asked Miss Minnesota if it would be in violation of her contract for him to pin one of his limited-supply "LOVE is a Johnson Skee-Horse" buttons on her. She thought about it a moment, smiled pleasantly, and said it would be. The Awards Banquet guests included not only the Misses Minnesota and North Dakota but also Miss Brainerd, Miss Little Falls, Miss Park Rapids, and the Princess of Silver Bay—almost all of them with tiny crowns perched on their heads. But the star was Miss Minnesota. She is known in the state for having won the talent competition at the Miss America Pageant, playing the flute, and before the banquet ended the master of ceremonies announced, "She's going to perform her talent for us tonight." Having dressed for the banquet in a gown that was totally without brand identification, Miss Minnesota first reminded those present that she and Miss North Dakota were sponsored by Ski-Doo, although they both hoped everybody had a good time, no matter what kind of machine he drove. Then she played the flute. At a hundred a day, Miss Minnesota is considered a bargain.

Brainerd is about a hundred and twenty miles north of Minneapolis and St. Paul, in what the snowmobile industry usually refers to as the Snowbelt—an area where the billboards are as likely to advertise Arctic Cats as Fords (on the Arctic Cats, imitation leopardskin seat covers are standard rather than optional), where sportinggoods stores sell snowmobile racing stripes made of contact paper, and where some small towns average more than one snowmobile per family. In Brainerd, which has nearby lakes that make it a summer recreation center, the word snowmobile enthusiasts often use to describe what life was like in winter before snowmobiles came along is "hibernation." Anyone who listens to a few snowmobilers talk about how dismal existence was in the old days begins to find it amazing that they managed to survive until someone discovered that a revolving belt and skis and a one-cylinder motor will propel a small vehicle over the snow at thirty or forty miles an hour. "I grew up around here," the employee of a snowmobile distributor told me as we sat in a roadhouse one dark, cold night. "And in the winter the only sound was the Grain Belt beer sign creaking in the wind." I shivered.

To businessmen, an area of hibernating people amounts to a block of dormant consumers just waiting for the right product to bring them to life. In the Snowbelt, no testimony of a snowmobiler on how glorious it is to have something to do all winter is quite as rhapsodic as the testimony of a banker on how glorious it is to have something to give loans on all winter. Snowmobiling has been marketed not as a sport but as a culture—a way to turn the former hibernation period into a time of what snowmobile marketers often refer to as Family Fun. Once winter is considered fun, the rest follows automatically. People in the Snowbelt enjoy being outdoors in groups, and now they can enjoy being outdoors in groups all winter merely by purchasing snowmobiles, snowmobile clothing, snowmobile trailers, snowmobile oil, and a drink called Snowshoe Grog. They like competitive sports, so there are snowmobile derbies every weekend. People who like to hunt can get to the hunting grounds in a snowmobile. People who like to drink can go from roadhouse to roadhouse in a snowmobile. The only adjustment necessary is to the cold, and snowmobilers are militantly oblivious of the cold. They like to talk about how explorers have proved snowmobile suits to be warm in temperatures as low as thirty or forty below zero, and they often stand outside when they could just as easily stand inside—the way little boys with new boots go out of their way to splash through puddles.

Snowmobile manufacturers are quite aware that their customers are, for the most part, small-town people—people who might like to go on outings pulling their kids behind them in a sled attachment, people who are more likely to be the townies of summer resorts than the owners of summer houses, people who, in the words of one snowmobile promotion man, "might feel uncomfortable in a ski resort."

"You might call them the Silent Majority," a spokesman for the industry told me at the derby, as we stood chatting just outside a heated tent.

"About the noise . . ." I replied, raising my voice enough to be heard over the sound of two passing Ski-Doos.

"It's terrible," he said. "Awful. Our worst problem."

Like the manufacturers of anything else, manufacturers of snowmobiles are organized to protect their interests—the International Snowmobile Industry Association has an executive secretary in Washington, the same man who serves as executive secretary of the American Golf Car Manufacturers Association, the Power Saw Manufacturers Association, and the Outdoor Power Equipment Institute—but even a trade association could never hope to persuade anybody that snowmobiles are anything but noisy. People in the industry admit that six or eight snowmobiles cutting through a back yard in the middle of the night can bring a homeowner leaping from his bed in the belief that, somehow, an anti-aircraft battery has just opened fire from his bedroom. They also admit—as they increase the power of some models to the point of being able to travel sixty miles an hour—that snowmobiles can be dangerous. On the theory that excesses could eventually result in a nasty backlash against Family Fun, the I.S.I.A. representative who makes the rounds of the Snowbelt legislatures acknowledges the need for legislation to prevent people from riding snowmobiles on highways or hunting from snowmobiles or using snowmobiles in populated areas late at night. He says his goal is "regulatory encouragement."

What nobody connected with snowmobiles will acknowledge is that the peaceful woods are being violated by snowmobiling—an idea they associate with people from big cities who know nothing about snowmobiles or woods. It is true that there is an automatic disdain for snowmobiles among the people I have always thought of as Abercrombie & Fitch Conservationists—sailing enthusiasts who complain about the noise the riffraff make with their outboards, people who build tasteful hundred-thousand-dollar houses on the unspoiled parts of the California coast and then talk about preserving the natural beauty of the area against the ugliness of tacky beach cottages. There are also serious conservationists who believe that, for a number of reasons, inaccessible woods ought to remain inaccessible, but their arguments have no effect on serious snowmobilers, who like to think that they are outdoorsmen and conservationists themselves. One snowmobiler I was talking with dismissed the idea that the noise of the machines frightens animals by saying that a snowmobile makes less noise in the woods than a chain saw. When I said that the comparison might not be the most felicitous to use with conservationists, he informed me that a chain saw attracts deer faster than a salt lick. Listening to a snowmobiler talk about the joy of riding through the woods at night, with the snow on the jack pines glistening in the moonlight, I found it hard to keep in mind that the scene would have to include the smell of gas fumes and the noise of an indoor go-cart race.

"I wouldn't have one of the things," a Brainerd citizen told me during a derby social hour at the Elks Lodge. "They just amount to a way of getting from one bar to the next, and I can get to a bar without a snowmobile."

It is true that some people in Brainerd use the snowmobile as a kind of pub-crawl vehicle—the pubs in this case being the restaurants and bars on the nearby lake shores. But going to a bar with a group of snowmobilers—and snowmobilers seem to go to bars only in groups—is not at all the same as arriving in a car. One of the promotion men at the derby told me that, in his view, the success of snowmobiling is due partly to the secret yen middle-class people in places like upper Minnesota have for the life of motorcycle gangs. But a snowmobile group entering a Minnesota roadhouse also carries the mystique of the Western—the Cartwrights riding into town and coming into the bar together, part of a good, strong outdoor group. In a bar, snowmobilers usually keep their snowmobile suits on—just getting out of the top half and letting it hang over their belts behind them as they talk about the bumpiness of the trail on the way over or about the relative virtues of a Polaris and an Arctic Cat.

The Saturday night of the Paul Bunyan Derby, I was in a roadhouse near the race track. Its parking lot seemed to have as many snowmobiles as cars. A few couples from Fargo, North Dakota, were there—people who had driven over in their cars for the derby, pulling their snowmobiles behind them on trailers—and there were a lot of local people making the usual Saturday night rounds in their snowmobiles. The place was jammed. A snowmobile promotion man I was with was talking about his company's spending a couple of hundred thousand dollars a year in racing, and about color-keying clothes to snowmobiles, and about putting out instructions to people on how to form snowmobile clubs. "Sometimes I think it's all a childish game," he said. "And sometimes I think we've rejuvenated these people." A lot of the snowmobilers were gathered around a piano bar. They were singing along with the piano player, and going over to the dance floor to jitterbug to the faster numbers, and drinking a lot of Grain Belt beer.

Kentucky, December, 1969

# The Logical Thing, Costwise

WHITESBURG

Once Bethlehem Steel had decided to begin large-scale strip-mining for coal in the mountains of eastern Kentucky, its public relations men might have been expected to advise picking a spot as far away from Whitesburg as possible. The *Mountain Eagle,* one of the few county weeklies in the United States that ever print anything that might cause discomfort to anyone with any economic power, is published in Whitesburg; it could be counted on to discuss Bethlehem's plans editorially in terms of mountains scarred, streams polluted, timber destroyed, and houses being endangered by floods and mud slides. Also, Whitesburg's best-known citizen is Harry Caudill, the author of *Night Comes to the Cumberlands,* and there is no subject that inspires Caudill to greater heights of acid eloquence than the subject of strip-mining—except, perhaps, the subject of out-of-state corporations that have managed to extract extraordinary riches from eastern Kentucky while the mountaineers who live there remain the poorest white people in the United States. More than any other man in Appalachia, Caudill can bring a controversy to the attention of the outside press and can muster the support of national conservation groups. He also happens to have the old-fashioned habit of assigning responsibility for a corporation's actions to the families that are said to own large chunks of its stock. "This may be the oldest forest of its kind on the planet," he says. "This forest was here when the Rockies rose up and when they went down and when they rose up again. It has withstood two great sieges by glaciers. But it couldn't withstand a single assault by the Mellons."

Bethlehem, through a subsidiary called Beth-Elkhorn, owns the mineral rights to about forty thousand acres of land in eastern Kentucky, but it happened to be convenient to start strip-mining at Millstone, in the southern end of Letcher County—not far from Whitesburg. The work, subcontracted to a local firm, began last summer. The letters from Caudill and his allies—to the governor ("I urge you to call upon Bethlehem to abstain from this act of greed"), to the president of Bethlehem Steel, to *The New York Times* and Charles Lindbergh and Arthur Godfrey and just about anyone else who had ever indicated an interest in conservation— began even earlier than that. Before long, the Louisville *Courier-Journal* ran an item pointing out that the Millstone operation appeared to be in violation of several provisions of a law Kentucky passed in 1966 to minimize the damage caused by strip-mining. Then the Division of Reclamation, the state agency responsible for enforcing the law, suspended the permit to mine at Millstone. The president of the state's Izaak Walton League—a young lawyer who had helped write the strip-mine legislation while working for the state—visited the site and eventually filed a two-million-dollar damage suit on behalf of one of the local landowners.

But in a few days Bethlehem's sub-contractors had corrected the violations to the satisfaction of the Division of Reclamation— which, the *Courier-Journal* wrote, had come to be so easily satisfied that its behavior "raised suspicions of political interference." Bethlehem took full-page ads in the *Mountain Eagle* and some other papers in the area listing its accomplishments in reclamation and beautification throughout the country. Thanks to Bethlehem's restoration programs, the ad said, "hundreds of acres of previously ugly terrain in various locations have been transformed into flowering fields and verdant slopes, pulsing with game and other wildlife." At Millstone, the strip-mining continued.

HELLIER

The question that occurs to someone seeing Hellier for the first time is what damage a strip-mine could do to it that hasn't already been done. Hellier and Lookout and Henry Clay and Allegheny are what remain of an isolated cluster of camps that various coal companies built in Pike County for their workers earlier in the century. The roads are accompanied by streams the color and consistency of old gravy, and dotted with the hardy roadside blossom of eastern Kentucky—abandoned automobile hulks. The creeks are spanned by decaying wooden bridges leading to dilapidated old coal-camp houses, many of them now occupied by retired or disabled miners. The lines of houses are broken occasionally by abandoned slag heaps—known locally as "red dogs"—which sometimes catch fire from spontaneous combustion and burn for years, giving off a putrid smoke. The second site scheduled for strip-mining by Beth-Elkhorn is not far from the old camps, and one of the protest letters sent to the president of Bethlehem came from the Pike County Citizens Association, a poor people's organization that has its headquarters in an old company store in Hellier.

The mineral rights to the land that many poor mountain people live on were sold to coal companies for practically nothing at the turn of the century under the terms of what is known as a "broadform deed"—giving the coal company the right to do any damage to the land it considers necessary for the extraction of the coal. Strip-mining happens to be the cheapest way of getting coal. In the dense mountains that cover eastern Kentucky, it amounts to cutting out a wedge all the way around a mountain, as if for building a very wide road—the purpose usually being to remove the outer edge of a seam of coal whose center has already been extracted by underground mining. If the dirt and rock that covered the coal are merely pushed off the cut into a pile on the mountainside, they can, with the addition of some moisture, slide down into the valley below, burying a road or a cornfield, blocking a creek, or destroying a house. The sediments can pollute rivers and alter the channels of creeks enough to cause flash floods. If the coal mined has a high sulphur content—which a small percentage of coal in eastern Kentucky does—the "acid mine water" formed from its exposure can get into a stream and kill every living thing.

In eastern Kentucky, there are fifty-five thousand acres of "orphan mines"—land that, having been reached before strip-mining regulations were established, was mined with no consideration whatever for the reclamation of the mountain or the life of the people below. "Right when they do it, it's not so awful bad," Edith Easterling, a local woman who runs the Marrowbone Folk School in Lookout, has said. "But when it rains, it's terrible. And after they've ruined your land, you still pay taxes on it. You can go to town, but you can't get a lawyer to represent you." In an eastern Kentucky county, most of the "town people"—particularly the public officials—have some financial interest in the coal industry, and it is sometimes said of the local lawyers, "If there's one who's not on a monthly retainer to a coal company, it's an oversight." The Applachian Volunteers and other poverty workers who came to eastern Kentucky at the beginning of the War on Poverty inevitably found strip-mining the most compelling issue among the poor—and the issue that brought the greatest hostility from the people in political and economic control.

In Pike County, opposition to strip-mining reached a climax in the summer of 1967. In a quiet place called Island Creek, a retired miner named Jink Ray told the Puritan Coal Company that its bulldozer was not going to come on the steep mountainside that rises in back of his house. Ray was supported not only by poverty workers but by a number of his neighbors, two of whom stood in front of Puritan's bulldozer when an attempt was made to come onto the property. After some arguing in court and a lot of arguing in the newspapers, the governor himself withdrew Puritan's permit. The incident is regarded by some local historians as the only victory for poor people in the history of Pike County, but the coal operators also seem to have profited from the experience. Landowners are ordinarily given a small royalty on the coal removed from their land, even if payment is not legally required, and if a man appears to be as stubborn as Jink Ray even after money is offered, coal operators skip his land rather than start a controversy that could stir up pressure for stricter regulations or could get somebody shot. The policy doesn't involve passing over much land. Although poor people in Pike County might point to Jink Ray as an example of how a mountaineer ought to act when his land is threatened, years of being poor and helpless have left many of them afraid to act that way. "Fear in poor people is one of the awfulest things," Edith Easterling says.

An organized effort of poor people against strip-mining in eastern Kentucky is hampered by the fact that there are practically no organizers left. Ten days after Jink Ray's victory, three poverty workers were arrested for sedition—attempting to overthrow the government of Pike County. Not long after that, the Appalachian Volunteers lost the grant from the Office of Economic Opportunity they were operating under. Eventually, the Kentucky Un-American Activities Committee—widely known as QUACK—came to hold hearings at the Pike County courthouse in order to ascertain how far Communists had gone in subverting established authority. When Edith Easterling was subpoenaed, she used the occasion to make known her opinion of the county's officials. "I went down to the courthouse," she recalls. "I told them, 'I've not done but one thing I'm ashamed of, and that's to vote for these dirty birds.' " About the only outside organizer left in Pike County is the director of the Pike County Citizens Association, and he and Edith Easterling don't get along—so the remnant of an organization is split into two remnants.

There are some people who believe that Bethlehem might run into violence in Pike County; strip-mining equipment has been blown up in the past. But anger in the past has usually been related to strip-mining that occurs right above people's houses, and the proposed Bethlehem site is rather remote. It's a section called Flatwoods, back in the mountains, where the auto bodies and the slag heaps and the grim, gray houses of Hellier can't be seen. It's so removed from Hellier, in fact, that it's still beautiful.

JENKINS

David Zegeer, the division superintendent of Beth-Elkhorn's operations in eastern Kentucky, talks a lot about blackberries. A visitor to Zegeer's office in Jenkins is almost certain to leave with a tiny jar of puce blackberry jelly—made, the label says, from blackberries "picked from the fruitful vines of Marshall's Branch surface mine." Beth-Elkhorn had never done any extensive strip-mining in eastern Kentucky, but several years ago, at a place near Jenkins called

Marshall's Branch, it did do some surface mining, mainly by augering—a method that is similar to stripping, although somewhat less severe. According to Zegeer, the results of Beth-Elkhorn's reclamation work at Marshall's Branch demonstrate that surface mining actually improves the land. For one thing, he says, the mining cut creates a flat area encircling the mountain (known in the trade as a "bench"), and "except for aesthetically, there is no commercial value to steep land." (Dave told me the bench would be good for cattle grazing," Harry Caudill likes to say, "and I told him when Bethlehem finished stripping all that land they will have created the longest, narrowest cow pasture in the history of agriculture—fifty feet wide and five thousand miles long.") Zegeer enjoys taking visitors around the mountain at Marshall's Branch, remarking on what a nice access road the flat bench makes, describing the *Sericea lespedeza* and crown vetch and Chinese chestnuts Beth-Elkhorn has planted, and, most enthusiastically of all, pointing out the blackberries. Because of Zegeer's enthusiasm, the Jenkins Kiwanis Club plans to dispense jelly jars to the women living near Marshall's Branch, buy the jelly they produce for a fair market price, and sell it at stores in state parks—after affixing a label that points out its origin. "Not to fight back, exactly," Zegeer says, "but just to show what people can do."

Although Zegeer says he is proud to have a hand in improving the land of eastern Kentucky and helping the economy of Jenkins, he emphasizes that the decision to begin strip-mining was made because it was "the logical thing, costwise." An area northwest of Jenkins that has been almost mined out by Bethlehem through one of its underground mines, for instance, still has about ten million tons of outcrop coal that can be reached through strip-mining, and Zegeer says that the time to mine it is obviously when it can be used to keep the underground mine's preparation plant operating. Zegeer points out that Bethlehem paid good money for the mineral rights to the land, and obviously has the right to get its money's worth by recovering all the coal in it. (It is common in the coal industry to talk about "recovering" coal, as if the mountain snatched the coal away from Bethlehem sometime in the past, and Bethlehem is obligated to get it back; a pro-strip-mining letter to the *Mountain Eagle* said, "I don't believe God would have put all this coal here if he hadn't intended for it to be taken out.") In an interview in the *Mountain Eagle* just after Bethlehem announced its strip-mining plans, Zegeer was quoted as saying, "If there's something wrong with my company, there's something wrong with the country."

There are, of course, disagreements between Zegeer and his opponents about the facts of strip-mining. According to Zegeer, for instance, the idea that strip-mining causes sedimentation in the streams is one of the many myths concocted by the conservationists; according to the conservationists, the idea that strip-mining is vital to the eastern Kentucky economy is one of the many myths invented by the coal operators. But Zegeer and the conservationists would disagree even if they agreed on the facts. The reclamation job that Zegeer proudly displays at Marshall's Branch—where the vertical side of the cut still forms a naked bluff that is thirty feet high in places—would strike most conservationists as a horror. And when Zegeer is told of some conservationists believing that Bethlehem ought to be satisfied with the millions of tons of coal it has already deep-mined from the area northwest of Jenkins, he shakes his head in amazement and says, "You can't just walk away from ten million tons of high-grade metallurgical coal."

LEXINGTON

The decision of Bethlehem to join the local firms that have been strip-mining in eastern Kentucky was bound to revitalize the anti-strip-mining efforts of Kentucky conservationists—partly because Bethlehem could be expected to be more sensitive to criticism than local coal operators. There is obviously an increasing national concern about problems of the environment, and Bethlehem, having been accused of doing more than its share to create the problems, has been active lately in trying to patch up its reputation. It is widely believed that public relations considerations might lead a corporation such as Bethlehem to stop doing anything that offended any vocal segment of the population—although in this case public relations considerations have so far merely led it to run full-page newspaper ads about good works and to give away jars of blackberry jelly while continuing to do whatever is logical costwise.

Not long after strip-mining was begun by Beth-Elkhorn at Millstone, the Kentucky Conservation Council passed a resolution calling for the prohibiting of strip-mining in eastern Kentucky—the feeling of many conservationists being that the steep terrain and heavy rainfall of that part of the state make reclamation impossible. When the council called a meeting in Lexington for people who were interested in lobbying to turn the resolution into law, those who attended did not appear to be particularly optimistic about their chances for success. From past battles, they are aware that the defenders of strip-mining have formidable economic and political resources. It is also possible that the most effective weapon conservationists had in the past—public opinion—may have been weakened by their own efforts. Even without strict enforcement, the 1966 law makes it much less likely that a poor mountaineer will lose his house to a strip-mining landslide, and the general policy of avoiding people like Jink Ray makes it much less likely that strip-miners will become involved in an embarrassing confrontation. The conservationists are left in the position of talking less about living, identifiable people and more about sedimentation and ecological balance and the obligation of the society toward generations unborn. "People!" Caudill said at the Lexington meeting when somebody mentioned to him that the human element in the controversy might have diminished. "We've already fought this on the people issue, and nobody cared. They said, 'They're just a bunch of paupers—let it go.' Nobody cares about people in this country. I think we're better off talking about the environment."

# Leave the Rest to Me

Before the first auction of the morning began, half a dozen old folks gathered across the Boardwalk from the auction gallery, in the shade of a frozen custard stand. It was a hot weekend in Atlantic City, but the men wore coats and ties and the women wore high-heeled shoes and dark print dresses. They looked like people gathering to catch a bus to the monthly dinner meeting of a Bronx senior citizens' club. "He said we shouldn't stand together," the last man to arrive said, glancing back toward the auction gallery. "What's the difference?" said a large man who had a hearing aid built into his glasses. "Nobody's looking." He moved a couple of steps away from a woman he had been talking to. "He's nothing but a horse dealer anyway," someone else said, and they began to share complaints about the hours they had to work.

*There are amusement piers in Atlantic City, and there is, of course, a wide white beach stretching between the Boardwalk and the Atlantic. But for most of the people strolling along the Boardwalk on a hot weekend—the men in slacks or Bermuda shorts, many of the women in bare-midriff blouses—the main entertainment seems to be purchasing. There are plenty of places to buy hamburgers or frozen custard or saltwater taffy or souvenir T-shirts. There are clothing stores—not just beach clothing but all kinds of clothing— and jewelry stores, and even fur stores. There are also a half-dozen or so auction galleries. They all look alike—doors that open the entire storefront, so that people can wander in off the Board-walk, rows of folding chairs, displays of porcelain figurines and silver tea services and the kind of paintings that might have been inspired by the Three Musketeers. The auction galleries lean toward English-sounding names like Lloyd's or Harper's, Ltd., or Shawe's Galleries, and every sign that has the gallery's name on it also includes the year it was established. All the galleries have signs say-ing that they act as agents for estates and insurance companies and private parties, and signs saying that everyone connected with the concern is bonded. "This is one of the oldest auction galleries on the Boardwalk," the auctioneer often says. "It's not like you're buying from someone on the street corner."*

The senior citizens stood in a tight group around a platform that had been placed just inside the auction gallery. A delegate from a Lions convention that was in town leaned against the wall. A coun-ter on the platform was lined with small appliances—a toaster, a radio, an iron, a coffee maker—and the man behind the counter was promising to auction off every appliance for which he received an opening bid, no matter how ridiculously low the bid was. "How many people ever heard of Polaroid?" he asked, holding up a Pola-roid camera. The hands of all the senior citizens shot up. "Oh, yeah, Polaroid," the man with the hearing aid said, in the tone of someone conversant with the names of camera manufacturers. "Sure. Polaroid." Eventually, the Lion drifted away. "How many people would pay me fifty cents for this Baby Ben alarm clock?" the auctioneer said. "You all know Baby Ben as well as I do." He gazed down at his audience. There were six senior citizens, all with hands raised. "What's the difference?" the auctioneer mumbled. Then he took a deep breath and began again. "It's hot as hell out-side and air-conditioned in here," he said. "What a great sale we're going to have today, ladies and gentlemen. G.E., Motorola, Sony. Everything must go."

*When the first auctions of the morning begin, at about ten-thirty, warmup auctioneers up and down the Boardwalk are standing on platforms near the entrances to their galleries talking to groups of elderly, formally dressed people. Atlantic City auctions have a ritual that varies from conventional auctions in about the same way that professional wrestling varies from the version approved by the Olympic committee, and the practitioners never stray from the ritual. The routines, the goods offered for sale, even the jokes are virtually identical every day in every gallery. Getting opening bids for appliances is always an occasion for auctioning off mystery packages that the high bidder doesn't have to take once the mystery is revealed—the auctioneer often decides not to accept any money for the item anyway—and for collecting quarters in exchange for tokens good for a gift later on. Until a crowd has gathered, while only a group of hyper-responsive senior citizens are pressed around the stand, the auctioneer just keeps talking toward the people on the Boardwalk—holding up toasters and electric knives, flipping on and off transistor radios, calling out brand names, sounding like a television talk-show host who has a minute and a half to kill between commercials.*

Gradually, about a dozen people were added to the crowd in front of the platform. The auctioneer asked them where they came from, and called them by their home towns. Queens was a relatively prosperous-looking man who maintained an expression of faint amusement; his wife, who appeared to be quite a bit younger than he was, bid eagerly on a couple of the appliances. There was a Negro couple—the wife rather interested in the sale, and the husband reluctant to let her invest a quarter, even when the auctioneer assured her that her money would be refunded if she didn't like the gift. Another Lion came in with his wife; he was a rotund, jovial man who wore not only his convention identification badge but also a "Keep Smiling" button. "Would you mind coming in out of the doorway, folks?" the auctioneer said. "I'm trying to gather a crowd. It don't take a professor from Pennsylvania University to see that."

*One of the ways that Atlantic City auctioneers try to dispel sus-*
*picions about their reliability is to bring the suspicions out in the*
*open and treat them as jokes. They regularly accuse some senior*
*citizen of accusing some blatantly authentic tourist of being a shill.*
*"I never saw you before in my life—did I, Tom?" the auctioneer*
*will say to the tourist, who, knowing himself not to be a shill, can*
*laugh about the ridiculousness of the suspicion. Sometimes auc-*
*tioneers even joke about collecting quarters from people in order*
*to keep them in the gallery for the few minutes the rest of the auc-*
*tion will take—a few minutes being the longest period of time ever*
*remaining at an Atlantic City auction, according to an auctioneer's*
*estimate. "Am I being fair?" the auctioneer will say. "Do you think*
*three dollars for a G.E. coffee maker is really starting low enough?"*
*There is immediate affirmation, led by the senior citizens. After a*
*while, the faintest interrogative tone in the auctioneer's voice seems*
*to bring up the hands of the senior citizens. Probably once a day in*
*Atlantic City there is the kind of scene in which the auctioneer,*
*about to begin a description of a man's gift, asks "How many people*
*here love their husbands?" and a sleepy-looking old gentleman*
*soberly raises his hand.*

After a while, the man behind the counter suggested that everyone
go on into the gallery and be seated for a few minutes so that he
could finish auctioning off the appliances and give away the quarter
prizes and open a mystery box that the Lion's wife had bought for
six dollars and eighty cents. Two or three more men from the gallery appeared between the crowd and the Boardwalk and began
herding people down the aisle toward the front rows of folding
chairs. Only a couple of people left. Somebody closed the doors. A
second auctioneer took over. He explained that the real purpose of
the day's auction was to advertise a sale to be held during the following week—a sale that happened to include three hundred and
eighty-five thousand dollars' worth of jewels. "Advertising costs
money," he said. "And we spend money to advertise." He opened
the box for the Lion's wife—it was a comb-and-brush set, which
didn't seem to excite her—and sold some of the appliances, all for
low prices and all to senior citizens. He shook his head sadly at the
sight of such merchandise going so cheaply. "How many people

like my auction sale so far?" he asked. Hands went up all over the room. "Well," he said, "I don't like it."

*An Atlantic City auctioneer, automatically becoming resigned to the hopeless penuriousness of the audience he has had the bad luck to draw, always manages to find some wry humor in his misfortune. "What is this—a conspiracy against me?" an auctioneer sometimes says. "Did you all get together next door and say 'Let's go aggravate the auctioneer?' " Auctioneers never permit an aversion to stinginess to alter their affection for the crowd. "It's not that you're not nice people," several auctioneers tell several audiences in Atlantic City every day. "Physically you're nice. Spiritually you're nice. But financially . . ." The auctioneer pauses and sighs. "Financially," he continues, "may the Lord have mercy on your stingy souls." When the auction moves from small appliances to diamond rings— and it always does—the auctioneer makes it clear that passing up a bargain can go beyond stinginess and become bad business judgment. He emphasizes that the people who get ahead—the people who own the yachts he sometimes sees as he gazes out over the audience toward the Atlantic—are willing to spend a dollar to make a dollar. In Atlantic City, a summer resort that sells fur coats, a bargain is no less a bargain because the purchaser doesn't happen to need it. The auctioneer always takes it for granted that nobody actually needs a diamond ring: "How many people out here in my audience who have no earthly use for it, who need it no more than you need water in your shoe, who have six on your hand, eight in a glove, and an aunt with twelve who doesn't feel very good—just as a gesture of good common sense, to invest a dollar to make a dollar (it's just as honorable, you know, to buy something at one price and sell it at another price as it is to drive a truck or dig a ditch)—how many people out here in my audience, for a carat-and-fifty-three fine white solitaire in platinum, would say the low, ridiculous bid—cash, check, or deposit—of one hundred dollars? Raise your hand."*

"Some people say, 'He rides an automobile and I have a bicycle. I never get a break,' " the auctioneer said when he finally got around to introducing some diamond rings, about forty-five minutes after

the auction started. "Did you ever think you didn't *make* a break?"
He had already collected a dollar apiece from people who wanted
one of the boxes he was saving for those who would trust him with
a dollar, and he had sold a couple more appliances to senior citizens. "How many people think this is a pretty diamond ring?" he
said, holding out a ring on a rolled-up piece of white paper. Most
people in the audience raised their hands, and one elderly man
said, "Oh, yes, beautiful. Very nice." The auctioneer turned to the
couple from Queens. "May I borrow your finger, my dear?" he said
to the woman, slipping the ring on her finger and holding it up to
the crowd. "Have you ever been a model?"

*In Atlantic City, the transition from toasters to diamond rings al-
most always comes about in the same way. During one of many
digressions, the auctioneer says something like "How many here
would give me five dollars for this box?" After only one or two
hands go up, the auctioneer opens the box to reveal glittering rows
of diamond rings and jeweled watches. "I'm sure you would," he
says. "It just so happens that this box contains one hundred and
thirty-five thousand dollars' worth of gems—part of our sale next
week." The auctioneer, it turns out, is willing to auction off three
diamond rings from the sale; trying to sell any more to such a crowd
would be futile—not that they're not nice people. But first he asks,
"How many people in my audience know that diamonds are an investment?" Diamonds are also, he assures everyone, "a symbol of
success, a sign of prestige—like a Cadillac, anyone who owns one
demands respect." The gallery's real business, he says, is diamonds. It sells more diamonds in a day than most stores sell in six
months to a year. It sells diamonds to people who sell diamonds. It
sells diamonds in a way that no other store does—accompanied by
a diamond certificate attesting to the diamond's exact specifications.
He waves the certificate—an impressive-looking document that resembles a correspondence-school diploma. The auctioneer talks
about the famous people whose estates the diamonds are from, and
the famous stores where they were bought for thousands years ago.
Atlantic City auctioneers love the sound of famous names and
famous stores and famous brands. Sometimes, during a pause in
his delivery, an auctioneer will look out into the crowd, shake his*

*head in wonderment and respect, and say, with simple reverence,*
*"Cartier's."*

"How many would give me a hundred dollars for this diamond ring?" the auctioneer said, in the manner of a man asking who would like to be offered the land under Rockefeller Center for fifteen hundred dollars, convenient terms to be arranged. It was the first of three rings, and the auctioneer had begun by asking who would like to pay nine hundred, or eight seventy-five, or even eight-fifty. During the silence that followed, one of the senior citizens had said he would give a hundred dollars. The auctioneer, looking pained, had explained almost angrily that the mounting alone was worth six hundred and that anybody would be happy to pay a hundred—a point he had proved by asking those who would to raise their hands. The Negro couple had left, the wife talking to the husband in harsh whispers on the way out. The Lion was still there; he had been joking along with the auctioneer about the low bids. Both he and the man from Queens raised their hands. The auctioneer counted seven hands. "Wrap me up seven special gifts," he said to his assistant. "For these people who had the courage to bid. Did you see which hands were up?" The assistant hadn't noticed, and the auctioneer asked the seven people to raise their hands again. He counted ten hands. A puzzled look crossed his face, and he began to ask each person with his hand up if he had really meant his bid.

*No assistant has ever noticed which hands were up. The second count is always higher than the first, and the attempt to straighten out that suspicious disparity is always an opportunity to discount publicly those people who don't really have the stomach to compete with the serious speculators. At this point in the auction, it has become clear that buying is an activity not merely for the shrewd but for the shrewd and courageous and manly. A few minutes after the second count, when the senior citizens have quickly increased the bid and the ring has gone to some elderly man or some little old lady for several hundred dollars, the auctioneer says, "Remember that there were people here who were afraid to pay a hundred dollars for that ring." He himself had told people who bid two or three hundred that he would personally buy the ring back for double the bid if they managed to get it at that price. "I'm not worried about this ring," the auctioneer says, toward the end of the bidding. "What worries me is, if I only get eight hundred dollars for this ring, what am I going to get for the second ring—the featured item, the big one?"*

"Do you want a hundred dollars profit right now or will you keep the ring?" the auctioneer asked an elderly woman after she had won the first ring with a bid of five hundred dollars. "Oh, no, I'll keep the ring," she said, a satisfied look on her face. The auctioneer asked everyone to give her a big hand, and an assistant led her to the back of the gallery to arrange payment. "Not to say anything against the first ring," the auctioneer said, reaching for another diamond. "But if I was going to buy a ring, this is the one I'd buy."

*The sale of the second ring—and perhaps a third and a fourth, and maybe a couple of watches, and sometimes a silver tea service—begins with the same futile attempt by the auctioneer to get an opening bid he considers suitable. The room is silent. When some senior citizen finally bids, say, two hundred dollars, those in the audience who have learned from the auction what diamonds are really worth smile at the auctioneer's stricken expression and shake their heads in amazement at anyone who could expect to buy a diamond ring at that price. Most people raise their hands when asked if they would pay two hundred dollars themselves. "If you wouldn't pay two hundred dollars for this ring," the auctioneer tells the rest of the audience, "you wouldn't pay two hundred dollars for the Holiday Inn." Their hypothetical two hundred dollars is soon being spoken of as a bid—eight or nine bids of the same amount— and the auctioneer has to remind everyone that although eight horses may begin a race, only one can win. An elderly man bids, say, two-fifty—far from a winning bid, judging by the sale of the first ring—and then the bidding seems to stop. The high bidder sits patiently while the auctioneer searches for a way not to sell him the diamond. Sometimes the auctioneer tells the audience that the elderly man is a dealer who will break up the ring and sell the results for an enormous profit. Sometimes he merely says that he would prefer to work something out with someone who has trusted him, or someone who would appreciate the ring. He always singles out a recipient—often, it seems, a Negro couple. "How little more would you pay?" he says to the man, holding the ring in front of the man's wife. "Two-sixty? Just call it out." Sometimes someone else from the gallery—perhaps a resident "gemologist" who has been called upon by the auctioneer to describe the ring—whispers to the chosen recipient that the ring is a steal; sometimes the whispering is done by the man's wife. "Just say two-sixty," the auctioneer will say, holding the ring out to the couple and nodding his head constantly while he talks. "Just say it. Don't worry—I have my reasons. Just say two-sixty. I know what I'm doing. Just call it out. Just call it out. Just say it, and leave the rest to me."*

Several people indicated that they would pay two hundred dollars for the second ring, and then an elderly man who had been enthusiastic about the appliances said he would pay two hundred and fifty. The auctioneer said he had promised to make at least one person happy, and he wanted it to be one of the people who had trusted him with a dollar. He asked for one person who had given him a dollar to have the courage to make a bid. The wife of the Queens couple looked at her husband, but he smiled and shook his head. The auctioneer was staring at the Lion. "Just say it," he said, holding the ring right in front of the Lion's wife. "Just say it, and leave the rest to me."

"Two seventy-five," the Lion said. The auctioneer tossed the ring up in disgust and let it drop to the floor. The Lion joined in the general laughter. The auctioneer shook his head sadly, and said that two hundred and seventy-five dollars was a disgraceful price for the ring. He talked for a few minutes about the value of the rings being offered for sale the following week and about the necessity of advertising the sale. Then he sold the ring to the Lion for two hundred and seventy-five dollars.

# The Sacred Projects

"TULSANS BUY THE PENN CASTLE HERE; TO MAKE IT 'SHOWPLACE' FOR CITY," a headline in the Eureka Springs *Times-Echo* read in July of 1964. For a town of about two thousand people in the Ozark Mountains, Eureka Springs has a surprising number of potential showplaces, and even a couple of buildings that might pass for castles. Known in its brochures as the Little Switzerland of the Ozarks or the Stairstep Town, it was created at the end of the nineteenth century as an elegant resort for people who wanted to "take the waters." ("Eureka Springs waters cure these ailments: kidney troubles, Bright's disease, rheumatism, catarrhal troubles, liver complaints, diseases of the stomach, paralysis, nervous diseases, diseases of women, scrofula, diseases of the eye, general debility, insomnia, diseases of the blood, dropsy, hay fever, rheumatic gout, epilepsy, skin disease," an advertisement said in 1909. "Write Secretary Commercial Club for further information.") Eureka Springs's principal hotel, the Crescent, which was erected in 1886 and completely modernized in 1902, is a castle—an imposing limestone castle perched on a heavily wooded mountain and visible for miles. The main street of Eureka Springs zigzags down a mountain, past springs marked with a tiny park or a gazebo or an old-fashioned outdoor bandstand. If there were such a thing as a Victorian hill town, it would look like Eureka Springs.

Penn Castle, although somewhat short of what is generally thought of as castle size, is one of the larger of the Victorian houses that are built on winding streets in a way that gives almost every house a spectacular view. Its new owners, the *Times-Echo* said, planned to refurnish it in the style of the eighteen-nineties, and, having been very active in Americanism movements throughout the years, they planned to include in the new furnishings personal correspondence from such people as General Douglas MacArthur and Henry Ford. "For example," the article said, "Mr. Ford's personal volume of the Dearborn *Independent*, his publication, will be placed in Penn Castle." The purchasers were identified as Elna M. Smith and her husband Gerald L. K. Smith.

A lot of people who live in Eureka Springs are old enough to know who Gerald L. K. Smith is. Before the First World War, the elegant spa had fallen before the early-twentieth-century advances in medicine like some particularly uncomplicated virus, and Eureka Springs, once the destination of daily Pullman cars, eventually came close to disappearing. After the Second World War, with the traditional industry of tourism restored only to the point of having some cheap package tours from Chicago at the Crescent, Eureka Springs partly made up for the migration of its young by attracting retired people. Eventually, middle-aged people from Arkansas were outnumbered by old people from Chicago. But even those older citizens who remembered that in the thirties Gerald L. K. Smith had been, as people in Eureka Springs tend to say, "controversial" did not become exercised at the prospect of his spending a few months in their town each year during his old age. (Smith is now seventy-one.) Once the Smiths had moved in, they behaved in a way that any elderly, distinguished-looking people who live in a place called a castle might be expected to behave: they smiled at everyone as they wound through the main street in their Lincoln, they spread their trade around to local merchants, they invited some of the town's businessmen in for dinner.

About six months after the purchase of Penn Castle, the *Times-Echo* ran a story headlined "A MONUMENTAL STATUE OF CHRIST

MAY RISE ON MAGNETIC MOUNTAIN." According to the *Times-Echo* account, about a hundred and sixty acres that included three mountaintops overlooking the city had been purchased by a Charles F. Robertson of Los Angeles, acting for "a committee of citizens in various parts of the United States" interested in erecting a "Christ of the Ozarks." The land had actually been bought by Gerald L. K. Smith. Charles Robertson is his assistant. Everett Wheeler, the man who runs the *Times-Echo,* had been told that Smith preferred to keep his name out of the project. The *Times-Echo,* like most weekly papers in the United States, will print pretty much anything that anyone furnishes as long as it doesn't offend anyone. A lot of daily papers in the United States are basically just as docile, but the *Arkansas Gazette,* in Little Rock, the morning paper that most people in Eureka Springs read, is not one of them. A few months after the *Times-Echo* announced Robertson's purchase, the *Gazette* ran a piece headlined " 'CHRIST OF THE OZARKS' STATUE IS PROJECT OF ANTI-SEMITE GERALD L. K. SMITH."

The *Gazette* said that the kind of Americanism movements that Smith had been involved in—the Americanism of Father Coughlin and the Protocols of the Elders of Zion—had been repudiated by virtually every public figure in America, out to and including Billy James Hargis. Everett Wheeler, at the *Times-Echo,* eventually obtained a current copy of *The Cross and the Flag,* the magazine Smith publishes in California. In the issue Wheeler read, there were some warnings about mongrelization and black rapists, an assortment of quotations about Jewish Bolshevism from such sources as the London *Morning Post* of 1919, a piece on the blasphemy of referring to Jesus Christ as a Jew, and one short item in a series of "Smith Missiles" that began casually, "Speaking of Jewish tyranny . . ." Wheeler did not trouble the readers of the *Times-Echo* with these controversial matters. He continued to print the releases of the Elna M. Smith Foundation, the official sponsor of the statue—sometimes with a contributor's line and sometimes without one. Wheeler is the only printer in town, and he was soon doing some of the printing involved in the Christ of the Ozarks project. "Smith is very clever," Wheeler will say to visitors. "He spreads business around town. The printing here, for instance, he could do cheaper in his own printing plant in California."

A number of people in Eureka Springs saw some financial advantage in Smith's presence. Since the elegant days of the spa, the town's economy has gone in peaks and valleys—mostly valleys and not very high peaks—depending on how many people come to see what the Stairstep Town looks like or to search out the five phenomena listed in Ripley's "Believe It or Not" or to shop in the gift shops and antique stores. "There will be no commercialism, there will be no admission charge, no collections and no merchandise for sale in relationship to the exhibit of this sacred object," a typical progress report in the *Times-Echo* said of the sponsors' plans for the statue. "It is their belief that nothing could be more sacrilegious than to bring gross commercialism into the presentation of the statue. It is believed and hoped that thousands of people will visit Eureka Springs just to see the statue, and if this has a constructive influence in the normal business operations of the community all concerned with the statue will be happy."

In letters to the *Gazette* and in an open letter printed in the *Times-Echo* to answer the *Gazette* story, Smith avoided any talk of Jewish tyrannies. "My life has been a very controversial life," he said in the open letter. "It struck us that nothing could bring us more joy during the sunset days of our lives than to pay tribute to our Lord and Saviour Jesus Christ. . . . It would be sinful and unrefined and un-Christian and un-American for anyone to use such a sacred project to promote any controversial activity." In a carefully researched article on Smith and Eureka Springs that appeared in the *Gazette* in May of 1965, Patrick J. Owens found that the citizens who thought one way or the other about Smith (anti-Semitism being a rather remote issue in Eureka Springs) tended to separate his past from his present. It was clear from Owens' pieces and *Gazette* editorials that the only difference between Smith's past and his present was the number of people paying any attention. But Owens had also found that the businessmen who expected the Christ of the Ozarks to start the boom that Eureka Springs had always waited for were determined to know as little about Gerald L. K. Smith as possible. The town does not have a tradition of being picky about who promotes what within the environs. Without provoking any great public outrage, Norman Baker, a notorious cancer-cure quack, turned the Crescent into his "hospital" for a few years in the thirties—before the federal government put him in prison for using the mails to defraud. Eureka Springs was founded, after all, on the financial implications in the belief that water from one spring could cure Bright's disease and water from another would clear up a case of scrofula. Unlike the usual tourist-attraction promoter, Smith hadn't approached the local businessmen for capital. Also, what could be wrong with a statue of Jesus Christ? "Oh, I got a little criticism," Norman Tucker, the man who sold Smith the land and the current president of the Eureka Springs Chamber of Commerce, said later. "Not criticism, really, but a few people kind of kidded me about selling that land too cheap."

The *Times-Echo* continued to print progress reports on the statue—that it would be seven stories high, that its arms would stretch sixty-five feet, that its hands were being hoisted into place. The Smiths let it be known that they had selected a small plot under one of Christ's outstretched arms as their burial place. Smith made his first appearance before a civic group—the Lions Club— and assured everyone that he did not intend to interfere in local politics or to move the headquarters of his publishing operation from California. "Smith . . . talks as though he had no plans at Eureka beyond the statue and a 'sacred museum' he says will be built on the statue's base," Owens had written. "But he talked when he came to Eureka last fall as though he had no plans except to live there."

At the dedication, in July of 1966, the man who was mayor at the time discarded the speech that the Elna M. Smith Foundation had provided for him. He said, instead, that Christ had taught the brotherhood of man and that the statue should be a mecca for all people, regardless of their racial or religious background. The speech was seen as an indirect denunciation of Smith's views on brotherhood—the closest anyone in Eureka Springs had come to denouncing Smith publicly. The revelation that Smith was behind the project had made little difference in press coverage during the statue's construction—the stories in Tulsa or Kansas City or Memphis or Joplin papers that bothered to identify him usually just noted that he had been controversial at one time—and the temporary plaque that went up at the statue carried the line "Project originated and instigated by Gerald L. K. Smith." The *Times-Echo* reported that art critics the world over had marveled at the statue, and the chief sculptor, an elderly man named Emmet Sullivan who had previously specialized in dinosaurs, soon began to build a dinosaur park for someone who owned property near Beaver Dam, a few miles from town. The owner of the dinosaur park had a mountain peak of his own, and he had begun to talk of the possibility of erecting a seven-story statue of General Douglas MacArthur.

The Christ of the Ozarks took its place in Chamber of Commerce brochures and tour books as just about the leading tourist attraction of the Stairstep Town—not as important as the odd look of the city itself but more important than the Miles Mountain Musical Museum or the Carrie Nation House or Quigley's Castle or Onyx Cave. The tourist business began to pick up in Eureka Springs. Local businessmen are not certain how much of the increase was due to the statue and how much to other developments that happened to take place about the same time: the creation of some recreation lakes nearby, the growth of tourism all over the Ozarks, and the development of such other attractions as Dogpatch and Silver Dollar City in the immediate area. There are even a few people in Eureka Springs who believe that Smith, who has managed to make the dissemination of his views to a decreasing number of people an increasingly sound financial proposition, foresaw the boom while vacationing in the area and merely rode along with it. But the stories in the *Times-Echo,* courtesy of the Smith Foundation, indicated that anyone who wanted to know what caused the increase in business, and even what caused the increase in real-estate values, need only glance up at the figure on the mountain. "VISITORS COMING TO SEE THE STATUE NUMBER IN SENSATIONAL THOUSANDS," a characteristic *Times-Echo* headline said.

The idea of a sacred museum evolved into something called the Christ Only Art Gallery, which opened in temporary quarters in a downtown storefront, admission fifty cents. The Smiths, local celebrities in a way, held occasional receptions at the Crescent, making it clear in the *Times-Echo* that everyone was invited regardless of social position, since "their acquaintances through the years have been made up of people of every walk of life from the humblest working men and women to the most prominent citizens of the nation and the world." The *Times-Echo* published articles by Mrs. Smith on the glories of living in Eureka Springs—one of the glories being the statue. Mr. Smith spoke at Rotary and Mrs. Smith spoke at the Women's Club. At a reception in November of 1966, Smith presented some awards to people who had restored Eureka Springs buildings and houses, and officially announced a project that had been hinted at in a progress report the previous February. The progress report, after commenting on the fact that the ministerial alliance had decided to hold its Easter sunrise service at the statue, had said, "There is a constructive ferment in certain areas toward the production of a Passion play on Magnetic Mountain at the scene of the statue."

There is reason to believe that the certain areas referred to were all in Gerald L. K. Smith's mind, and that the idea had been constructively fermenting there for some time. Smith has always said that the inspiration for some kind of Easter tableau came to him as he stood on the mountain one day when the statue was about half finished, and that the inspiration gradually developed into the idea for a Passion play. But as early as January, 1965, about the time the *Times-Echo* ran the first story on Robertson's plan to build a statue, Smith mentioned, in a private letter to Everett Wheeler, the hope that the statue would lead to a Passion play "which might make Eureka Springs the Oberammergau of America." Oberammergau is the Bavarian village in which a medieval Passion play evolved into an event treasured equally by ideological anti-Semites and local tradesmen. The *Arkansas Gazette* took the trouble of reminding everyone that the Passion play, a rendition of Christ's last week on earth, was a device that had been used by anti-Semites for centuries, and that it might not be a coincidence that the one proposed for Eureka Springs was being sponsored by Gerald L. K. Smith. But people in Eureka Springs, most of whom knew nothing about Passion plays except that they are based on the New Testament, preferred to consider the play the same kind of religious project as the statue—maybe even another act of old-age repentance for all of that political controversy. The foundation began to refer to the play, the statue, and the gallery as the Sacred Projects, and people in Eureka Springs continued to assure outsiders that Smith was careful to restrict his controversial activities to California. A new round of progress reports began to appear in the *Times-Echo*. A three-thousand-seat amphitheater for the play would be built directly across from the statue, on a mountain that Smith had named Mount Oberammergau. It was announced that the people of Jerusalem would be played by the people of Eureka Springs—with the aid of dialogue recorded on stereophonic tape—and that local women would help make authentic Biblical costumes.

At the reception where Smith had announced his plans, he had introduced Robert Hyde, a specialist in outdoor drama, who had written the script and had supervised its recording (by actors who, Smith later assured everyone in a *Times-Echo* ad, were all believing Christians). Hyde, it turned out, was also in charge of designing the City of Jerusalem set, helping to build it, producing and directing the play, and appearing in the role of Jesus Christ. "Less than ten acres sold not long ago for more than we paid for the entire 167 acres on which the statue rests," the Smiths wrote in an open letter headlined "GOD BLESS EUREKA SPRINGS AND HER PEOPLE. THANK GOD FOR EUREKA SPRINGS AND HER PEOPLE." And they went on, "One million people have visited the Christ of the Ozarks statue since it was dedicated June 25, 1966. What will the motels and the hotels do when the Passion play opens and we release at 11 P.M. on Mount Oberammergau from 2,000 to 5,000 people for 100 nights during the summer of 1968?" The same letter said, "Builders who miss the opportunity to buy vacant lots within view of the statue and sell modest homes to retired people on the grounds that the front porch or the front deck is in view of the statue will miss one of the greatest development opportunities in the history of any community."

Opening night was July 14, 1968. The presentation was as grandiose as the progress reports had suggested. The street of Jerusalem was four hundred feet long and had real buildings; part of the action was played in the natural setting of the mountain itself; there were real horses and real donkeys and real camels; the prerecorded voices were thrown to the proper place in the huge set so that they matched whatever movements of the actors' lips could be seen from the great distance. Hyde was the only professional in the cast, and the ranks of both the apostles and the scheming Jewish Sanhedrin included a number of Eureka Springs businessmen. A few months before, the National Council of Catholic Bishops had listed a half-dozen or so ways in which a Passion play might be subverted into an exercise in anti-Semitism—portraying Pilate as a more or less innocent bystander, for instance, or presenting the enemies of Christ as caricatures, or highlighting "those texts of the gospel narrative that are amenable to misinterpretation by uninformed audiences, such as: 'His Blood be upon us and upon our children' "— and Hyde's version contained just about all of them.

The *Times-Echo,* in its coverage of opening night, said, "One outstanding newspaperman who flew in from Miami, Florida, to see it and who is thoroughly familiar with the presentations of Hollywood and New York said, 'It is the greatest thing by far of its kind that I have ever seen. . . .' This comment came from Captain George Maines, who was for years with the Hearst organization and is even now the press agent for the great entertainment star Jimmy Durante." An editorial in the *Arkansas Gazette* on July 14th said, "We were never surprised by Mr. Smith's having the nerve to try it. We were surprised, faintly, by Eureka's falling for it, and suppose that, in the end, it was local boosterism that was largely responsible. It has occurred to us before that the local booster spirit in America is such that some Chambers of Commerce would jump at landing the annual reunion of Sepp Dietrich's old *Waffen SS* outfit if it meant a little something in the till."

The Passion play is now the preeminent Sacred Project in Eureka Springs. "Ladies and gentlemen, you are about to witness a dramatic production unexcelled in the history of the Christian Era," the voice over the loudspeaker says at the beginning of each performance. "As the story unfolds, in complete harmony with the scriptural account, you will become increasingly gripped to the point of silence." A plaque at the entrance to the amphitheater commemorates those who have donated a thousand dollars or more to the project. Hyde, who has said that more than fifty per cent of his best friends are Jewish, continues to oversee the production, appear nightly as Jesus Christ, and take a percentage of the gross. Full-page newspaper ads, even in the *Arkansas Gazette,* carry a list of facts about the play—that "special lighting effects facilitate what appears to be an actual ascension," that "one important daily newspaper reporter said that he almost felt the earth shake as the darkness of death enveloped the Cross and Golgotha's Hill," that the play uses "imported camels."

At a booth where visitors to the Christ of the Ozarks register (they are later sent a letter requesting contributions), high-school girls hand out literature for the Passion play. The literature and reprints of the newspaper ads are displayed in most Eureka Springs stores; programs are for sale at the Crescent desk, along with a book on the Sacred Projects by Smith and picture postcards of the play by the Crescent's co-owner. The Christ Only Art Gallery is now in its permanent headquarters on Mount Oberammergau in an adobe-style building next to the Passion play box office—a matching adobe-style building, where tickets are available at two, three, and four dollars. In the gallery, Christ appears not only on canvas but also on china plates, in lava, out of black walnuts, on copper, in porcelain, in needlepoint, in chinquapin wood, out of a cedar tree, and in a reproduction that is given to anyone who makes a twenty-dollar maintenance contribution. The gallery is not actually Christ Only: there is one picture, on velvet, of Robert Hyde as Christ, there is one large oil portrait of Mrs. Smith, and there is one large oil portrait of Mr. Smith.

The Passion play itself is not an issue in Eureka Springs. Even those in town who consider themselves opponents of Smith tend to complain not about the play but about the fact that, like the statue, it is being sponsored by a man who publishes hate literature in California. People in Eureka Springs either do not make the connection between the Passion play and Smith's other activities or have made the connection and prefer to put it out of their minds. It is not unusual for people who refer to Smith as a hatemonger to appear occasionally or even regularly in the Passion play—because its success means business for the town or because "it's something to do." The use of townspeople in the play is sometimes discussed in Eureka Springs as a way to keep teen-agers off the streets in the summertime or a way of giving retired people some activity and a little extra money. (Those who appear receive a share of the gate receipts for themselves or charity—a share that amounts to little more than a token but provides *Times-Echo* headlines like "$2,000

HAS BEEN DISTRIBUTED TO LOCAL CHURCHES AND TO CHARITIES.")
One Eureka Springs clergyman says that three couples from his
congregation who don't particularly care for Smith and have no
business interests in the town regard their regular appearances in
the play more or less as their contribution to the community, that
they considered the *Gazette* attacks on the play and Smith as attacks on Eureka Springs, and that the attacks caused one couple to
cancel their subscription.

Last year, Charles Robertson, who is officially the coordinator
of the Sacred Projects and is listed as editor of the magazine Smith
publishes and has served Smith in tasks that have ranged from taking care of clerical details to running for Vice-President of the
United States, was elected to the board of directors of the Eureka
Springs Chamber of Commerce. After four or five years in which
the Smith Foundation has taken an increasingly important role in
the community, the election seemed natural—as natural as the
Chamber of Commerce advertising the Passion play in its brochures or directing Girl Scout groups and Sunday-school classes to
the box office. The current mayor, co-owner of the Joy Motel, also
named Robertson to the town planning commission. The Sacred
Projects are, after all, considered significant elements in the future
expansion of the town. In fact, the county recently applied through
the Economic Development Administration, which was established
to help generate jobs in economically depressed areas, for about
two hundred thousand dollars in federal money (another fifty thousand to be furnished by the county) with which to rebuild the road
that goes from the highway through Smith's property to the statue
and Passion play. According to the application, the Elna M. Smith
Foundation (Gerald L. K. Smith's name is not mentioned) has
some Sacred Projects to come. "Plans of the Foundation for expansion of the complex over the next ten years include construction
of a replica of the Sea of Galilee and sets depicting the happenings
around it as described in the New Testament," the application says.
"The sets will be animated on the order of animated scenes in Dis-
neyland."

When picking his way through the Victoriana in Penn Castle
with visitors, Smith likes to display a plaque presented to him by
Eureka Springs citizens at a testimonial dinner in appreciation for

what he has done for the town. "It's very provincial, of course," he says of the plaque. "But sometimes something like this can mean more than something more sophisticated." For their part, the Smiths began thanking Eureka Springs profusely for the warmth of its welcome almost before the citizens realized that the Smiths were in town. In an open letter after he announced that there had been a threat to dynamite the statue, Smith wrote, "We have felt so sheltered and so chaperoned that somehow we believe that the whole community constitutes a committee of protectors for our lives and the project that we had the honor to inaugurate." Some people in Eureka Springs maintain that Smith is constantly thanking the community for a warm welcome that doesn't extend past the businessmen who hope to profit from the presence of the Sacred Projects. A Smith Foundation plan to have the churches furnish the actors for the Passion play and receive the actors' share of the gate —a plan that would have assured a steady supply of participants and would have given the churches a financial stake in the play's success—was politely turned down by the ministerial alliance. And this year the alliance did not officially sponsor the Easter sunrise service held at the statue, although some ministers participated as individuals. The foundation has had difficulty this season recruiting enough regular participants to make the bloodthirsty Jerusalem crowd look truly menacing every night. Eureka Springs businessmen say that the organization of the testimonial dinner was another one of the many services performed for Smith by Charles Robertson. "He would approach people publicly to sign up, and they either had to say yes or be rude," a woman who dislikes Smith told a visitor recently. Then she paused for a while. "You know," she went on, "it's a pretty sad day in this town when the worst crime is being rude to a bigot."

There are some people in Eureka Springs who are irritated at the town's increasing connection with Smith, but they have never made their opposition a public issue. There are no activists in Eureka Springs except Gerald L. K. Smith. The people who consider themselves the most sophisticated people in town argue—in the manner that sophisticated people in so many other places where people like Smith operate have argued—that Smith has not really been accepted by the town because, despite his efforts to assume the baronial role, the Better People would never think of asking him to dinner. Many of the businessmen who support the Sacred Projects in one way or another are always happy to share a mildly critical remark to two about Smith. They like to emphasize that they are not, as they say, "in his pocket." Some of them say that they disagree with Smith's views and don't care if he knows it. Some of them say that they would draw the line if Smith tried to interfere in local politics and tell them how to run the town. They enjoy telling visitors that during the latest foundation reception at the Crescent, Smith, apparently forgetting himself for a moment, departed from the benign Christian remarks that have been his Eureka Springs trademark in order to launch a lengthy tirade against the Communist plot to get sex education in the schools—and that a couple of citizens walked out. People who appear in the play—often being a couple of hundred feet from the audience and free to chat among themselves while the words of Christ or some crafty Jewish high priest come over the tape—make mildly sacrilegious comments about who is going to be crucified that evening or what is on the menu for the Last Supper. At one performance, the woman who bathed Christ's feet put green dye in the water, and the woman who played Mary accompanied the line about shedding one last tear over the body of her son by wringing out a sponge of cold water on Hyde.

Although many people in Eureka Springs prefer to talk as if the town merely tolerates Smith and the Sacred Projects or as if Smith is retired or is not really an anti-Semite, a number of businessmen take pains to speak cynically about their participation. "If the Devil came here and brought business and money to the town, I wouldn't complain," a real estate man told a recent visitor. "It's Smith's land. And it's not like he's putting out his magazine. He's drawing people here. A man'd be a damn fool to be against it."

"Then you wouldn't object unless he started putting his magazine out here?" the visitor asked.

"His magazine?" The real estate man smiled. "Well," he said, "we'd have to cross that bridge when we came to it."

# BLACK AND WHITE

# A Hearing: "In the Matter of Disciplinary Action Involving Certain Students of Wisconsin State University—Oshkosh"

After the events of November 21st, ninety-four of the hundred and fourteen black students enrolled at Wisconsin State University— Oshkosh were suspended almost immediately. They were told that a hearing could be requested by filing written notice within ten days. On December 9th, Federal District Judge James E. Doyle, finding that the suspensions had been imposed without due process of law, ruled that the university would have to reinstate the students unless it conducted the hearing on a specific charge and announced the results by December 20th. The Board of Regents of State Universities, which had assumed jurisdiction over the cases, chose to maintain the suspensions, and a hearing was held. In his opinion, Judge Doyle summarized what had happened at W.S.U.O. on November 21st, and then wrote, "The events described in these affidavits cannot be recounted without evoking deep sadness; sadness in the memory of decades, even centuries, of injustice, the fruits of which are now so insistently with us; sadness that this legacy seems now to be producing a profound sickness in some of our people, and specifically some of our younger black people; and sadness that some of them appear so unaware that there is a sickness there."

ROGER E. GUILES, PRESIDENT OF THE UNIVERSITY, TESTIFIES TO BEING THE VICTIM OF UNDESIRABLE ACTIONS IN HIS OWN OFFICE:

GUILES (*A distinguished-looking man with a remarkable resemblance to the actor Fredric March, he speaks slowly from the witness stand and twiddles his thumbs slowly as he speaks.*): I looked up somewhat surprised to find students standing in the doorway or moving through the doorway. . . . I looked up and asked if they had an appointment. . . . As I looked again, I noticed that they were in front of a much larger group of persons, who moved in through the office until there seemed to be no more space available. . . . I was presented with an eight-and-a-half by eleven-size sheet of paper on which were listed a number of demands, and I was told that I was expected to sign the statement. I was reminded that this was not to be a session for discussion or dialogue, that it was my signature that was being demanded and I'd better sign. . . . The students were crowded very tightly against all sides, and other students were sitting on the desk. . . . I pointed out that, Number One, I could not sign the statement. . . . I also asked the students to consider the fact that they were acting in a very undesirable manner and it was not to their advantage to remain in the room. This, however, was not accepted by them, as evidenced by the fact that they did not move. . . . After some fifteen or twenty minutes—a time during which I was unable to really communicate because my statements were interrupted—someone gave the signal of "Do your thing." . . . At that time, the room exploded. . . . In a relatively few minutes, the interior of the office became a shambles, as did the adjacent offices in rapid succession.

Just about everyone in Oshkosh was outraged by the property damage. It was originally reported, erroneously, at about fifteen thousand dollars. The Oshkosh Chamber of Commerce circulated a petition demanding that the students be expelled and be required to pay for the damage—then recalled the petition when it was pointed out that this uncharacteristic participation in collegiate crime and punishment might be misinterpreted as reflecting some animus toward Negro students. A newspaper reporter who collected public reactions in Oshkosh a couple of days after the event found most citizens so angry and astonished that they could explain the destruction only in terms of outside influence, perhaps Communists. It was Oshkosh's first experience with modern student unrest—unless one counts some springtime trouble a couple of years ago when the legislature was considering raising the legal beer-drinking age.

Even people who considered themselves particularly sympathetic to the black students were shocked. "Nobody could understand why they did it," a local reporter told me. "I'm not sure that they understand why themselves." The university, after all, had consciously recruited Negroes and had established a special committee to assist them—the Advisory Committee for Culturally Distinct Students. The demands given to the president on November 21st were basically the same demands that had been turned over to the committee five weeks earlier—demands for an Afro-American cultural center, and black instructors, and courses on the black experience in America—and the university said later that the committee had actually been making considerable progress toward meeting the demands. An old house, due to be torn down next summer, had been offered as a temporary cultural center, but was rejected; a couple of courses concerning black Americans were planned for the spring semester; letters had been sent to predominantly Negro colleges expressing interest in hiring Negro faculty members. Even before the demands were made, the university library had begun to stock *Ebony* and the plays of LeRoi Jones. "I think we did pretty well for five weeks," the committee's chairman told me. "After all, this is a bureaucracy."

PRESIDENT GUILES TESTIFIES TO THE PRESENCE OF BLACK STUDENTS AT THE UNIVERSITY:

LLOYD BARBEE (*the lawyer for most of the suspended students —a bearded, frail-looking man, who is the only Negro in the Wisconsin state legislature*): President Guiles, when you first came to the university here, it was known as a state college, is that not correct?

GUILES: That's right.

BARBEE: And at that time did you have any black students?
GUILES: I believe that we've always had black students. I'm not absolutely sure of that, but as far as I can recall we've always had black students.

They were Africans. When Guiles arrived in Oshkosh, in 1959, after seventeen years at the state college at Platteville, there were about two thousand students enrolled. There may have been a few black African students among them, but until a few years ago black African students were the only kind of black students who came to Oshkosh. In 1964, the new director of admissions, Donald D. Jorgenson—now the registrar and the chairman of the Culturally Distinct Committee—mentioned to Guiles that the university ought to have some American Negroes, and was encouraged by the president's response. The following year, some Negro high-school seniors in inner-city Milwaukee, ninety miles away, began to receive visits from Jorgenson and even free bus tours of the W.S.U.-O. campus; Negro high-school seniors as far away as Newark, New Jersey, began receiving W.S.U.-O. applications in the mail. In 1967, a federally supported educational-opportunity center was established in Milwaukee and began channeling dozens of black students toward W.S.U.-O. The white enrollment had also been growing at an extraordinary rate. W.S.U.-O. now has eleven thousand students. About half of them are studying education—the university was called a teachers college before it was called a state college, and was called a normal school before that—but the university has promised a "sustained thrust toward various forms of interdisciplinary studies." Through its interdisciplinary program in international affairs, W.S.U.-O. made some arrangements with universities in Ghana and Sierra Leone and, this year, began sending students off for a junior year in Africa.

PRESIDENT GUILES TESTIFIES ON THE DIFFICULTY OF ESTIMATING THE BLACK POPULATION OF THE CITY OF OSHKOSH:

BARBEE: Doctor, do you know what the black population of the city of Oshkosh is?
GUILES: I haven't exact information. I have some idea. . . .
BARBEE: What is that idea in terms of numbers?

GUILES: I do not know exactly, because that's not in my realm of responsibility.

BARBEE: Is it large or small?

GUILES: Well, I don't want to get involved here with relative terms—what you mean by small, what you mean by large. I would assume that if you leave off the university population it would certainly be a very small percentage of the population.

If you leave off the university population, there aren't any black people in Oshkosh. There are very few Negroes in any of the cities along the Fox River Valley, from Oshkosh to Green Bay, but Oshkosh, a city of fifty thousand people, has been known for its singular whiteness. Before a few African students began coming to W.S.U.-O., about the only black people Oshkosh citizens ever saw were some who came up from Milwaukee on summer weekends to fish from the bridges. Off the campus, black students have occasionally run into fights and have regularly heard shouts of "Nigger!" from passing cars. In some bars, they have inferred that their patronage wasn't really welcome. More important, they have constantly felt stared at, strange, alone. "In Milwaukee, you go downtown and at least you see some black faces, even behind the counters," one of them told me. "Here everyone looks at you like you're some kind of freak."

Some of the black students didn't feel a lot more comfortable on the campus. The style and experience and dialect of the Milwaukee inner city did not provide an easy bridge for contact with middle-class white students from middle-class white towns in central Wisconsin. "This semester, everything seemed to go wrong," one of the black students told me. W.S.U.-O. is not a particularly demanding college—admission is automatic for any state resident in the top three-quarters of his graduating class; one undergraduate summed the university up as "a high school with ashtrays"—but graduates of black inner-city high schools are likely to have difficulty at any college, and the attrition rate of black students has been high from the start. This fall, a number of them also seemed to be running into administrative problems with the scholarships and loans that had been arranged through state and federal programs. The black students—almost all of them freshmen and sophomores—felt a long way from home. They tended to go around together in groups, and to keep their own counsel. (The white liberals on the faculty who denounced their suspension became close to them only after November 21st.) Few of them took part in the ordinary student activities. Every Wednesday, they got together for a meeting of the Black Student Union and talked of demands that black students should make. "That cultural center was important to us," one of them told me. "It would be a psychological symbol that we exist."

PRESIDENT GUILES TESTIFIES ON THE COMMITTEE THAT HAD BEEN GIVEN THE DEMANDS IN OCTOBER:

BARBEE: Dr. Guiles, what could this . . . committee do in view of the demands that the black students had given it?

GUILES: Well . . . it is true that a large part of their responsibility hinges upon the art of persuasion, but that's not uncommon on a university campus.

"If the university was serious, they would have given the demands to a committee that had some power and money," one of the black students told me. In the opinion of one faculty member sympathetic to them, the black students had a sense of urgency about the demands which the administration never understood—and a need to assert themselves. They found the normal language of academic bureaucrats maddening. They considered the committee a stall, and events since November 21st have tended to convince them that they were right. Despite the talk about hiring black professors, for instance, the students have been told by white liberal faculty members that the departments felt no serious pressure to do so, and the one black instructor now at Oshkosh—a Nigerian —has said that when he gave the university some leads they were ignored; at a university convocation held a couple of days before the hearing Guiles said, "Here faculty is selected on the basis of background and ability for the position to be filled. Race should have nothing to do with it." At the same convocation, university officials replied to accusations that the then accepted damage figure of twelve thousand dollars was inflated by perhaps five hundred per cent. It was explained that the figure had reached the press by mistake—being not the actual damage but the total of an accounting that the university had made, for some reason, to show what the cost would be if every piece of furniture involved were replaced, so that a tipped-over desk showed up as a new desk. "They were really thorough about adding up the damage," one of the black students said. "What they're not interested in is what really caused the damage."

PRESIDENT GUILES TESTIFIES TO PROBLEMS OF IDENTIFICATION IN A LARGE UNIVERSITY:

A STATE ASSISTANT ATTORNEY GENERAL (*acting as prosecutor for the regents*): Now, Dr. Guiles, were these students all black?

GUILES: All of these students who were in the offices—all the students I observed—happened to be black.

ASSISTANT ATTORNEY GENERAL: Now, do you recall any particular student who was in your office on this morning?

GUILES: I think I would have to say, first of all, that with an enrollment of eleven thousand students . . .

It is agreed by the eyewitnesses that only a certain number of the students who were present participated in damaging the president's office, but the eyewitnesses are unable to say which students they were. The damage was what had outraged everybody—that, and the idea of students presenting demands rather than requests to the president—but the hearing had to be held on the charge of blocking the use of a university office. All the students had been arrested for refusing to leave the suite of offices, and the police arrest list had provided the names for the mass suspension—even the names, it turned out, of a few students who, perhaps not having been present the previous evening, when the Black Student Union decided to stage the demonstration, had been in class during the time the damage was done and had only joined the crowd in the presidential suite later in the morning. It is agreed by both sides that many students merely stood in the office all morning, and that some stood there only through the pressure of racial solidarity. (The solidarity was eventually carried further: the black students remaining at W.S.U.-O. presented Guiles with a statement saying that they would not return next semester if any of the suspended students were expelled.) The suspended students say they weren't asking that their demands be met immediately but that the president sign the paper immediately, as an indication of his good faith.

"You know," I was told by a girl who had been present, "we were just praying he would sign that paper."

E. O. THEDINGA, VICE-PRESIDENT FOR STUDENT AFFAIRS, TESTIFIES TO WHAT HE DID UPON HEARING THAT THE BLACK STUDENTS HAD TAKEN OVER THE PRESIDENTIAL OFFICE:

> THEDINGA (*He has been at Oshkosh since 1936 and is as distinguished-looking as President Guiles. The students call him the Silver Fox.*): I immediately picked up the phone and dialed for Mr. James McKee. He responded. I said, "Do you know that the black students have taken over the presidential office and the executive suite?"

The plans for attracting black students to W.S.U.-O. did not establish any office or program to give them special attention once they arrived. Last February, after it was brought to the attention of a W.S.U.-O. faculty member that a number of the black students were carrying unrealistic class loads, he organized an ad hoc committee that was eventually made into the formal Advisory Committee for Culturally Distinct Students. This fall, the university hired James McKee, a Negro, to co-ordinate its efforts for the culturally distinct, and hired one of the first Negro graduates of W.S.U.-O. as his assistant. The committee considered the hiring of McKee a solid accomplishment and considered McKee its link with the students. Testifying at the hearings, McKee went out of his way to indicate his sympathy for the students, but on November 21st he had been as surprised as E. O. Thedinga to hear that they were occupying the president's office. "The students thought of me as part of the administration," McKee told me. "I hadn't talked to them in weeks."

SERGEANT DISCH OF THE OSHKOSH POLICE, AND SERGEANT MISCH
OF THE WINNEBAGO COUNTY SHERIFF'S DEPARTMENT, AND OTHERS
TESTIFY THAT THEY TOLD THE STUDENTS TO LEAVE, IN THE NAME
OF THE STATE OF WISCONSIN, AND LOADED THEM ON TWO HERTZ
RENTAL TRUCKS AND TOOK THEM TO JAIL. BARBEE THEN MAKES
SOME CLOSING REMARKS:

> BARBEE: The university administration here is used to operat-
> ing a certain type of higher-educational institution that it has al-
> ways run and that has not become flexible enough to meet the
> realities of the current generation . . . the university attempted
> to handle the situation in the normal middle-class administrative
> way of appointing a committee . . . and engaged in the kind of
> vague semantic language that was no substitute for action.

What a college administrator might expect from black students
at a predominantly white Northern university was, of course, quite
a bit different in 1964, when the idea of recruiting Negroes came
up at W.S.U.-O., from what it is today. "I think a lot of people here
thought it would be a good idea both for the black students and for
the broadening of the white students, a lot of whom come from
pretty parochial backgrounds," a faculty member told me. "I think
that even after students were being recruited directly from the
ghetto there was some feeling that they would just be black versions of our middle-class white students. It was hard to accept the
idea that they had different patterns of behavior, different expecta-
tions." Some of the black students I spoke with during the hearings
had reached the conclusion that the entire program was cynical—a
way to qualify for federal grants. (The university says there is absolutely no federal money in question.) A lot of the black students,
though, think the administration wanted to do the right thing. "I
think they were sincere," one of them said. "They just didn't know
what they were being sincere about."

ROBERT SILVERSTEIN, A LAWYER REPRESENTING SEVERAL OF THE
STUDENTS, MAKES SOME CLOSING REMARKS:

These students were trying to tell us something . . . obviously
the signing of that paper by the president was nothing more than
a symbol—a symbol saying "Yes, we realize we haven't listened.
We're listening."

THE ASSISTANT ATTORNEY GENERAL MAKES SOME
CLOSING REMARKS:

I'm not going to engage in a philosophical or a sociological argument. . . . However, I don't believe that any group of students,
whether they be black or white, has the right to present such an
ultimatum as was presented to President Guiles on the morning
of November 21st. No group has that right.

Two days after the hearing ended, the Board of Regents, adher-
ing to the time limit set by Judge Doyle, expelled ninety of the
ninety-four suspended students.

# Categories

The position of the Church of Jesus Christ of Latter-Day Saints affecting those of the Negro race who choose to join the Church falls wholly within the category of religion. It has no bearing upon matters of civil rights.—*The First Presidency, Church of Jesus Christ of Latter-Day Saints. December, 1969.*

Most Americans believe that a moral issue can be contained within a category, and they often find themselves astonished or irritated by those Americans who do not. A lot of university trustees can't imagine why students who are receiving a perfectly peaceful liberal education should concern themselves with the fact that some other department of the same institution happens to do research for the Department of Defense. Most Americans do not hold a Rockefeller in New York accountable for what kind of regime his family's bank helps support in South Africa. But a lot of young people and black people insist on considering everything connected. Brigham Young University, which is operated by the Mormon Church, happens to be one of the few places in the country where even the students believe in the sanctity of categories, making it difficult for nearly everyone there to understand how objection to a Mormon religious belief could be translated into rudeness to the B.Y.U. basketball team. In reaffirming that the priesthood which every male

Mormon must hold in order to participate fully in the Church, would remain closed to Negroes, the First Presidency clearly stated not only that the matter was wholly within the category of religion but also that in the civil category the Church specifically teaches that all of God's children should have equal constitutional rights. Furthermore, the University's president has pointed out, the Church has nothing to do with arranging athletic events; and, furthermore, the coaches often say, some of the players are not even Mormons and the athletic field would obviously not be the place to argue politics or religion even if they were. Yet B.Y.U. basketball players can hardly appear anywhere without being hooted at as racists, and Stanford University announced last fall that it would no longer meet B.Y.U. in athletic contests. Keeping the argument within its original category, Ernest L. Wilkinson, the president of B.Y.U., called Stanford's action "flagrant religious discrimination."

Since the demonstrators obviously have no interest in joining the Mormon Church, it follows to any strict categorizer that they are insincere troublemakers who have merely chosen B.Y.U. athletics as a shortcut to national publicity. B.Y.U. distributes an article from the N.C.A.A. newspaper in which the editors, in their first venture into political undercover work, report being reliably informed that revolutionaries were laying their plans against B.Y.U. last summer. B.Y.U. also makes available reprints of an anti-Mormon article from a Communist newspaper—a get-the-Mormons signal to the Communist Conspiracy, according to an accompanying analysis by W. Cleon Skousen, a former Salt Lake City police chief who is a member of the B.Y.U. religious instruction department. It is assumed by nearly everyone at B.Y.U. that even if the Communists are not behind the demonstrations the people who are behind them have chosen an innocent party for their abuse, and the result is often described around B.Y.U. as "persecution." Mormons have been persecuted for their religious beliefs before, of course, and some Mormons explain the current difficulties almost completely as more of the same—an unpleasant and unfair but not unexpected attack from the Gentiles. What strikes the B.Y.U. administration as particularly unjust about dragging the B.Y.U. basketball team into the argument from four or five categories away is that B.Y.U.

students are not merely innocent but demonstrably more innocent than any other students. "The students are hurt and angry," I was told by a University public relations man. "There's probably not a higher-type student body in the United States. Look at that campus! Not a drop of paper on it. No cigarette butts. When the flag goes up, the students come to attention. On other campuses, the students burn the flag. Our students are patriotic and they're well dressed, and these are the people who are being persecuted. The kooks, the hippies, the filthy people—they're not persecuted."

If a B.Y.U. student acknowledges that any of the black students demonstrating against the basketball team are sincere, he usually explains their actions as a failure to understand. It is said they fail to understand that Mormons have nothing to say about Church doctrine, since a belief central to the religion is that doctrine comes, through a process of continuing revelation, from God to the president of the Church and from the president to the membership. There is a feeling among students and administrators that the press has not fairly presented the University's position that the restriction on Negroes holding the priesthood is purely a religious matter and has no connection with the University's policies on race—the complete whiteness of every basketball team ever fielded by B.Y.U. having been explained at length within a separate category. I often asked B.Y.U. students about the possibility that a black student at Arizona or Colorado State might not believe that such distinctions were important compared to the presence of yet another institutionalized implication of his inferiority. Most of the B.Y.U. students I asked would pause for a few moments, as if they had never considered that possibility, and then acknowledge that a sincere black student might understand everything perfectly well and decide to demonstrate against the B.Y.U. basketball team anyway—even though the result would be persecution of an innocent party.

The Mormon Church leaves little room for loyal dissent, and Brigham Young University leaves practically no room at all. Mormonism has not only a strong belief in revelation as the only source of doctrinal change but also an authoritarian structure and a tight sense of community and a history of outside pressure that sometimes makes disagreement seem the equivalent of ammunition for the Gentile enemy. Yet there are Mormons who manage to express disagreement about the denial of priesthood to Negroes—to argue about its origins and point out its contradictions—and still stay within the Church. At B.Y.U.—where ninety-five per cent of the students and virtually all of the faculty are Mormons, and mostly churchgoing, orthodox Mormons—there are few people who hold such views, and fewer still who might want to express them publicly, and no one at all who does. The student newspaper, which reports on the demonstrations and has devoted a lot of space to the University's protestations of innocence, has been instructed to print no discussion of the Church doctrine that is presumably causing all the trouble, and most students agree that there is no reason to argue about something they have no control over. Although the man-in-the-street interviews in the student paper's special issue on the Stanford decision included one or two with students who thought there might be some prejudice at B.Y.U., the rest of the issue was virtually identical to a special issue of the alumni paper on the same subject—a collection of official statements about the absence of discrimination at B.Y.U., a series of answers to such commonly asked questions as why there are only three or four Negroes among the University's twenty-five thousand students ("their decision, not our policy") and a supportive column by Max Rafferty. B.Y.U. faculty members have always had difficulty distinguishing the positions of the University administration from the positions of the Church—the Church's General Authorities also serve as B.Y.U.'s board of trustees—and normally express no disagreement with either. At B.Y.U., no one on the faculty has tenure.

Although the young men who serve tours as missionaries for the Church are known for wearing ties and neat white shirts, a Mormon with long hair and a beard could be married in the Salt Lake City temple—unless, of course, one of his great-grandfathers was a Negro. At B.Y.U., someone with long hair and a beard would not be allowed to register for classes. Although Mormons undoubtedly tend to be politically conservative, there are liberals as well as conservatives in the Church leadership. At B.Y.U., Wilkinson regularly lectures student assemblies on the federal government's having become a Socialistic monster, and a few years ago it was revealed that there was a network of student spies reporting to the administration on what was said in the classroom by a few professors suspected of holding liberal political views. At B.Y.U., peaceful picketing is not permitted, the Young Democrats are the most leftwing political group allowed on campus, and the two political bumper stickers available at the bookstore of the Ernest L. Wilkinson student center say "I'm Proud to Be an American" and "I'm a Member of the Silent Majority."

The strain of political conservatism is sufficiently strong in the Church that under Wilkinson's emphasis it becomes practically Church doctrine to B.Y.U. students. Among the Mormon religious pamphlets displayed at the bookstore is one called "Civil Rights— Tool of Communist Deception," by Ezra Taft Benson, one of the twelve apostles of the Church. Not long ago, when the campus Young Americans for Freedom were criticized for displaying the Book of Mormon among such books as Skousen's *The Naked Communist,* someone sent a letter to the student paper pointing out that David O. McKay, who was president of the Church until his death in January, had recommended *The Naked Communist* to the faithful as an "excellent book." The most politically conservative department at B.Y.U. is the religion department, some members of which are said to have quit worrying about the Communist Conspiracy and switched their concern to something called The Illuminati, an ancient cabal that supposedly still looms S.M.E.R.S.H.-like above even the Red Menace.

The University does permit a weekly free forum during the lunch hour in one of the lounges of the student union, although there have been some complaints that it amounts to no more than the handful of campus radicals (Young Democrats) talking to each other. The day I saw it, all but a few people in the lounge just happened to be studying or chatting there when the forum started. The radicals were arguing that the Mormon tradition included an intellectual search for the truth and that people should be judged for themselves rather than by the length of their hair; the only applause was for speakers who praised the University or defended its dress regulations. During the discussion of dress, one young man in the audience said that the reason for strict control of student appearance was obviously not religious—the prophets of the Church, after all, wore beards—but economic, the realities of the marketplace having led the University to use the uniquely respectable dress and behavior of its students to raise money. He wasn't objecting; he thought it was obviously worth shaving his beard if shaving helped build a new field house.

The largest single gift to the University—a thousand-acre ranch in San Clemente said to be worth several million dollars—was presented in 1967 by Ray Reeves, the inventor of the air-wedge sole, and his wife Nellie. The University invited the couple to Provo for the official presentation, and students were given "Thanks, Ray and Nellie" lapel stickers to wear for the ceremonies. "Some time ago my wife, Nellie, and I read a syndicated newspaper article describing Brigham Young University as a place where youngsters still had ideals, still cut their hair, still believed in God," Ray Reeves said. "We had to see it, so we drove to Provo, Utah. The young people at B.Y.U. were all clean-cut, good-looking. We didn't see any miniskirts. There was no beatnik atmosphere. Those students had their feet on the ground. Instead of finding fault, they were accepting leadership. In short, we liked the way the University was being run. Our association with the people at B.Y.U. has been marvelous. To show our support, we've given the University our ranch."

The reaction of B.Y.U. to the continuing demonstrations is not likely to diminish the reputation it has acquired among those who are pleased to find one university that stands up to Minority Pressure Groups. The football coach has recruited B.Y.U.'s first black football player, after making it clear to him that interracial dating is not allowed. But according to the Provo paper the coach recently told a local Chamber of Commerce breakfast, "A lot of people are mad at me right now because they feel we are giving in." There are a few people at B.Y.U. who are considering suggesting to the administration that the University prove the sincerity of its statements about the civil category by recruiting Negro students for the same kind of special-help program that B.Y.U. runs for American Indians, but Wilkinson says that limitations on the University's space preclude recruiting of any kind. At the strong urging of the administration, students who organized a nighttime, non-credit Student Academy at B.Y.U. this semester reduced their proposed courses in Afro-American history and literature to one composite course;

until the planned curriculum was made public, the faculty members involved were under pressure from the administration to teach no course at all on the subject.

Intellectuals who try to remain within the Church have always had to face the tension between their faith and their intellectual curiosity, and the few students at B.Y.U. who have such problems find them more acute these days. Wilkinson talks of the priesthood restriction on Negroes as if it were some isolated religious practice like total immersion among the Baptists; he often says that Stanford's decision was the equivalent of B.Y.U. refusing to play Notre Dame because of different ideas on divorce. But the B.Y.U students who tend to approach official statements questioningly know that those students who have been on missions in the South proselyte only among white people, that the traditional attempts by Mormons to explain the restriction on Negroes all contain some implication of inferiority, that the Church is noted for giving its official support to right-to-work laws rather than civil-rights legislation, that the elderly men who preside over Mormonism have sometimes made remarks that would cause the least conspiratorial Negro to shout at B.Y.U. basketball players. (The current president of the Church, who completed his college education in the ninetenth century, was quoted a few years ago as saying that "darkies are wonderful people.") A Mormon social scientist has done an attitude study in which he concludes that Mormons in California are no more prejudiced against Negroes than other whites are, but neither side of the argument is heard at B.Y.U.

The vast majority of B.Y.U. students accept the official statements of the University administration as unquestioningly as they accept official statements of the Church authorities. It has never occurred to most of them to compare the statement of the University that black athletes are recruited "under exactly the same terms as any other athletes" and the public acknowledgment by coaches that they have warned Negro prospects that a black athlete may not be happy at B.Y.U. because of the lack of "social life." B.Y.U. has never appeared to place the stimulation of intellectual curiosity high on its list of priorities The lack of tenure and of a faculty senate have meant some problems with accreditation and the loss of the kind of professors who obviously wouldn't teach in a university that didn't take those institutions for granted, but there has been an accompanying absence of faculty dissent. In the tension between faith and intellect, the University has been a strong supporter of faith. Although the Mormons—people who have placed great value on education—have created what they often call the largest privately operated university in the United States, it is not really the intellectual center of the Church. The center of serious discussions about the race situation and the Church is the state-supported University of Utah. The principal forum for Mormon intellectuals—a fascinating quarterly called *Dialogue*—is published in California rather than Provo, and includes hardly anyone from B.Y.U on its board of editors. B.Y.U. has presumably chosen to make its reputation on instilling its students with religious faith and patriotism and high standards of personal morality. As far as "building character" is concerned, Wilkinson said in a speech not long ago that universities such as Harvard and Yale—and, of course, Stanford—have "passed their zenith." In its own terms, B.Y.U. has assumed leadership in the field.

# Doing the Right Thing Isn't Always Easy

JAMES PERRILL AND FRANK SOUTHWORTH SAID THE ISSUE WAS
FORCED BUSING

When Martin Luther King was assassinated, the Denver Board of
Education resolved to integrate the schools. The vote was five to
two. The supporters included the only Negro board member, who
had offered the resolution; Edgar Benton, a lawyer in his early forties, who had been the city's most articulate advocate of school
integration for a half-dozen years; two relatively conservative
board members whose views on integration had changed during
their tenure; and a state senator named Allegra Saunders, who
sometimes seemed to interpret majority rule to mean that she was
obligated to go along with the majority, wherever it happened to be
going. In the Denver public schools, the twenty per cent of the
students who belong to the Spanish-surname population usually referred to as Hispanos have, as a group, the lowest academic achievement and the highest dropout rate. But it is the black children—
about fifteen per cent—whose schooling is most restricted by *de
facto* segregation and whose parents have been the most insistent
about the need for change. As a first step toward integration, the
school board eventually resolved, by the same five-to-two margin,
to adjust the ratio of black to white in the schools of one area next

fall by changing some attendance boundaries and transporting some children by bus—devices that are familiar to the white citizens of many Northern cities under the name of Destroying Neighborhood Schools by Forced Busing.

The school board held public hearings on the resolutions. Most of the people who testified—many of them members of an integrationist coalition that had been formed after King's death—expressed approval of the integration plan or criticized it for being too mild. They became known in Denver as A Vocal Minority— the assumption being that most people (at least, most white people) would express a contrary opinion if they happened to be the kind of people who testified at school-board hearings. There was a lot of talk in Denver about how the school board had been pressured by A Vocal Minority into acting contrary to the desires of The Silent Majority. This spring, about a year after King's death, a simple remedy presented itself to The Silent Majority. The seats held by Ed Benton and Allegra Saunders came up for election. Two conservative Republicans named James Perrill and Frank Southworth announced that, in the interests of giving the citizens a clear choice, they were running for the school board as a team committed to combining with the board's two dissenters to form a majority that would rescind the integration resolutions. The integrationists organized behind Benton and Monte Pascoe, a young lawyer with similarly strong views about the necessity of integration, and the Democratic Party officially endorsed the ticket—an endorsement that failed to prevent five more Democrats from running as independents. The clear choice Perrill and Southworth had in mind concerned forced busing. Their campaign advertising started with billboards proclaiming them to be FOR neighborhood schools and AGAINST mandatory busing—a position that also served to sum up the educational philosophy of most of the independent candidates—and it ended with a newspaper advertisement that asked, "Why Mr. Benton, are you for Forced Busing which will Destroy the Neighborhood Schools?" In their public appearances, Perrill and Southworth managed to elaborate on that limited theme with a kind of creative redundancy. Mandatory busing and forced busing combined to become mandatory forced busing. They also mentioned crosstown busing, massive busing, and massive crosstown busing. By the end of the campaign, Southworth was talking about "forced mandatory crosstown busing on a massive scale."

## ALL THE CANDIDATES EXCEPT BENTON AND PASCOE SAID THE ISSUE WAS NOT INTEGRATION

All the candidates said that they personally believed in integration —the general rule in such campaigns being that a nominal commitment to integration is expected from everyone involved except the voters. Perrill said integration would come about when the economic status of Negroes improved and when some changes were made in men's minds—the kind of changes that could not be dictated by laws or resolutions. He and Southworth said that voluntary busing would be fine—another rule being that any time white people are expected to associate with black people they ought to have a choice in the matter. All of the candidates who were running against forced busing said they were distressed at the implication that they harbored ill feelings against other men on the basis of race, creed, or color. The implication seemed particularly galling to Nathan Singer, the most entertaining of the independent antibusing candidates, an aeronautical engineer who read intently from set speeches that included dramatic proclamations and an occasional rhyme ("Be aware, vote with care," or "Some may choose not to accuse, but I shall"). At one of the many P.-T.A. meetings addressed by all the candidates, Singer offered as a proof of his tolerance the fact that Sammy Davis, Jr., belongs to his fraternity. "And anyone who wants to check that," he told the McMeen Elementary School P.-T.A., "can call the national headquarters of Tau Delta Phi, in Chicago."

## BENTON AND PASCOE SAID THE ISSUE WAS NOT FORCED BUSING

The Benton-Pascoe campaign recognized that there were genuine concerns about the inconveniences or educational disadvantages that busing might bring, and about whether or not busing was really the best way to provide equality of education, and about integration itself. Benton-Pascoe advertisements did not attempt to explain the board's intricate plans for integration, but in answering questions in smaller groups the candidates explained that the racial composition of each school would reflect the entire school district's population, so that white children would be bused to schools that would become predominantly white and black children would be bused to schools with a substantial black minority.

By the end of the campaign, though, a lot of the Benton-Pascoe canvassers came to believe that most of the questions people raised about the problems inherent in busing were not meant to be answered. Benton repeatedly pointed out that the Denver school board had, for one administrative reason or another, employed forced busing in the schools to some degree for at least forty years —a process that had involved hundreds of thousands of schoolchildren without provoking any citywide controversies about the length of the ride or the provisions made for taking care of a sick child. (Nine thousand children are now bused—about half as many as would have to be bused in the final stage of integration. As it happens, Destroying Neighborhood Schools is an old habit of the Denver school board, which used to manipulate boundaries to avoid having to send white children to predominantly black schools; in fact, some of the children in the area most bitterly opposed to the proposed destruction of neighborhood schools would actually be transferred to schools closer to their homes.) Late one night, a few people were at Pascoe's house talking over the evening's meetings when the phone rang. The caller shouted an obscenity at Pascoe and called him a nigger-lover. Pascoe smiled when he repeated the conversation to his guests. "I've probably met that guy at some meeting," he said. "And he's told me he's all for integration, but what about the effect busing will have on after-school activities or parent participation?"

BENTON AND PASCOE SAID THE ISSUE WAS DOING THE RIGHT THING

What else could they say? Candidates normally try to appeal to the voter's self-interest, and Benton and Pascoe could hardly argue that sending children to school out of the neighborhood on a bus was a convenience that every taxpayer had been looking forward to. White people opposed to busing didn't have to be racists but merely people who didn't feel a strong enough commitment to integration to make any personal sacrifices for it. As a minor theme, the Benton-Pascoe campaign linked the integration plan to the future health of the city. Compared to other cities of similar size, Denver still has a small Negro population, and a relatively high percentage of it is middle-class; by chance, the expansion of the Negro neighborhood has been toward solid neighborhoods that have houses desirable to whites. Benton and Pascoe argued that Denver still had time to prevent the inner-city decay and separated societies that are found in Eastern cities—the first step being the school board's plan to prevent East High School and Smiley Junior High School, the most important schools on the edge of the Negro neighborhood, from becoming all black. But nobody in the Benton-Pascoe campaign really believed that the white people who live in, say, the outlying middle-class residential districts of southeast Denver actually consider their future linked to the state of the inner city or that they feel any urgency about preventing the creation of separate societies. When Pascoe visited a high school in the area, the complaint expressed about the Negroes who had come to the school by bus under a small experimental program was that only two of them had joined the Pep Club.

The appeal to white people that Benton and Pascoe were left with was an appeal to do what is right in reversing the inequalities existing in Denver schools. "Doing the Right Thing Isn't Always Easy," their brochure said. "But Doing the Right Thing Is Always Worth Doing." The issue, Benton said in one speech, was whether "there is enough humanity and enough charity among the majority to hold out a helping hand to these children, not to say, 'We believe in holding out a helping hand, but there are many reasons why we can't do it.' "

PEOPLE IN PARK HILL SAID THE ISSUE WAS PARK HILL

A few years ago, the customary housing pattern of Negro expansion and white panic selling may have been reversed in the southern part of an area called Park Hill—an attractive, convenient area that was once considered the place to live in Denver—mainly because of the efforts of a neighborhood organization called the Park

Hill Action Committee. The houses that come up for sale in Park Hill now are bought by white people as well as black people—young people of the type who prefer a solid old house to life in the subdivisions, or liberals who welcome the opportunity to live in an integrated neighborhood, or just people looking for a good buy. East High School and Smiley Junior High School, which would both be given large white majorities by the integration plan, serve Park Hill. Without the plan, East, which is about forty per cent black, and Smiley, which is about seventy-two per cent black, represent the most serious threat to Park Hill's future as an integrated neighborhood. A number of Park Hill people—black and white—considered the Benton-Pascoe campaign the culmination of a nine-year fight. The campaign presented a rare opportunity, one resident observed during a huge Park Hill fund-raising party for Benton and Pascoe. People could work for their beliefs and their property values at the same time.

### MOST OF THE CANDIDATES SAID THE ISSUE WAS THAT THE BOARD HAD FORCED ITS WILL ON THE PEOPLE

In the North, integration is now almost invariably an elitist movement. The more democratic the decision-making process, the smaller the chance any plan for purposeful integration has of being put into effect. There had been no clear-cut integration vote in Denver, but the results in the previous school board election and the defeat of a school bond issue a few years ago were both interpreted as being caused partly by anti-integration sentiment. People who serve on a school board in a city like Denver—seeing ghetto schools at first hand, studying the difference in achievement between the average Hispano child and the average Anglo child, reading reports about a national crisis in race, feeling themselves responsible for the future, listening to A Vocal Minority—are bound to take some actions that are difficult to explain to The Silent Majority. The school board election became partly an argument about the extent to which public officials should represent their constituents—whether, a Denver *Post* article said, the public preferred school board members who lead or "school board members who, in effect, follow the wishes and feelings—including prejudices—of the voters who elected them." Perrill often said that "power comes from people, not from ideas," and that the integration resolutions had to be rescinded in order to clear the air and restore the confidence of the people in the board. All the anti-busing candidates emphasized that the people had not been given a choice—that forced busing for forced integration had been forced on them.

In Denver, both school integration and the preservation of neighborhood schools have been white-collar movements; with little heavy industry, Denver has a relatively small working-class population. But the Benton-Pascoe campaign—in its formulation of the issue as something approaching noblesse oblige, and in the backgrounds of its candidates and its staff—had a kind of Ivy League tone. When one independent candidate, a truck driver named Robert Crider, finally lost his temper near the end of the campaign, the first thing he thought to say was that the problem on the school board for the past eight years had been that Ed Benton thought he knew more than anyone else.

SOME NEGRO LEADERS SAID THE ISSUE WAS BASIC SYMPATHY

Black separatists were said to be treating the election as merely the final frivolous delay before serious talk began on who was to control the schools of each neighborhood. But even the integrationist Negroes who supported Benton and Pascoe seemed reluctant to go into details about a program whose premise is that the way to improve the performance of black children is to expose them to white children. About a week before the election, the most influential Negro adviser to Benton and Pascoe suggested that campaigning in the Negro areas should concentrate not on the complicated arguments about busing but on the fact that Benton and Pascoe would be basically sympathetic to minorities. During the last weekend of the campaign, the handbills passed out in the Negro neighborhoods contained a simple statement of why Negroes should vote for Benton and Pascoe: "They're for us."

### THE HISPANOS DIDN'T SAY MUCH OF ANYTHING

In Denver, Hispanos are noted for being politically silent. They vote Democratic, but they often don't vote. The most visible and by far the most militant Hispano leader, Rudolfo (Corky) Gonzales, is a separatist who believes that Negro pressure for integration is just a manifestation of the black man's inferiority complex; the few conservative leaders who exist to form a link with the Anglo community would probably agree. In between, there is no equivalent of the usual Negro integration organization—and little organization of any kind. The Hispanos, many of them migrants from the isolated farming villages of northern New Mexico and southern Colorado, are generally worse off economically than Negroes in Denver. But those Hispanos who think about such matters tend to believe that neither the causes nor the cures for the Hispanos' plight have much in common with those usually associated with the problems of the black community. Most Hispanos don't appear to be concerned with such issues one way or the other. The only approach that the Benton-Pascoe forces could think of to make to them was an appeal to party loyalty. One Benton-Pascoe brochure had on the back page a long explanation of busing under the headline "TO-DAY'S SCHOOL IS A WORKING MODEL OF TOMORROW'S SOCIETY." In the version distributed in Hispano neighborhoods, the equivalent space was taken up with block letters saying "ENDORSED BY THE DENVER DEMOCRATIC PARTY."

### BENTON SAID THE ISSUE WAS EDUCATING THE PUBLIC

From the start, Benton and Pascoe knew they would probably lose, but everyone in their campaign seemed surprised at the magnitude of the defeat. Soon after the polls closed, it became obvious to the people who had gathered in Benton-Pascoe headquarters that Southworth and Perrill would win by a margin of at least two to one. A heavy Perrill-Southworth vote was expected in outlying white neighborhoods, but it also came in some white areas closer to the center of town. One Benton-Pascoe worker pointed out an area in the East High district and said that in that neighborhood it was logical to expect even pure bigots—at least, bigots with some fore-sight—to vote for Benton and Pascoe on grounds of self-interest; the integration plan would mean increasing the white enrollment of their children's school and, probably, increasing the value of their property. "That precinct went two to one against us," the worker said. "Reason has nothing to do with this."

In a speech at the party for campaign workers that night, the Benton-Pascoe campaign manager said that Ed Benton and Monte Pascoe had had the courage to step out in front of the community and try to lead. Benton was asked by a local radio station what the results indicated. They indicated, he said, that it was difficult to present complicated issues concerning inequality to the public, and that it was difficult to persuade people to change established ways of doing things—ways of doing things that had become convenient for one section of the population and devastating for another. "It's always difficult to educate people," he went on, "whether it's children in the classroom or people in the community."

# Metaphors

Martin Luther King, Jr., was a great man for metaphors. Among Southern Negro ministers in general, of course, the metaphor has always been indispensable to human communication, but King used it with unique effectiveness. In the early sixties, the civil-rights movement in the South included almost nightly mass meetings in Negro churches, and sometimes, as I sat listening to King explain how the long, dark night of discrimination was going to give way to the great dawn of emancipation, bringing a bright new day of equality and freedom, it occurred to me that the easiest way for white Southerners to cripple the movement would be to pass city ordinances against the use of metaphors in public. Their lawyers would argue solemnly that the ban was strictly non-racial in character, although everyone would know that white-segregationist orators would be unaffected, since their indispensable figure of speech was the simile ("Why, that ole boy was just as happy as a turkey on the day after Thanksgiving").

I was reminded of all that a few days ago when a reporter asked Ralph Abernathy if members of the Poor People's Campaign were responsible for throwing rocks through some windows in the Supreme Court building and he said that the only rocks his people were concerned with were "the rocks of injustice that we are bang-ing against until they come crumbling down." For anyone who sat through those church meetings in the South, Resurrection City, the encampment that the Poor People's Campaign has strung along the parkland between the Lincoln Memorial and the Washington Monument, sometimes seems like not only the implementation of a Martin Luther King idea but the materialization of a Martin Luther King metaphor—some elaborate, resonant, five- or six-sentence construction about the community of the impoverished being a crumbling eyesore among the shiny monuments to American democracy.

One of the problems of making a metaphor visible is that it becomes an issue itself. When the mud in Resurrection City became so thick that overshoes were sucked right off people's feet, I half expected to hear something about the poor people slogging along through the thick mud of despair and desperation while the affluent whisked by them on the broad throughways of indifference; instead, most of the talk in Washington was about how muddy it was in Resurrection City. Andrew Young, the executive vice-president of King's Southern Christian Leadership Conference, tried to tell reporters that the important point about the mud was that the poor people in America—at least, the poor people in small towns and rural areas—live in mud all of their lives, but the news stories were about whether or not Resurrection City had become a health hazard. Young told me that the S.C.L.C. had taken a medical survey of the four hundred people who came to Washington from Memphis and had found that a hundred of them were sick. "Everybody said that there were sick people on the march," he said. "The point is that on any given day a quarter of the poor people in this country are sick."

Abernathy tried to redirect attention one day when reporters were asking about some stress between the Negroes and the Mexican Americans in the campaign. "The issue is not Resurrection City," he said at a press conference. "The issue is not any kind of dissension or strife that might arise in Resurrection City. The issue is poverty." But Washington has not accepted Resurrection City as a metaphor. Having agreed that Congress is unlikely to be affected by the sight of a few thousand poor people, commentators tend to blame the Poor People's Campaign for a futile demonstration rather than blame Congress for being unresponsive to the needs of the poor. The poor in Resurrection City have come to Washington to show that the poor in America are sick, dirty, disorganized, and powerless—and they are criticized daily for being sick, dirty, disorganized, and powerless.

Around Resurrection City, everyone is addressed as Brother or Sister. The habit is so widespread that I even heard one of the Indian spokesmen referred to as Brother Mad Bear. When Jesse Jackson, the first city manager of Resurrection City, began leading demonstrators to the Department of Agriculture every day, the man chosen to handle the situation for the Department was the Assistant Secretary for Administration, an erect, businesslike, tight-lipped man named Joseph M. Robertson; Jackson merrily greeted him as Brother Joe or Brother Roberts. The Secretary of Agriculture himself is referred to as Brother Freeman. Members of one of a variety of peace-keeping organizations in Resurrection City are identified by stenciled letters on the back of their jackets as Peace Brothers. "Brother" and "Sister" are used more or less in the black-ghetto sense of "Soul Brother" and "Soul Sister"—in fact, "Soul" is another popular word in Resurrection City, and the most prominent chant of the movement is 'Soul Power"—but there are echoes of the "Brother" and "Sister" heard in Southern Negro churches. The S.C.L.C. is still dominated by ministers, and when one of them begins to speak an invisible pulpit often seems to slide into place in front of him, melting a news conference or a private conversation into a mass meeting. The demonstrations are another reminder of the days when Negro ministers led boycotts and sit-ins and marches. At one point, the issue between the Poor People's Campaign and the Department of Agriculture was—in addition to how the program for feeding the poor was being administered—whether or not the demonstrators could eat in the Department of Agriculture cafeteria that day. When negotiations had been carried past two o'clock and the Department could report that the cafeteria had closed, Abernathy told the demonstrators that the Department had turned them away in the rain, that the rejection showed how difficult their task would be, and that they therefore must all attend a meeting the next night at the John Wesley A.M.E. Zion Church.

After the poor people had gone back to Resurrection City, the Department of Agriculture held a press conference so that Joseph M. Robertson could tell reporters, "This cafeteria is not a public cafeteria and is run primarily for the benefit of the employees of the Department of Agriculture." It might have been a scene from the South in the early sixties—a businesslike white manager carefully explaining why normal business practices happened to preclude serving Negro demonstrators, and the demonstrators planning to retaliate with a mass meeting at a Negro church.

In using the same techniques to demonstrate in Washington for an end to poverty as they used in the South to demonstrate for an end to segregation, S.C.L.C. leaders have to get along without some useful old enemies, such as Bull Connor and Jim Clark, and have to get along *with* some independent new friends, such as Appalachian whites, Mexican-Americans, and Indians. Resurrection City was overcrowded when the first large contingent of Mexican-Americans and Indians arrived, and, in what later turned out to be a matter of ideological as well as physical convenience, the Mexican-Americans settled in at a private school in Southwest Washington and the Indians moved into a nearby church—giving everyone a principality from which to dispatch emissaries. No one really thought than an instant New Populism was going to spring from the participation of the various groups; Young sees a certain amount of friction as part of the nature of the poor ("You have to get used to the fact that poor folks are fussy") and the nature of the country ("I think the relationship is good, considering that we've been brainwashed for two hundred years by racism").

It is also true that, despite the ritualistic reconciliations, the specific needs of the Negro poor and the Mexican-American poor and the Indian poor do not necessarily coincide. The most prominent Spanish-speaking leader in the Poor People's Campaign is Reies Lopez Tijerina, who has been leading a group of people in New Mexico in a bitter and occasionally violent effort to regain what they claim is land stolen from their ancestors. In style and rhetoric, Tijerina is closer to Stokely Carmichael than to Ralph Abernathy, and he is interested not in jobs and housing but in land—specifically, the land in New Mexico that was dealt with in the Treaty of Guadalupe Hidalgo of 1848. There is no subject from which Tijerina cannot make his way logically to the Treaty of Guadalupe Hidalgo within two or three minutes. He is not interested in seeing Brother Freeman; he wants to see Brother Rusk. The urban Mexican-Americans, of course, have problems that have nothing to do with land, and the Indians are interested in treaties the Mexicans never heard of. When a priest at the church where the Indians were staying told me one rainy day that most of them had gone to the Smithsonian Institution, I asked if a tour had been arranged so that they could pass the time by seeing some of the sights of the capital. "No," he said. "They arranged this themselves. They say there are some relics there that belong to them."

The various groups of poor people have what rich people call communications problems. At a public meeting in the Resurrection City "cultural tent" one day, a young white man with hair down to his shoulders—a member of the California delegation—listened to plans for forming a city council, rose to say that "we don't want to play the white man's game," and suggested, to the horror of the organization-minded Negroes present, that Resurrection City might better be run on some tribal arrangement borrowed from the wonderfully sophisticated governmental structure of one of the great Indian nations. Another day, I saw Abernathy at a meeting in which Negro leaders joined with Mexicans in supporting a cause of the Indians—or, as Abernathy would say, "joined with our brown brothers in supporting our red brothers." The issue was a Supreme Court decision against some Nisqually and Puyallup Indians who were in a fishing-rights dispute with the State of Washington. Abernathy told the audience—largely Mexican—that denying fishing rights in Washington was the same as denying food to poor people in Mississippi, and he reminded everyone about the mass meeting at the John Wesley A.M.E. Zion Church. "That's easy to remember," he told the Mexicans. "John Wesley, the famous Methodist preacher. Then African Methodist Episcopal Zion."

The next day, Abernathy was marching arm in arm with Indian and Mexican leaders to demonstrate against the decision—undoubtedly the first Negro civil-rights leader to be in the front line of a demonstration against the Supreme Court. At demonstrations, the issues—the fishing rights of Indians, the size of the delegation allowed in—become less important than the mood of militancy. At the end of the day, Tijerina, standing on the steps of the court, orated against "this criminal conspiracy called the Supreme Court of the United States," and a Negro in the audience shouted, "Preach, brother, preach!"

A few days after the Supreme Court demonstration, a group of Indians went to the National Press Building to protest the coverage —most of which was concerned more with the broken windows than with the fishing rights of Indians. The demonstration was, in fact, a good illustration of how difficult it is for Indians to make their grievances known by public protest. The cameramen present descend on somebody in Indian regalia, the reporters hunt down some Indian with a strange name, somebody makes a joke about the Indians being on the warpath again—and that is usually that.

The Poor People's Campaign in general has a problem with the press. In a way, it exists for the press—the press is the means of making the metaphor visible all over the country—and at a Senate subcommittee hearing Abernathy was told by Senator Gaylord Nelson, of Wisconsin, that the Campaign had already been a success by inspiring so much coverage of poverty by magazines and television. But relations with the press have been complicated. Neither the press nor the residents of Resurrection City are ever quite certain if a picture of a little boy standing in mud is going to be considered a matter of showing the nation the plight of the poor or exploiting a child's misery. When organizations like the S.C.L.C were demonstrating in the South, reporters who didn't come from overtly racist papers often seemed to feel that they deserved a bit of special consideration for taking the trouble to be there, and those who come to Resurrection City with that attitude are quickly offended. Perhaps because the opportunities to display militancy are limited in a nonviolent campaign of poor folks asking for food, there is a kind of territorial ferocity in Resurrection City. White reporters who are curious about what it must be like to be a young Negro constantly harassed by the police learn more than they want to know about the subject after a couple of days of being harassed by young Negro marshals in Resurrection City. Although almost everybody seems to assume the role of a marshal occasionally, the best-organized group is called the Tent City Rangers. Its members wear blue-jean outfits, work boots, and the kind of hat identified with Stewart Granger in African movies—with a leopardskin band and the brim snapped up on one side. To visitors—who are usually reporters—they sometimes take on the appearance of a kind of Wild West *tonton macoute*.

The S.C.L.C. has sent some of the more hostile young Negroes back to Chicago and Detroit, and on the steps of the Supreme Court both Abernathy and Young spent some time trying to persuade the Mexican marshals to leave cameramen alone. Both of them hold frequent press briefings. But the real problem cannot be solved by better relations with reporters. The S.C.L.C. has found that the advantage of having the huge Washington press corps on hand is also a disadvantage. Something has to be written about or photographed every day, and the more visible the metaphor gets the more vulnerable it becomes. Young talks about how everyone in America is on some kind of welfare except the poor, and reporters ask him if Abernathy has been sleeping in Resurrection City. Abernathy talks about current policies toward the poor being genocide, and reporters ask him why his demands to Congress are not more specific. Reporters are assigned to examine the phenomenon —to find out how well it's working and what it might accomplish. And the ministers of the S.C.L.C. will never be able to persuade them that a minute examination of Resurrection City is like a minute examination of one of the Martin Luther King metaphors that was not made visible—as if a press conference had been held and reporters had asked, "Which mountaintop did you say you've been to, Dr. King?" or "Tell us, Dr. King, exactly what night was it that you first started having this dream?"

## About the Author

CALVIN TRILLIN was born and raised in Kansas City, Missouri. He is the author of two previous books, *An Education in Georgia* and *Barnett Frummer Is an Unbloomed Flower*. Mr. Trillin has been a staff writer on *The New Yorker* magazine since 1963 and lives in New York with his wife and daughter.